Crypto Basics

A Nontechnical Introduction to Creating Your Own Money for Investors and Inventors

Slava Gomzin

Foreword by Ken Westin

Apress®

Crypto Basics: A Nontechnical Introduction to Creating Your Own Money for Investors and Inventors

Slava Gomzin
Frisco, TX, USA

ISBN-13 (pbk): 978-1-4842-8320-2   ISBN-13 (electronic): 978-1-4842-8321-9
https://doi.org/10.1007/978-1-4842-8321-9

Copyright © 2022 by Slava Gomzin

Managing Director, Apress Media LLC: Welmoed Spahr
Acquisitions Editor: Susan McDermott
Development Editor: Laura Berendson
Coordinating Editor: Gryffin Winkler

Distributed to the book trade worldwide by Springer Science+Business Media New York, 233 Spring Street, 6th Floor, New York, NY 10013. Phone 1-800-SPRINGER, fax (201) 348-4505, e-mail orders-ny@springer-sbm.com, or visit www.springeronline.com. Apress Media, LLC is a California LLC and the sole member (owner) is Springer Science + Business Media Finance Inc (SSBM Finance Inc). SSBM Finance Inc is a **Delaware** corporation.

For information on translations, please e-mail booktranslations@springernature.com; for reprint, paperback, or audio rights, please e-mail bookpermissions@springernature.com.

Apress titles may be purchased in bulk for academic, corporate, or promotional use. eBook versions and licenses are also available for most titles. For more information, reference our Print and eBook Bulk Sales web page at http://www.apress.com/bulk-sales.

Printed on acid-free paper

To Svetlana
and our daughters Alona, Aliza, and Arina.

Table of Contents

About the Author

Slava Gomzin is a cybersecurity and crypto enthusiast, full-stack technologist, and entrepreneur. He is the author of multiple publications on information security and technology, including the books *Hacking Point of Sale: Payment Application Secrets, Threats, and Solutions* (Wiley, 2014) and *Bitcoin for Nonmathematicians: Exploring the Foundations of Crypto Payments* (Universal Publishers, 2016). *Hacking Point of Sale* became a handbook and the primary reference for many professionals in the payment, retail, and cybersecurity industries. Slava has designed and co-created two cryptocurrencies. GRAFT (GRFT), a CryptoNote blockchain-based two-layer payment network, was launched in 2018 and allowed secure, private crypto transactions with less than two-second confirmations. Lyra (LYR), a new generation blockchain for secure private closed-loop payment solutions, was launched in 2020 and was designed and coded from scratch using recent advances in crypto technologies. Lyra is based on DPoS and block lattice technologies and allows instant (less than one second) on-chain transaction confirmations. Slava is currently the director of software development at Toshiba Global Commerce Solutions, focused on payments R&D, product security, and cloud technologies.

About the Technical Reviewer

 From Switzerland and currently working for AWS in New York, **Norbert Funke** has more than 20 years of industry experience with demonstrated success in all aspects of software engineering and information architecture. He has leading expertise in crypto, emerging data technologies, big data, and natural language processing (NLP), combined with deep industry experience in financial services and health care. He has worked in Europe, the United States, Australia, and China.

About the Foreword Author

 **Ken Westin** is a security researcher who has been helping organizations with security analytics, threat hunting, and insider threat programs for the past 15 years and has aided law enforcement in investigations, unveiling organized crime groups in the process. His work has been featured in *Wired*, *Forbes*, *New York Times*, *Good Morning America*, and others, and he is regularly reached out to as an expert on topics including cybersecurity, insider threat, privacy, and surveillance.

Acknowledgments

Writing a book is not easy and one cannot succeed without help from other people. First of all, I would like to thank Susan McDermott for bringing this project to reality. Thanks to the entire Apress team, especially to Gryffin Winkler, for flexibility and support during this project. Thanks to my colleagues at Toshiba for establishing and maintaining a creative work environment. Also, I would like to thank my past and current colleagues in the crypto industry, especially Dan Itkis and Wuzhou Yang – without their dedicated work, I would have nothing to write about.

I would like to thank Val Abelhouse, whose questions helped inspire me to write this book. Thanks to Norbert Funke for his enthusiastic support and contribution. Special thanks to Ken Westin for his brilliant and genuine foreword. And finally, I want to thank my wife, Svetlana, for her continuous support and understanding.

Any opinions, findings, conclusions, or recommendations expressed in this book are those of the author and do not necessarily reflect the views of his respective employer.

Foreword

I met Slava Gomzin a decade ago; at the time, criminal hackers were successfully targeting major retailers' point-of-sale systems, harvesting credit cards en masse with customized malware specifically designed for these systems. The industry was in a panic and looking for help. At the time, I was working for a security vendor who specialized in monitoring the security configurations of these systems and wanted to learn more about how they are compromised. That is when I learned of Slava Gomzin's first book, *Hacking Point of Sale*, and I reached out to him with some questions, and he responded. Slava and I even did a joint webinar on the topic of point-of-sale malware, and we have been friends since. Slava is a great teacher and knows the ins and outs of payment systems unlike anyone else I know, from how transactions are made to how they're secured, and has a clear understanding of both the history and future of payment systems.

Like my interest in point-of-sale systems, my interest in cryptocurrencies was piqued when I saw it was being used in underground forums and by criminal syndicates who were taking advantage of the pseudo-anonymous nature of Bitcoin to evade detection by regulators and law enforcement. It has been disturbing to see how cryptocurrency and the underlying blockchain technology quickly became overhyped in mainstream media as a "get-rich-quick" scheme fueling a craze of speculative investment, often by individuals who did not understand the underlying technology or risks associated with such a venture.

This hype reminds me of another hype cycle in cybersecurity when every cybersecurity vendor claimed to have "Artificial Intelligence" solutions that would replace the security analysts, mostly in attempts to land large rounds of funding from VCs. The promise of AI replacing security analysts not only turned out to not be true but also took attention away from the real and practical research that has been done utilizing machine learning which is a tool of AI to aid security analysts in their work, versus replacing them.

Similarly, the speculative investment hype around cryptocurrencies fueled by countless initial coin offerings and exchanges has taken attention away from the practical use of cryptocurrencies as actual currency, facilitating the decentralized exchange of goods and services. Instead, cryptocurrencies became centralized through exchanges and further diminished by associating with overpriced NFTs and Web3, all of which have made the crypto space appear to be more of a Ponzi scheme from the outside than a revolutionary egalitarian technology for the masses to circumvent existing centralized currency and controls. The unfortunate result of this speculative investment and hype is that the original intention of cryptocurrency, as laid out by Satoshi Nakamoto in the original "Bitcoin: A Peer-to-Peer Electronic Cash System" paper which gave rise to Bitcoin, is lost. Nowhere in the Satoshi Nakamoto paper is there a mention of investment in cryptocurrencies, mechanisms to exchange for fiat currency, or even tying Bitcoin's value to fiat currency; this all came later and was driven by greed and speculation.

It is important for businesses to understand how cryptocurrencies work to better understand where they can be used not as a speculative investment but how and where they can be used as a legitimate payment method. Many companies now accept cryptocurrencies such as Bitcoin, including AT&T, Microsoft, and Tesla, to name a few. Security professionals should be familiar with how cryptocurrencies work, as they are the de facto currency of cybercrime, whether it's used by cybercriminals to pay for services and tools or ransomware gangs demanding payment in cryptocurrency, taking advantage of their pseudo-anonymous nature. Financial professionals also need to know how cryptocurrencies operate as there are increasing regulations related to the use of cryptocurrency due to its capability for financial crimes such as money laundering, as well as tax implications of trading cryptocurrencies.

In this book, Slava walks through how cryptocurrencies work, from how cryptocurrency is created and traded to how it is secured. He provides a history of currencies so the reader understands how cryptocurrency fits within a historical context and highlights how some of the popular cryptocurrencies, such as Bitcoin and Monero, work and how they are different from each other. This book isn't a get-rich-quick scheme like you may find with some other books that hype cryptocurrencies as an investment vehicle, but more a guide to explain how cryptocurrencies operate and function to demystify them so that you, the reader, can make educated decisions on how and why to make use of them.

—Ken Westin

Preface

I was exposed to the idea of Bitcoin for the first time relatively late, back in 2014, after I finished writing my first "full size" book, *Hacking Point of Sale* (Wiley, 2014), and right before I joined HP as security and payment technologist. I remember it very well because writing a big book for a big publisher for the first time is a disaster you never forget. So, after I finished the book and it was published, I felt like a free man once again and decided to leverage the short break between my jobs and learn something completely new. Bitcoin, fortunately, was the best candidate at the time.

I was fascinated by the genius of a person or a group behind Bitcoin. It's too bad we still don't know their real identity. Given my extensive background in electronic payments and cybersecurity, which are still my two passions in addition to crypto, I immediately started thinking about adapting Bitcoin and other cryptos to the real world of retail business so that they could break into the mainstream. Unsurprisingly, my research resulted in another book, this time about crypto. *Bitcoin for Nonmathematicians* (Universal Publishers, 2016) was my first attempt to reveal the dangerous gap between traditional payment systems and cryptocurrencies. But the book started identifying some issues and did not offer any solutions.

Fast forward one year, and I was fascinated for the second time by the power and beauty of cryptography behind another breakthrough in the crypto world. Monero (XMR), a privacy coin based on the CryptoNote protocol, in a "bitcoin style," was also designed by an anonymous person or group. Unlike Bitcoin, Monero hides all the details of payment transactions from the public view while keeping intact the main advantage of crypto – decentralization.

The cryptography behind Monero is a perfect fit for what Arthur Clarke meant when he said that "any sufficiently advanced technology is indistinguishable from magic." Despite remaining issues with scalability (ability to process multiple payments simultaneously) and transaction processing time (the time it takes to validate and approve a single payment), I felt crypto is ready to go primetime for the first time. So, my friend Dan Itkis and I came up with the idea of a new cryptocurrency called GRAFT (GRFT), aiming to elevate the crypto payment processing to the level acceptable for the big retail but without defeating the very foundation of the crypto – decentralization. I was so thrilled by the opportunity to disturb the industry and consumed by the project that I left my day job in a prestigious predictive analytics startup and interrupted my promising career path as a cybersecurity executive.

The first version of the GRAFT network was successfully launched on January 16, 2018, and GRFT, at some point, was among the top 25% of cryptocurrencies by market capitalization. However, the initial success was shadowed by the complexity of development, weak market demand, and crypto winter 2018–2019.[1] In addition, over the course of the development process, I realized that GRAFT would not resolve all the issues associated with the long-term goal of entering the mainstream payment processing. Scalability was one of them, but another was the lack of flexibility as GRAFT was a "solo" blockchain that could not carry other tokens. That's how the idea of new crypto, which we later called Lyra (LYR), was born.

I wrote the Lyra white paper, created a design, and wrote the initial proof of concept code by myself, from scratch, while Dan helped to form the idea. But the actual, working version of Lyra (we call it *mainnet* in crypto) wouldn't happen without Wuzhou Yang, super-programmer and Lyra co-creator.

---

[1] Max Yakubowski. What's Next for the Industry as 'Crypto Winter' Thaws? https://cointelegraph.com/news/whats-next-for-the-industry-as-crypto-winter-thaws

Lyra's design has been based on a combination of more advanced technologies, very different from Bitcoin or Monero: *block lattice* and *delegated proof of stake* (DPoS). This completely new tech stack allowed us to resolve all the preceding issues while enabling even more features. Thousands of transactions with various coins, tokens, and NFTs (non-fungible tokens) can be processed within milliseconds, with the wallet software's footprint so small that it can even be placed on a smartcard chip.

Lyra mainnet was successfully launched on September 30, 2020, and it is still in development. I believe Lyra has its unique niche in the crypto specter, and one day, once all the proposed features are implemented, it will demonstrate its full power. I also believe that my good and bad experiences, which I sincerely share with the readers of this book, will help them succeed in their own crypto journey.

Introduction

I am not in the business. I am the business.

—Blade Runner: The Final Cut. Director: Ridley Scott

For many centuries, creating money was a king's privilege. Money was (and still is) associated with the higher power, and so monarchs were marking their reign by minting new coins with their portraits, like a golden *Louis d'or* coin first created by King of France Louis XIII in 1640 (Figure 1).

Figure 1. *Half Louis d'or coin minted in 1662*

Later on, state governments took over the right to mint and print new money. But things still change, faster and faster these days, thanks to industrial and technological revolutions. The invention of cryptocurrencies pushed the borders of possibilities even further: it allowed virtually any group of people, or even individuals not associated with any government or corporation, to create their own money. They typically don't call it money and put various explanations around their "tokens" utility. But in reality, it is what it is: money. Crypto tokens can be counted, divided, transferred, exchanged, and even minted, so they have all the necessary attributes of money.

With recent developments in crypto – an introduction of NFT (non-fungible token) – you can even put your face on your coin if you wish, similar to kings' coins. But I leave open the discussion about the nature of crypto and where it belongs and let other people decide whether crypto is, in fact, money or not. I would instead focus in this book on how to use it and, yes, how to create it – just in case you'd like to create your own... crypto.

I learned at least three things while speaking about crypto on multiple occasions.

First, most people are fascinated by the whole idea of crypto, but at the same time, they are typically interested in different aspects of it. The two major areas are technical and financial, which are also fragmented. For example, the technical side includes massive subdivisions such as cryptography, decentralized networking, and distributed consensus. But there are other aspects: economic, political, humanitarian, and psychological.

Second, it is impossible to explain the crypto phenomena in only technical or economic terms. The genius of the bitcoin creator (or creators?) is that she/he/they compiled multiple mandates for ultimate digital money in a single outstanding invention, which includes a decentralized payment network and economic policy on top of blockchain and distributed consensus with all the math around them.

And finally, the third thing I realized is that most people don't fully understand what crypto really is and how it works. Some of them get the basics of crypto financials but don't understand – and, as a result, underestimate and don't trust – the power of cryptography, distributed consensus, and, most importantly, the decentralized nature of crypto. This is, by the way, one of the main reasons for crypto to remain outside of mainstream payment and banking industries.

But I am still optimistic – after all, it's been less than 15 years since the Bitcoin white paper was published. It took us centuries to switch from metal to paper to electronic money, so 15 or 20 years would be a reasonable time to move from plastic to crypto. It's worth mentioning that this transition is not just about going from plastic cards to digital wallets. There is much more to that – moving from a centralized banking system controlled by national governments and corporations to decentralized financial networks, which are open across borders and do not belong to anyone!

Why Do We Need Crypto?

To get a definitive answer to this question, let's first look at the Bitcoin white paper – the document that proposed the first crypto. This is the first (but not the last) time I am going to cite the original Bitcoin white paper, which defines the very first crypto as an "electronic payment system based on cryptographic proof instead of trust, allowing any two willing parties to transact directly with each other without the need for a trusted third party."[1] The two key declarations here are *payment system* and *without the need for a trusted third party*. In other words, crypto is a decentralized financial system that any national government or corporation does not control. Thus, the two prominent use cases for crypto are *peer-to-peer payments* and *frictionless funds transfer* (which is a superset of payment, but there is a vast difference which will be described in Chapter 7). Let's review some examples for these two use cases.

---

[1] Satoshi Nakamoto. Bitcoin: A Peer-to-Peer Electronic Cash System. 2008. https://bitcoin.org/bitcoin.pdf

Imagine you own some real estate in Russia or Argentina, and you want to sell it and transfer proceeds to your US bank account. Many real estate deals in these countries are still done using cash. So, you need to open a local bank account, deposit the cash, exchange it for US dollars, and then transfer it to the US bank. While technically, it is a relatively simple operation, which can be done using SWIFT (an international banking funds transfer system) or Western Union (another system for international money transfers), it's not an obvious task given the relatively large amounts of real estate transactions, the current state of the political and economic relationships between some countries, and local financial regulations and cultural differences.

With crypto, however, money transfer is simple: buy Bitcoin (for example) in one country and sell it in another country (or just spend it without even exchanging it for the local fiat[2] currency). Most countries today have legal and unofficial exchanges, both online and physical, where local fiat currency can be exchanged for crypto, and then crypto can be converted to different fiat currency in another country. Crypto does not recognize national borders and exists everywhere as long as there is access to the Internet.

Typical payment use cases differ from funds transfers, but payments can also be made using crypto, especially when traditional payment methods are unavailable. Here is, perhaps, not the best example, but at least very well known: ransom payment to ransomware attackers. One of the significant ransomware attacks on the oil pipeline resulted in a 75 BTC (bitcoins) payment, equivalent to $4.4 million.[3] Given the amount and nature of such payment, it would be impossible for the attackers to process

---

[2] Fiat currency is the money issued by a national government and is not backed by any commodity such as gold. Examples: US dollar, Euro, the British pound.

[3] Tom Robinson. Elliptic Follows the Bitcoin Ransoms Paid by Colonial Pipeline and Other DarkSide Ransomware Victims. May 14, 2021. www.elliptic.co/blog/elliptic-follows-bitcoin-ransoms-paid-by-darkside-ransomware-victims

it via regular bank wire transfer or credit card. But crypto payment can be made regardless of the physical location of the payer and payee, who can also stay anonymous. However, there is only a certain degree of anonymity that can be provided by "regular" crypto, such as Bitcoin – we will review this issue in detail in Chapter 5.

Finally, another use case was not even foreseen (or at least not described) by the genius Bitcoin creator(s) – trading and investment. The fact that crypto prices fluctuate attracts short-term traders, while the common trend of historically growing crypto prices attracts long-term investors. We will review crypto trading and investment in Chapter 11.

What This Book Is About

This book has been written for a broad audience. The title, ambiguous at a glance ("Creating Your Own Money"?), in fact, is double-barreled, which is also hinted at by this phrase: "For Investors and Inventors." Yes, you understood it correctly. I will show you both how to use crypto (buy, store, transfer, trade, and invest) as well as how to create your own one – depending on your goals, not to mention the fact that you need to know how to handle crypto before you can create a new one, don't you? Also, in both cases, you need to understand how crypto works, first, on a high level, and then even more in depth.

You own your crypto money no matter who you are – user or creator. Think about it. When you simply buy crypto, you get the money that does not belong to any government or corporation, and it only belongs to you. You own your money created by someone for you and other people. When you create new crypto (maybe it sounds like a very hypothetical case to you right now, but I will show you how relatively simple it is in reality), you own new money that others also can use. With that said, the title is not just double-barreled but also a little bit sarcastic because, let's face it, you cannot just create your own money entirely out of thin air.

Creating money is not just a technological act. While crypto is a pure product of technology, money results from the collective consciousness. Everyone can potentially create their own crypto. Then, it can or cannot become money. I will show you how to create your own crypto, and I will explain how some crypto might or might not become money, but I cannot guarantee that the crypto you have created will ever become money. If you are eager to create your own crypto project, I'm not going to demotivate you, but you should build the right expectations. There will be a comprehensive review of this process in Part III.

Another goal of this book is to explain crypto while reviewing its integral parts in detail. This book is focused on two top aspects of crypto: technical and financial, and their subdivisions such as cryptography, decentralization, distributed consensus, monetary policy, security, privacy, and payment processing capabilities.

When you finish reading this book, you will understand all these elements and how they work together. You will understand Bitcoin and any other cryptocurrency and be ready to start doing a business with crypto. To become savvy enough about crypto, you don't have to learn the math behind cryptography and distributed consensus. In addition to explaining the crypto basics in layman's terms, this book also offers different parts for various audiences.

While Part I gives an overview of the technologies around crypto, Part II provides practical knowledge necessary to dive into the crypto business, such as investment, trading, and even creating your own crypto project, which is covered in detail in Part III. Just check out the table of contents and select what you want to learn.

What This Book Is Not About

Before we dive into the depths of the crypto ocean, it's also important to mention what this book does not cover, just to help the readers build the right expectations.

First, this book is not a "how to get rich" guide. While it contains an analysis of financial and economic aspects of crypto, because it is almost impossible to conduct an intelligible conversation about crypto without mentioning money, it still puts a more significant emphasis on the technical side when it comes to crypto creation schemes. And, once again, as you will see, not every crypto ends up as money.

Another important "not" is the use cases not associated with the payment or financial systems. The Bitcoin white paper defines Bitcoin as a payment system. But just as not all cryptos are based on the original blockchain technology proposed by Bitcoin creators, not all blockchains are payment systems. There is an army of inventors who fanatically try to apply blockchain database technology to all aspects of our life, no matter if it's appropriate or not. It often looks like an attempt to use a jet rocket engine in a car: it will drive (or fly?), perhaps faster than a traditional car, but no one would use it in real life because there are less expensive and safer gasoline or electric engines that are more suitable for cars. In the same way, there are traditional relational or NoSQL databases that are more suitable in most cases for solutions outside of FinTech. Even though some attempts to use a blockchain database and decentralized tech outside of their original intended area might be pretty successful, they will remain out of scope for this book which is focused solely on crypto.

And finally, I am not a professional investor or trader but rather living on the "opposite" side of the barricades. So, this book cannot be viewed as a professional crypto investment or trading guide but rather as a starter and helper. There are many books on trading and investment, and some books in this area explicitly target crypto. With that said, when you deal with crypto projects day to day, from the very beginning to coding to the actual listing of the trading pair on an exchange, you must understand the motivation and behavior of the "other side" – people who view the crypto as a purely financial instrument.

Besides being an amateur investor and trader by myself, I know some professionals in this area. They don't need anyone to teach them to do what they know to do well already. They are looking for a guide on getting started that answers some basic but essential questions: What is crypto? How does it work? And finally, what are the right things to begin with, and what is no go? They will find answers to those questions in this book. In addition to understanding what's under the hood, an insider's overview of crypto technology and economy should help investors and traders estimate the potential of a particular project and even try to predict its future.

Some Basic Terminology

Before we continue, let's agree on some basic industry jargon.

First, *crypto* is the same as *cryptocurrency*. We simply save some time, ink, storage space, power, and paper by using crypto instead of cryptocurrency. Cryptocurrency is also a shortcut for *cryptographic currency*, which is essentially a money and payment system combined together and based on cryptographic algorithms. Now try to count how much more ink and paper we just saved.

Next, *blockchain* is not the same as crypto. Most cryptos are based on blockchain, but other essential technologies are required for crypto to exist, and blockchain is just one of them. Blockchain is just a type of database where records, financial transaction records in the case of crypto, are stored in chained blocks. Another name for such a database is *distributed transaction ledger*. The blocks are linked one after another to form a chain. It's worth mentioning that all crypto use some kind of database to store transaction records. Still, it's not always the same blockchain technology invented by Bitcoin creator(s), and it's not even always called a blockchain. Read more about types of distributed transaction ledgers in Chapters 2 and 3.

A *network node* is another important term. It's often simply called a *node*. This is typically a computer, server, or a group of servers running crypto software. The nodes are linked to each other through the Internet and comprise a crypto network, often called the *mainnet*. Each node maintains its own copy of the transaction ledger (such as a blockchain). The nodes constantly sync with each other to make sure their copy of the blockchain is up to date.

Another exciting term associated with crypto is a *fork*. The fork is created when two parallel versions of blockchain are started from the same original blockchain, for example, when developers release a new version of crypto node software. The fork might create two temporary versions of the same blockchain or even a new cryptocurrency. In many cases, the fork is the standard way to upgrade the cryptosystem or maintain the distributed consensus. There are different types of forks: *soft fork*, *hard fork*, and *temporary fork*.

In simple words, a *soft fork* is a minor update, while a *hard fork* is a major network update that creates a new version of blockchain that is not compatible with the old one. Typically, the new version of the blockchain gradually replaces the old "forked" version as node operators update their nodes.

The hard fork is also the way to create new crypto from the existing one. For example, Bitcoin Cash is a hard fork of Bitcoin. New crypto based on another crypto code base is also called its fork. For example, Litecoin is a fork of Bitcoin because its code is forked from Bitcoin code. And finally, a *temporary fork* can be created during the *mining* process, which we will review in Chapter 2.

The crypto community creates much more industry jargon, but we will introduce it gradually in the following chapters as we move forward by describing different aspects of crypto.

Why New Crypto Is Born Every Day

As of the time of writing this text, there are more than 20,000 cryptocurrencies listed on CMC (short for the cryptomarketcap.com website), the popular source for statistics and real-time status of the entire crypto market. Yours truly had co-created two out of those 20,000 cryptos, and one of the reasons for writing this book is my experience with crypto, not just as a user but as an inventor.

Each crypto has an inventor (or inventors), a team of developers, a supporting community, and a community of users (investors, traders, and simply consumers) behind it. Each crypto also has some idea behind it. Sometimes, it offers a unique technology or financial instrument, and sometimes it's trivial and a copycat from another crypto. I have experience creating both.

But there is a third way which became very popular after Ethereum introduced an ERC-20 token standard back in 2015.[4] Before the Ethereum era, the only way to create your own crypto was launching a new blockchain with a new network of nodes that would handle this blockchain, which is a pretty complex project. Ethereum was the first crypto that allowed multiple custom tokens running on a single Ethereum blockchain and network, which created a revolution in crypto. Thousands of new crypto were created using this pattern. We will review this process in detail in Chapter 12.

Now back to "classic" crypto. My first project, GRAFT, was a copycat (also known as "fork," which sounds more scientific and less trivial) from existing crypto – Monero. But unlike simple forks, when creators just duplicate the original functionality of the source project, GRAFT offered a quite sophisticated technology on top of the Monero protocol, which was supposed to make it suitable for processing payments in near real time.

---

[4] ERC-20 TOKEN STANDARD. https://ethereum.org/en/developers/docs/standards/tokens/erc-20/

Unfortunately, the way from the idea, even a brilliant one, to its implementation is too long and very bumpy. On the way, you sometimes realize that the downsides outweigh the benefits. That's how the idea of my second project called Lyra was born – creating new technology from scratch. Lyra was designed to have all the missing features in GRAFT and other cryptos.

However, like in any other startup, there are multiple components in every crypto project, and even a brilliant idea or breakthrough technology is not enough for success. In some cases, it is even the opposite – the projects that do not offer any new technology or don't have any practical purpose become very successful financially. There are many examples of such projects, and Dogecoin is just one of them. Dogecoin was created as a joke. But it was supported, for unknown reasons, by some influential people like Elon Musk, which sent its price to the sky and put it into the enormous financial success category.

No matter what the idea behind crypto is (or no idea at all), one of the keys to skyrocketing development of the crypto industry is *open source* philosophy. Even completely new technologies like Lyra, with the source code primarily written from scratch, still use some open source libraries created for other crypto projects, not to mention forked projects like GRAFT, which were entirely made possible by the open source nature of crypto. The reason for such altruism of developers is not their generosity – after all, any crypto ecosystem is all about money. The real reason is the decentralized nature of blockchain-based FinTech.[5]

Real crypto cannot belong to any individual or group of individuals, not to mention government organizations such as a central bank or corporations such as PayPal. Therefore, the source code must be visible to everyone and can be reused by anyone, which is enabled by open source licenses. For the same reason, crypto technologies are rarely patented.

---

[5] FinTech stands for Financial Technology, which includes all new businesses based on innovative technologies that compete with the traditional banking system, including crypto.

Patents would link crypto to particular individuals or entities, which would defeat its decentralized character. We will talk about different degrees of decentralization in Chapter 3. And, of course, there are detailed instructions for creating your own crypto in Part III.

I sincerely envy you because learning and understanding crypto's various concepts and capabilities are fascinating. Enjoy!

A Note About Volatility...

At the time I was writing this book, there was a significant uptick in crypto volatility. I speak about this in more depth in Chapter 11, but I wanted to say a few words here as well. Volatility in crypto markets – as compared to traditional financial markets – is actually quite common, mainly because crypto is a very young technology, a new financial instrument, but already a part of a global market and, as such, is influenced by standard economic processes. Therefore, there is much uncertainty about its current and especially future state.

Even though the common trend – once again, like with traditional stocks – is a "bull" market, that is, rising prices, there were several times when the crypto value fell significantly. But based on the historical data, the prices eventually returned and grew even more.

Crypto volatility is contradictory and ambiguous. On the one hand, it is one reason cryptocurrencies are still not accepted as a payment method by mainstream businesses. On the other hand, some groups of users (think traders) can even benefit from frequent ups and downs. In any case, one should be careful when entering the crypto game and always remember a simple thing: *crypto prices are volatile!*

PART I

Understanding Crypto

CHAPTER 1

How Cryptography Works

Bitcoin is the most amazing mathematical miracle.

—Steve Wozniak, Apple co-founder

When I was a kid, my parents often took me on a trip to "The South" during the summer breaks. I grew up in St. Petersburg, the big city in Russia's northwest. It's very close to the border with Finland (yes, Santa Claus lives there nearby). Summers there are not very cold, and sometimes you can even get a decent sun tanning and enjoy swimming in rivers, lakes, and even the Gulf of Finland (Baltic Sea). However, you still cannot compare it with the subtropical climate of the south regions facing the warm Black Sea, which are simply called by Russians "The South."

For people living in northern and central Russian regions, traveling to "The South" was like a trip to Florida for Canadians. It was associated with all kinds of resort activities and bloomy subtropical flora. Who knows, maybe an attempt to restore the collapsed Soviet empire to revive old memories is one of the reasons why the totalitarian Putin regime is so desperate to seize the southern Ukrainian territories.

© Slava Gomzin 2022
S. Gomzin, *Crypto Basics*, https://doi.org/10.1007/978-1-4842-8321-9_1

I can't tell for sure now whether it was my idea – may be inspired by the heroes of Jules Verne's novels (remember Jacques Paganel?[1]) – or just a summer school homework, but on one of such trips, I decided to make an herbarium. I remember, though, that back then, I was sure that this was simple work: just collect the leaves and stick them into the album – everyone can do it! How wrong I was. Now I realize that, in fact, it was real scientific work.

Collecting and classifying information is what authors do when writing nonfiction books. But after reading such a book, readers sometimes leave reviews like "information in this book can be found online." Of course, it can be found – everything these days can be found online, including this book! But keep in mind that this information needs to be selected, sorted, verified, digested, validated by comparing with personal experience, and finally presented in a way understandable by the readers.

So yes, maybe some information here can be googled, but in the same way, you can prepare your dinner instead of going to the restaurant. However, you still go to the restaurant to get your favorite food prepared for you by a professional chef. So welcome to my restaurant. The first main course on the menu today is Bitcoin cryptography!

First Ciphers

Even though most of the information in this chapter is related to Bitcoin, most of the things you will learn from it apply to all crypto. I would even name it "How *Crypto* Cryptography Works," but I believe you agree that it wouldn't sound good... Like "salt is salty." But on the other hand, the reason for crypto to be called crypto is precisely this – *crypto* is a shortcut for *cryptocurrency*, and *cryptocurrency* is an abbreviation for *cryptographic*

---

[1] Jules Verne. In Search of the Castaways (French: Les Enfants du capitaine Grant, "The Children of Captain Grant"). 1865.

currency. Crypto is called crypto because it simply wouldn't exist without cryptography, or, more precisely, without relatively recent breakthroughs in that domain of science.

Cryptography has existed for centuries in the form of ciphers. People always need to protect their secrets from what's called in cybersecurity *unauthorized access*. This discipline has been developing as a continuous cat and mouse game, which is what it still is. As soon as someone comes up with a new way of protecting information from public view, someone else starts trying to break it.

It all began from primitive methods, which, however, used to be quite effective back in their times. The first "cryptographers" were not even using ciphers – they were simply hiding messages, which we now call *steganography*, from the Greek words *steganos* and *graphein* (meaning *covered* and to *write*, respectively). By the way, the word *cryptography* itself is also composed of Greek words: *kryptós* (*hidden* or *secret*) and also *graphein*, as it is in steganography.

It's not a coincidence that Greek words are used in crypto terminology. Perhaps, the first description of cryptographic methods has been found in Greek sources. In his *The Histories*, Herodotus, the Greek historian, describes how Greeks protected their messages from Persians and how these secret messages helped Greeks win the long-running war.[2] As I mentioned before, the methods they used to safeguard their information were not even ciphers.

The Greeks were hiding their secret messages by writing them on the folded wooden wax tablets, which were used back then as the way to write and transmit the postal letters. Usually, the message was written with a stylus by scraping the wax surface. So what the Greeks did was they removed the whole wax surface and wrote their messages on the wood itself instead. Then they recoated the tablets with the new layer of wax, so

---

[2] Simon Singh. The Code Book: The Secret History of Codes and Codebreaking. Ted Smart, 2000. Page 4.

they looked like just brand-new empty tablets. It sounds like a primitive trick, but it allowed the Greeks to prepare for an attack and defeat the Persians!

The difference between steganography and cryptography is that while the former uses various hiding techniques to protect the message (like the Greeks' wax tablets described earlier), the latter does not hide the message text itself but "scrambles" its characters using a particular *encryption algorithm* (or *cipher*) to make the final text (or *ciphertext*) unreadable for unwanted readers. The only way to *decrypt* (restore the original *clear text* to make it readable again) such a ciphertext is when you know the cipher.

But in most cases, it's not enough to know what cipher has been used, so you also need to know the *key* used to *encrypt* the original text. Thus, modern ciphers can be endlessly reused because each new key is generated for any further algorithm usage, and that key is what you keep in secret – not the algorithm itself.

This is a fundamental characteristic of encryption, which is also called Kerckhoffs's principle: the security of the encryption scheme must depend only on the secrecy of the key and not on the secrecy of the algorithm.[3] Whenever someone tries to hide the encryption algorithm itself and, to do that, comes up with some kind of new, homegrown cipher, the chances are such an algorithm will be cracked. Only a handful of strong ciphers were tested by enormous amounts of attempts to crack them and, therefore, safe enough to use.

One of the first well-known ciphers is named after Roman emperor Julius Caesar.[4] This cipher uses a *shift* as the main cryptographic technique. The letters of the input message are shifted several positions (usually 3) using the alphabetic sequence, so letter A, for example, is

---

[3] Niels Ferguson, Bruce Schneier, Tadayoshi Kohno. Cryptography Engineering: Design Principles and Practical Applications. Wiley, 2010. Page 24.

[4] Robert Churchhouse. Codes and Ciphers: Julius Caesar, the Enigma, and the Internet. Cambridge University Press, 2002. Page 13.

replaced by D, B by E, Z by C, etc. Here is the example of the ciphertext produced by Julius Caesar cipher:

ELWFRLQ

To decrypt the message, we need to shift each letter by three positions using the Latin alphabet so that E will be B, L will become I, etc. The result will reveal the original message in clear text:

BITCOIN

As you can imagine, Julius Caesar's cipher could be practical in ancient Rome, but it is too primitive to be helpful today. Many other ciphers have been created since then, but the most sophisticated ones emerged with the development of computing. Over time, ciphers evolved from primitive methods to the modern designs in current crypto implementations.

Modern Cryptography

Massive development of cryptography can be attributed to the emergence of the Internet. Initially, the global network was not designed to be secure. The Internet creators were so excited about the very possibility of communicating freely with other people around the world that they did not consider any privacy and security concerns. In fairness, it should be noted that no one (in the field of computers, of course) cared much back then about security or privacy.

But both computers and networks evolved and expanded from the universities to the real world of business and government, which started demanding new standards for secure and private communication. That's how the *Secure Socket Layer* (SSL) protocol was born, along with security *certificates* and *Public Key Infrastructure* (PKI). You may ask how it's all related to crypto. It's very related because crypto uses similar algorithms and protocols – the building blocks used to secure the Internet but evolved into more sophisticated mechanisms. For example, *public key (asymmetric) encryption* schemes are necessary to secure the Internet by SSL (now renamed TLS – *Transport Layer Security*) and cryptocurrencies. *Hash functions* are also used in both PKI and crypto.

Another example is the *Diffie-Hellman* (DH) algorithm used by the *Diffie-Hellman key exchange* algorithm, employed in SSL/TLS. Privacy cryptocurrencies based on the *CryptoNote* protocol, such as Monero, also use DH to make their transactions private (there is more info about privacy and privacy-centric cryptos in Chapters 5 and 6). Now let's review all these algorithms one by one. Since SSL/TLS and PKI are out of scope for this book, we will learn mainly about the cryptocurrency applications of the hash function, DH, and public key (asymmetric) encryption.

Hash Function

We'll start from the *hash function* since it is a fundamental algorithm for cryptocurrencies and perhaps the easiest one to understand. It is simpler than symmetric or asymmetric encryption (which we will review next). Strictly speaking, the hash function is not even an encryption algorithm in practical terms because it cannot be used to scramble the communication transmissions, which we reviewed previously (such as Julius Caesar cipher). The issue with the hash function is that you *can encrypt* a message with it, but you *cannot decrypt* it. That's why it is also called *one-way encryption*. This useless at first glance feature found a tremendous application in cryptography because it made possible a *digital signature,* the primary enabler of any blockchain and any cryptocurrency. But before we dive into its application, which is described in the next chapter, let's see how the hash function works.

I just mentioned that the hash function has another name – one-way encryption. In fact, there is a third name – *message digest* – which is a kind of self-explaining. The truth is that the hash function knows to take any message (clear text) as an input and generate the short ciphertext as an output. Short is the keyword here because the length of the output ciphertext always remains the same, no matter how long the clear-text input is. This is an ideal feature for blockchains, of course, where every extra *byte* of information (the minimum portion of the information required to code a number or Latin alphabet character) costs much money because the copies of the blockchain are distributed thousands of times between multiple nodes and require more and more disk space to store them.

Another essential feature of a hash function is its ability to produce unique output for any individual input. It means two things. First, the output ciphertext uniquely identifies the original input message. Therefore, no matter who, where, when, and how many times runs the hash function on the same input, the result (output) will be always the same (as long as the input remains the same!). Second, it is impossible to run the hash function on two different messages and get the same result. Thus, blockchains use the hash function to "replace" long messages when the original message itself does not matter. And the primary use case for this is when you need to make sure that the original input message was not altered.

SHA-256

One popular hash function used by Bitcoin is called *SHA-256*.[5] The algorithm is a variant of the SHA-2 (Secure Hash Algorithm 2), developed by the National Security Agency (NSA).[6] Without going into the math, which you can find in the following references if you are interested, I just

---

[5]What is SHA-256? https://coinmarketcap.com/alexandria/glossary/sha-256
[6]Descriptions of SHA-256, SHA-384, and SHA-512. https://web.archive.org/web/20130526224224/http://csrc.nist.gov/groups/STM/cavp/documents/shs/sha256-384-512.pdf

want to mention that its name contains "256" simply because it creates a 256-bit output. As we said, no matter the input message's length, the output is always 256 bits (one bit is 0 or 1).

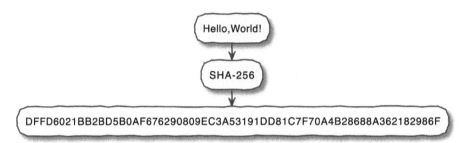

Figure 1-1. *Example of SHA-256 hash function*

You can see an example of SHA-256 in Figure 1-1. If you noticed, the length of the message digest is 64 characters. This is because we use a *hexadecimal* encoding (HEX) to represent *bytes* in the printable text (one byte contains eight bits). In hexadecimal representation, each symbol (a number from 0 to 9 or a letter from A to F) can carry 16 values or 4 bits of information. So 64 HEX symbols are enough to represent 256 bits. By the way, you can try it by yourself using some simple online hash generator.[7] Bitcoin, however, uses even more "compressed" encoding, which is called BASE58. Yes, it uses 58 Latin alphabet characters (instead of the 16 used by HEX) to encode the binary data. So the size of the resulting message will be even shorter. For example, the SHA-256 of the "Hello, World!" phrase encoded in BASE58 will be 72k1xXWG59fYdzSNoA – only 18 characters![8]

Now, to illustrate the power of hash, let's remove the exclamation mark at the end of the sentence and rerun the hash function. You can see that the resulting message digest is entirely different (Figure 1-2).

---

[7] SHA256 Hash Generator. https://passwordsgenerator.net/sha256-hash-generator/

[8] Base58 Encoder/Decoder. www.appdevtools.com/base58-encoder-decoder

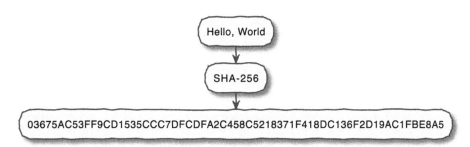

Figure 1-2. *SHA-256 of the modified input (without exclamation mark at the end)*

This feature of the hash is used in crypto to maintain the immutable nature of the blockchain, meaning that once the blockchain update is created and the majority of the network validates and agrees on this update, it can never be changed.

RIPEMD160

There are many different hash functions, but Bitcoin uses two of them. One is SHA-256, which we reviewed in the previous section, and another is RIPEMD160. RIPEMD (RACE Integrity Primitives Evaluation Message Digest) is a group of hash functions developed by Hans Dobbertin, Antoon Bosselaers, and Bart Preneel in 1992.[9]

The reason for using RIPEMD160 is apparent: it creates a much shorter message digest – right, with a fixed 160-bit length (Figure 1-3).

---

[9] RIPEMD Hash Function. www.geeksforgeeks.org/ripemd-hash-function/

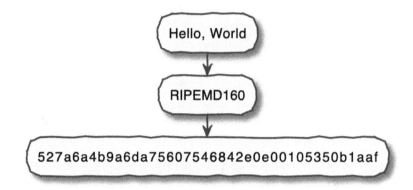

Figure 1-3. *RIPEMD160 example*

But what is the reason for Bitcoin to using two different hash functions – both SHA-256 and RIPEMD160? While I don't think there is an exact answer to this question, we will see how these two hash functions are used in Bitcoin in Chapter 2.

Merkle Tree

Before moving to the next important part of this chapter designated for public key encryption and digital signatures, I would like to mention another fundamental mechanism used in Bitcoin – the *Merkle tree*, or *tree of hashes*. It is not precisely a cryptographic algorithm but rather a mathematical tool, but it still belongs to this chapter since it is based on hash functions. The Merkle tree was invented by Ralph Merkle.[10] The idea is simple: one hash can represent multiple hashes which represent various data objects (transaction records in our case with cryptocurrencies). The tree of hashes makes the process of integrity validation more efficient, which is very important when applied to cryptocurrencies.

---

[10] Ralph Merkle. A Digital Signature Based on Conventional Encryption Function. https://people.eecs.berkeley.edu/~raluca/cs261-f15/readings/merkle.pdf

The critical element of the Merkle tree is the *Merkle root*, which is the single hash that represents all records in the tree. The tree of hashes is formed by combining the hashes in groups of two. Let's say we have four transactions, represented by hashes A, B, C, and D (Figure 1-4).

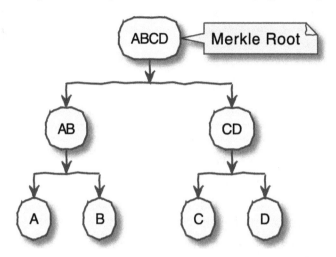

Figure 1-4. *Example of the Merkle tree*

The tree is created by combining A with B and C with D first, creating hashes AB and CD. Then AB and CD are calculated into a single hash ABCD, which is the Merkle root. The Merkle tree and Merkle root allow Bitcoin nodes to validate a specific transaction without recalculating all the hashes, using the transaction hash and the Merkle root of the transaction block. We will see how it's used in Bitcoin in the next chapter.

Asymmetric (Public Key) Encryption

If we tried to classify the encryption algorithms, the result would be presented in Table 1-1.

Table 1-1. *Classification of Encryption Algorithms*

Encryption Type	Encryption Keys	Can Encrypt	Can Decrypt	Used in Crypto	Example
Hash function	0	Yes	No	Yes	SHA-256, RIPEMD160
Symmetric	1	Yes	Yes	No	AES
Asymmetric	2	Yes	Yes	Yes	RSA, Elliptic Curves

First go hash functions, as a "simplest," one-way encryption mechanism. Then go symmetric encryption algorithms out of scope for this review. Why? Simply because they are not used in Bitcoin and other cryptos! But we must briefly talk about symmetric just to understand the difference between hash, symmetric, and asymmetric. In two words, here is the difference: hash function (one-way encryption) – no key; symmetric encryption – one key; asymmetric (public key) encryption – two keys. That's it.

There is no encryption key in hash functions – there is only the algorithm itself, like in Julius Caesar cipher. But hash functions are a billion times more secure than Julius Caesar. You input the clear-text message and get the secure message digest as the output. The (significant) "side effect" – there is no way back; the result cannot be decrypted.

Unlike hash functions, symmetric encryption has the key, which can be used to encrypt the original clear-text input and decrypt the resulting ciphertext back to the original. Symmetric algorithms are used mostly for encrypting data at rest (like file systems and databases) and data in transit (like network communication). Since we are not interested in these areas, let's move straight to the asymmetric.

Unlike symmetric encryption, asymmetric encryption has two keys: private and public. These keys are different; that's why it's called asymmetric. It's also often called *public key encryption* because the public key is used to encrypt the message when it is sent through the open communication channel.

When you think about it, it is very convenient – the public key is not a secret, so it can be openly shared with anyone and sent through public networks. The private key is the secret one. Hence, it's called private. So, let's say we want to use asymmetric encryption as a cipher in our favorite use case – encrypt the secret message sent through the open channel. Although both public and private keys can be used for encryption and decryption, it does not make sense to use a private key to encrypt the message in our case because then everyone can decrypt it with the public key (remember, the public key is not a secret). So we use the public key to encrypt and the private key to decrypt.

Let's say Alice wants to send a secret message to Bob. First of all, Bob generates a pair of keys, shares the public key with Alice, but saves the private key for himself (Figure 1-5).

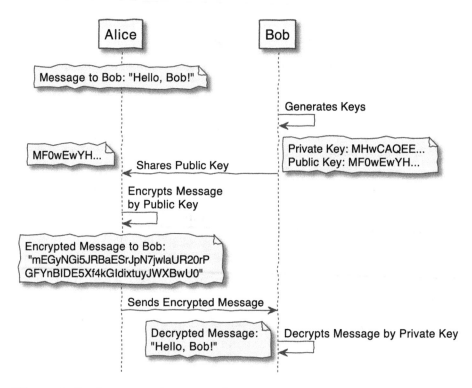

Figure 1-5. *Asymmetric encryption*

Alice takes Bob's public key, encrypts her message, and sends it to Bob. He receives the encrypted message and decrypts it using his private key. Very simple and secure!

Unlike symmetric encryption algorithms, where the same key is used for both encryption and decryption and must be kept secret by both sides, Bob can openly share his public key with anyone who wants to send him an encrypted message! Once the public key encrypts the message, the same public key cannot be used to decrypt it, so only Bob can read that message using the private key that only he knows.

The power of asymmetric (public key) encryption is enormous, but our example is just the beginning. There is another extremely important application of asymmetric encryption: *digital signature*.

Digital Signatures

Blockchain (and so all crypto) would not be possible without digital signatures as they are used to authenticate the owners of the funds and authorize them to make funds transfers between wallets. Now, let's see how a digital signature works using public key cryptography.

Unlike our previous example with Alice sending an encrypted message to Bob, using the public and private keys in the digital signature is precisely the opposite. The private key is used to encrypt, and the public key is used to decrypt. However, instead of encrypting the message itself, it will encrypt its digest – the hash function which we reviewed previously.

Let's say Alice wants to send a message to Bob once again. But this time, the content of the message itself is not a secret. More than that, Alice wants to make sure that everyone can read this message, not just Bob. Maybe Bob is not the only recipient of this message. Perhaps the message contains important information about a new security vulnerability (just the first example that comes to the head of the security guy). But what's important for Alice, and especially for Bob, is to make sure that the message that Bob receives is authentic, that is, it was not modified by anyone during transmission.

Looking ahead, I will reveal that, in fact, the content of that message, when it comes to crypto, can be the number of coins that Alice sends to Bob. Hence, Bob needs to make sure this is the correct number of coins that Alice originally sent, and everyone else (observers and validators) needs to make sure that Alice sends no more than she has.

In reality, this process is more complex, but we will "decipher" its complexity in the next chapter. Now back to a digital signature.

To digitally sign the message, Alice needs to perform the following steps. First, generate the pair of keys, and share the public key with Bob (or anyone else who wants to be able to validate her digital signatures). Note that, unlike the previous example with asymmetric encryption, where Bob

generated the keys, this time Alice does it instead and sends the public key
to Bob. She also saves the private key for herself because it will be used to
sign all her future messages (Figure 1-6).

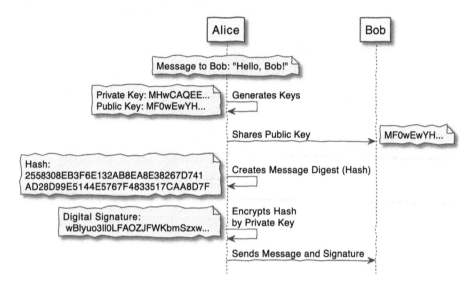

Figure 1-6. *Digital signature*

Now she takes her favorite message, "Hello, Bob!", and runs a hash
function on it to get the digest. Next, she encrypts the digest using her
private key. The resulting ciphertext is the digital signature!

Alice now can send both the message and the signature to Bob.

Note that she does not need to send the digest because they previously
agreed on the hash algorithm (let's say SHA-256). She also does not need
to send any keys because the hash function does not require a key. The
only thing Bob needs to know is the type of hash function she used, which
never changes.

Now Bob receives the message and needs to validate its signature to
ensure this is still the original message and was not modified during the
transmission. Bob first runs a hash function on the message to validate
the signature, then decrypts the signature using Alice's public key and

compares the two results. If they are the same, the new message digest (created by Bob) is identical to the original digest created by Alice (and encrypted into the digital signature). Done!

Note that actual implementations of digital signature algorithms can be different, but my goal here was just to explain the idea behind it. We could stop here and move to the next chapter to see how all this cryptography is applied to create crypto ecosystems. However, a story about bitcoin cryptography would not be complete without some description of elliptic curves, which is one of the best asymmetric encryption algorithms. As you can guess, yes, it is the one used in Bitcoin and most other cryptos.

Elliptic Curves

Unfortunately, the math behind the elliptic curves algorithm is so complex that it is beyond this book's scope. I tried to explain it in layman's terms, with minimum math, in my previous book about Bitcoin, so if you are interested in the details, you can find them there.[11] It also contains some source code illustrations in C# and Python. But here, I would like to try again and provide another very brief explanation, this time with no math and no source code, of course. The beauty of this cryptography is worth it.

Elliptic curves cryptography starts, as you can guess, from the elliptic curve – Figure 1-7 shows what it looks like.

---

[11] Slava Gomzin. Bitcoin for Nonmathematicians: Exploring the Foundations of Crypto Payments. Universal Publishers, 2016. www.universal-publishers.com/book.php?method=ISBN&book=1627340718

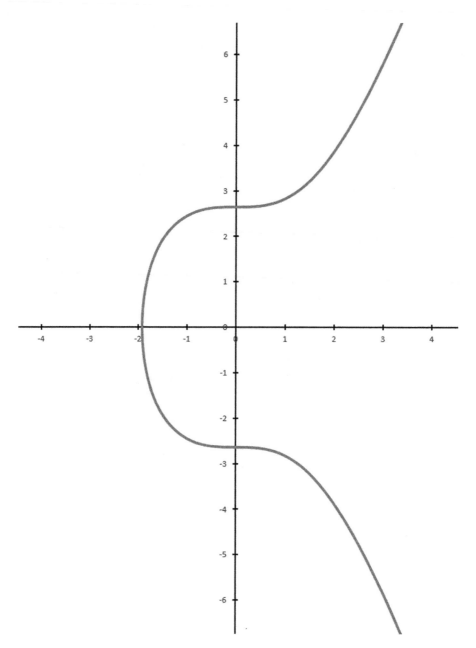

Figure 1-7. *Elliptic curve used by Bitcoin*

There are different forms of elliptic curves, and their shape depends on the formula (equation) behind them. Without going into the math, I will tell you only that this is precisely the curve that Bitcoin uses.

As you know already, to use it as asymmetric encryption, we should be able to generate private and public keys. So let's start with the private key. In elliptic curves, this is very simple – you just generate a random number. The primary condition is that this number should be very large. In alphanumeric encoding, which we studied previously, such a number will look like this:

```
MHwCAQEEIQDj1Kdz0l4VgnHCmHDLDMI3Pakg6ZzKe5Bo5ekzvn3INqAKBggqhkj
OPQMAEKFIAOYABJbO3zzbH/EN23LhfJCzfPrDQU44qrSkeiGkElJ7NbeCu8nhwW
90ian1jHia4jszuM7ze876euPGDxbWYY1Ah+FjaNIV
```

Now let's generate the public key. This is going to look... differently. The thing is, public keys in elliptic curves cryptography are not numbers; they are points. That's why we need the curve – to use points on that curve. This point, of course, has horizontal and vertical coordinates x and y (not math, I promised, I just wanted to say that instead of one number, it is going to be two numbers; that's it). Now let's see how we get the public key.

Here, it is necessary to mention that elliptic curves have exciting features (that's why they were selected for this important mission in the first place): you can add and multiply points on the curve. So, for example, if you have two points A and B, you can add A to B, and the result of this operation will be another point, C (Figure 1-8).

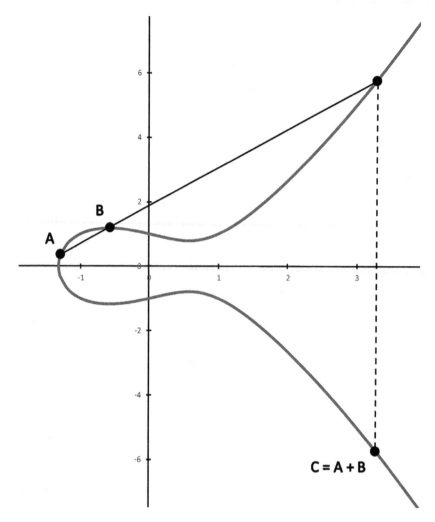

Figure 1-8. *Point addition*

I think it's pretty clear so far, even without math, right? Just one more thing, and we are close to the finish, I promise. Another operation you can do with points is multiplication. So if you have point A, you can add A to itself multiple times, and the result will be, once again, another point. For example, D = 5A. I am not going to illustrate multiplication with a diagram because it is a little bit more complicated than addition. I only say that those features of elliptic curves allow one to generate a public key by selecting a random point on the curve and multiplying it by the private key (which is a very big number).

As with the hash function and asymmetric encryption, the result of such multiplication cannot be reversed back if you don't know the initial point. It means that the private key cannot be reconstructed from the public key.

That's pretty much it. Of course, there is a lot of math that allows us to encrypt and decrypt data using these keys or create a digital signature using them. But as I said, we are not going to go there; this is beyond the scope of this book. We have a lot of other exciting things to learn. But I hope at least you got the basic idea of elliptic curves cryptography!

Cryptography and Security

At the beginning of this chapter, I mentioned Kerckhoffs' principle, which tells us that the security of the cryptographic system should not rely on hiding the implementation details. Another essential security principle says that the *security of the cryptographic system is only as strong as its weakest link*. This rule works for any cryptographic system, and cryptocurrency is no exception. Here is what it means when applied to crypto. Let's say your crypto uses the best encryption algorithm in the world, like elliptic curves used by Bitcoin. There are two potential weak areas where your crypto can fail, even if it's using fancy elliptic curves.

The first is the implementation of the algorithm itself. If the code is written from scratch just for the project, the odds are that this implementation is far away from being ideal and has bugs. In cryptography, even minor bugs mean cracked encryption, which in turn means the end of the world for the project. So, it is crucial, especially for a new crypto project written from scratch, to reuse some well-known, open source cryptographic library that was previously tested on multiple other projects.

Even in the case of a forked project (when you create new crypto by copying and branching another crypto project's open source code), it is still essential to ensure that the original project uses well-known cryptographic libraries and not reinventing the wheel. You cannot just rely on other project developers, even if the original project is famous and super successful.

Sometimes, cracking encryption takes time. It's possible that the cryptographic community and hackers simply do not pay attention when the project is still young. But once it becomes more popular, its valuation rises, and cracking its cryptographic code suddenly becomes a profitable business – for both "white hat" (good guys – cryptographers and security researchers) and "black hat" (criminals) hackers. White hats will just publish the results of their research to draw another "kill mark" on the side of their fighter jet,[12] while the black hats will try to monetize their victory by either blackmailing the project team or even crashing the crypto's market. In either case, there is no good outcome for the project.

Another important way of failure is using weak algorithms and implementations surrounding the main algorithm, even if it is very strong and proven. For example, the new crypto developers can use the same elliptic curves for digital signatures used by many other projects, which gives you some degree of insurance. But they suddenly decide to use some exotic hash function instead of the well-known SHA-256. So the digital signature can work just fine. Still, the hash, which is used to represent the transaction record uniquely, can be cracked because a forged transaction (the one that a hacker places instead of the original one created by the actual sender) produces the same hash (it is called *collusion*). The result can be disastrous.

---

[12] Bruce Herman. Painted Warbirds. www.pbs.org/wgbh/antiquesfyi/features/warbirds/index.html

You can say that this kind of detail is too deep to be important for an average crypto user, and only creators of new crypto projects must pay attention to them. This might be true unless your money is at stake, meaning that you are an investor. In this case, you should know about the project you are investing in as much as you can before putting your money into it! Try to find some professional third-party independent reviews or ask developers questions directly. If their implementation is correct, they will be willing to respond and will be OK to do it publicly.

What's Next?

In this chapter, I just scratched the surface of the cryptography domain. Still, this information should be sufficient for you if you are an investor, trader, or entrepreneur who wants to create your own crypto project. If you are a developer, you probably need a deeper understanding of cryptography, but it depends on your project. For example, if you are forking the code of existing, well-known crypto, you can decide to rely on its developers' work and that it was most probably already tested in the wild by white hats and black hats.

But if you decide to write your code from scratch, you need a higher level of cryptographic education. Fortunately, there are many books about cryptography. In fact, yours truly published a book called *Bitcoin for Nonmathematicians*, which I already referenced in the previous section. Among other things, it explains how cryptography works but still tries to use minimum math (thus the name of the book). I have described how both RSA and elliptic curves work, step by step, by providing the layman's instructions and reference implementation with source code in Python and C#.

By the way, RSA is never used in cryptocurrencies because of its large key sizes – yes, cryptocurrencies do care about the space. However, it is much easier to understand; that's why I described it first to show how public key encryption works. Honestly, a complete comprehension of the elliptic curves is not an easy task that requires concentration and some basic math knowledge. I must mention that some readers still complained about excessive math – I am sorry, that was the minimum necessary to understand those very complex algorithms!

You don't really need to fully understand the cryptography behind crypto if you are just a user or even a developer. After all, encapsulation is one of the best development principles, which means that implementations of complex things like elliptic curves can be used as a black box.

Modern programming is basically a series and hierarchy of such black boxes, starting from the CPU commands and going to the operating system code to application libraries. Developers just need to take the right bricks and put them in the proper order. No one knows the entire stack, and this would be impossible given the complexity of today's computers. Nevertheless, developers still need to know what features these black-box bricks provide and how they interact.

With that said, for some of you who want to take a deeper dive into the theoretical jungle, there are many books about cryptography, and some of them are referenced throughout this chapter. But for the rest of the audience, it's time to move forward to see how Bitcoin (and many other cryptos derived from it) actually works!

CHAPTER 2

How Bitcoin Works

In a way it is even humiliating to watch... miners working. It raises in you a momentary doubt about your status as an 'intellectual' and a superior person generally.

—George Orwell. *The Road to Wigan Pier*

The former Soviet Union used to be the largest country in the world, with its territory occupying about one-sixth of the entire Earth's land surface and controlling about half of Europe (all the modern Eastern European countries). As we can see today, most subjects of the "Evil Empire" were not joined voluntarily. Therefore, the communists also had to have the biggest army in the world to be able to watch over such a vast territory. So, they had a draft, a mandatory enrollment into the armed forces, when every young man (well, almost everyone) had to spend two or three years (depending on the military branch they were drafted into) at the most dangerous place you can even imagine.

Think of not seeing your family for years in severe weather conditions, often accompanied by hazing, hunger, abuse, and humiliation. Many people never came back; some returned disabled, physically or mentally. There were ways, however, to avoid the duty. The universities linked to the military had special courses that "replaced" the military service. Getting into such educational institutions was not easy – serious knowledge and grades were required. Most people who graduated from these universities

© Slava Gomzin 2022
S. Gomzin, *Crypto Basics*, https://doi.org/10.1007/978-1-4842-8321-9_2

eventually worked in research and development for the military-industrial complex in then prestigious areas like space, aviation, and navy. Many were selected to work for the KGB (the main Soviet security and intelligence service).

The communist regime, realizing the high risk of losing these elite people, was defending them from the service in its own army, which, by definition, was supposed to be the main protecting body of this very regime. It sounds like a paradox, but it's really not. The system was heavily flawed yet self-healing. In other words, it was smart enough to know how to safeguard itself from its own vulnerabilities!

The Bitcoin system is also self-healing and self-protecting in a way. It's not perfect as designing and implementing such a decentralized, distributed payment network, where participants don't know and don't trust each other without issues, is quite tricky. There is also a price for it: long confirmation times, low scalability, and high transaction fees. But what's most and more important is that the system knows to continuously adjust itself and always gets back on track when things go out of sync. Let's see how it works.

Problems Solved by Bitcoin

Bitcoin is the very first crypto, and most other cryptos are derivatives of Bitcoin (well, at the very least, of the idea of Bitcoin). Therefore, it's fair to say that you understand crypto if you understand how Bitcoin works. That's why we start to study crypto by learning Bitcoin design principles.

To understand Bitcoin, you need to learn about two main design principles (and associated mechanisms): blockchain and distributed consensus (a.k.a. proof-of-work, or PoW). These two principles are the mechanisms that solve two big problems of any payment system, either centralized or decentralized: the double-spending problem and the Byzantine Generals Problem (Table 2-1).

Table 2-1. *Problems Solved by Bitcoin*

Problem	What It Means	Solution
Double-spending problem	Unlike paper money, one can create an unlimited number of absolutely identical copies of the digital record. So how to prevent spending the same digital money twice?	In traditional banking: centralized database In crypto: a copy of transaction ledger (blockchain) is stored by each network node. But the majority of the nodes must reach a consensus on the right version of the blockchain (see Byzantine Generals Problem)
Byzantine Generals Problem	How to ensure consensus on a single source of truth between untrusted participants in decentralized distributed network?	Proof-of-work – a distributed consensus mechanism that requires participants to invest their computing and electric power to demonstrate their "loyalty" and provides incentives (rewards) to loyal participants ("miners")

Both problems have been previously solved for centralized payment systems such as banking, credit cards, or PayPal. They simply use their central database and server farm to maintain a single source of truth. But unlike centralized payment systems, decentralized ones do not have the luxury of central arbitrage (which is also their main advantage!). So Bitcoin was the first decentralized payment system that offered solutions to double-spending and consensus problems. We will be learning about Bitcoin by reviewing those problems and their solutions.

Double-Spending Problem

In the banking system, when you run a credit card transaction, for example, the authorization request message goes through multiple routers and gateways. Still, eventually, it comes to the bank server connected to the bank database, which contains up-to-date information about your credit card. The bank computer decides to authorize or decline your transaction based on this information. Without going into the details of implementation, the process is straightforward.

In a decentralized network like Bitcoin, the situation is very different. There is no central server or database, but there are thousands of Bitcoin nodes that don't know and don't trust each other. So if I have some Bitcoin, what prevents me from spending the same coins twice? I could, for example, create two transactions – one is a payment to a merchant for something I would like to buy, and another one is a transaction to my second wallet. This way, I could buy something and get my money back. That's precisely the double-spending problem. Bitcoin solves this problem through blockchain technology.

Distributed Peer-to-Peer Network

Although Bitcoin is often associated with blockchain as a synonym, and blockchain is probably the most important part, another necessary part supports blockchain – a network of bitcoin nodes or a distributed peer-to-peer network. Any computer in the world with an Internet connection can become a Bitcoin node and connect to the Bitcoin network.

That's the main difference and advantage of Bitcoin compared to traditional banking – not every person in the world, and I would even say very far away from every person, can become a bank customer – open a bank account and get a debit card. You must have at least documents confirming your identity, permanent address, citizenship, national insurance (like social security in the United States), and location in a particular jurisdiction – typically, within the borders of the state where the local subsidiary of the bank operates, even if it's an international bank (Table 2-2).

It's even more challenging to receive a credit card for many people. You must show some proof of a good job and credit history. And it is almost impossible for an average person to become an accredited investor to be able to invest in startups, hedge funds, and other attractive forms of equity. In the United States, for example, to become an accredited investor, you have to have a gross income exceeding $200,000 in each of the two most recent years or a net worth that exceeds $1,000,000! Becoming an investor in foreign markets can be even more difficult.

Table 2-2. *Prerequisites for Access to Different Payment and Financial Services*

	Bank Account	Credit Card	Accredited Investor Working with Broker	Online Brokers like E-Trade	Retail Investment Apps like Robinhood	Bitcoin
Identity (legal name that matched government ID)	Yes	Yes	Yes	Yes	Yes	No
Email	Yes	Yes	Yes	Yes	Yes	No
Phone	Yes	Yes	Yes	Yes	Yes	No
Permanent address	Yes	Yes	Yes	Yes	Yes	No

(continued)

Table 2-2. (*continued*)

	Bank Account	Credit Card	Accredited Investor Working with Broker	Online Brokers like E-Trade	Retail Investment Apps like Robinhood	Bitcoin
Residence in particular jurisdiction	Yes	Yes	Yes	Yes	Yes	No
National insurance (social security)	Yes	Yes	Yes	Yes	Yes	No
Job/income information	Yes	Yes	Yes	Yes	Yes	No
Good credit history	No	Yes	No	No	No	No
Income > $200K or $1M net worth	No	No	Yes	No	No	No

Of course, there are tricks and workarounds around these rules. For example, people without bank accounts can use preloaded (stored value) payment cards instead of debit and credit cards, but those cards have a lot of fees associated with them and are not as convenient as credit cards. People who do not qualify to become accredited investors can use crowdfunding to invest in startup projects. But you still need to be eligible with proof of identity, bank account or credit card, and other documentation.

Bitcoin does not have all these barriers. The only thing you have to have is some kind of device (desktop computer or mobile phone) and access to the Internet. You don't even have to run a bitcoin node to use bitcoin, as there are bitcoin wallets implemented as mobile apps. But it goes even further than that. You don't have to have a wallet or Internet connection just to store bitcoin – a piece of paper is what you need to write down the private key or mnemonic phrase that uniquely describes your wallet. It's called "cold storage," and we will discuss it in Chapter 8.

But there are advantages of running the node for many people and companies and even incentives for some people. The primary motivation is the ability to mine Bitcoin (although you can participate in mining without running a node). Another reason is security and privacy. Companies like crypto exchanges must run the nodes to ensure they have the up-to-date "snapshot" of the Bitcoin ledger to ensure the security of their users and themselves. Some users can also run a node independently from third-party hosting providers, ensuring maximum security and privacy of their transactions.

According to some monitoring tools, the number of active Bitcoin nodes currently fluctuates between 7,500 and 13,300.[1] In general, the more nodes participate in the network, the more secure Bitcoin is. At least, that is how the system was originally designed by Satoshi Nakamoto (whose identity we still don't know). However, we will see that this is not exactly true these days in later chapters while reviewing the details of the mining process.

Bitcoin node is just a piece of software running on a computer with Internet access, typically some kind of server, but it can be just a regular consumer-grade desktop or laptop. The difference between consumer-grade computers and server is that the latter normally has a more powerful and faster CPU (often multiple CPUs), more RAM (memory), and hard drive space. Servers are also typically located in a unique environment

---

[1] Bitnodes. https://bitnodes.io/dashboard/?days=365

such as a server room or data center, with high physical security, fast network circuits, and redundant power supplies that ensure uninterrupted service.

It's important to note that Bitcoin is a distributed and untrusted network, which means its nodes are not required to follow either of these conditions provided by enterprise-grade servers. Bitcoin was designed as a peer-to-peer network relying on simple computers and imperfect Internet. However, things have changed since the Bitcoin launch, and some network functions like mining and real-time transaction validation cannot be done without special equipment. But once again, I would like to say that the beauty of Bitcoin is that you can still run a full bitcoin node on your laptop!

How Bitcoin Blockchain Works

Since understanding the blockchain mechanism is probably one of the most fundamental insights about the entire crypto, let's try to study it in several stages, starting from the very basic example. To make it even simpler, we will also compare the blockchain with the traditional financial and payment systems side by side.

Cash and Bank Transactions

Let's assume our two old friends, Alice and Bob, want to exchange some assets they store in their homes. Their assets are gold bars. Alice has four gold bars, and Bob has one. Alice wants to share with Bob and send him two gold bars. Alice and Bob store their gold bars in boxes in their home safes, as shown in Figure 2-1.

Figure 2-1. *Alice's and Bob's gold bars stored at home*

To give gold bars to Bob, Alice takes two bars from her box and gives them to Bob, who puts them in his box. That's how *cash* works, and this relatively simple process of taking and putting is called a *transaction*. Figure 2-2 shows their boxes after their cash transaction is complete.

Figure 2-2. *Alice's and Bob's boxes after cash transaction*

I said that the transaction is a *relatively* simple process because there is nuance: the transaction is started when bars are removed from Alice's box but considered finished only after they are placed in Bob's box. In the real world, it's possible that the gold bars are taken from Alice's home safe but never make it into Bob's home safe. That's why people started using banks – to simplify and secure their transactions. The bank guarantees that the transaction is committed, that is, the bars eventually make it to the new owner. In many cases, the bars are even stored in the same bank safe (Figure 2-3). If something happens in the way and bars cannot make it to Bob's box, they will be automatically returned to Alice's box, that is, the transaction will be *rolled back*.

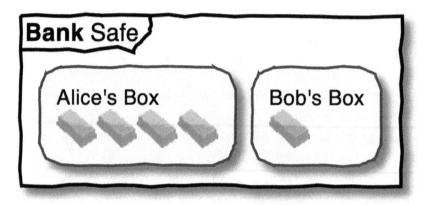

Figure 2-3. *Alice's and Bob's gold bars stored in a bank*

Blockchain vs. Bank Transaction Ledger

Now let's see how such a transaction would happen on the blockchain. Alice's and Bob's gold bars on the blockchain are also stored in different "virtual boxes," but unlike the bank, where each customer has all their bars in their own box, they may have multiple boxes on the blockchain, as shown in Figure 2-4. So, the boxes do not belong to any particular person, but each gold bar in every box is marked by the previous owner with a special label containing the new owner's address (just a name in our simplified example).

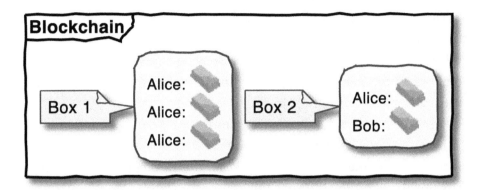

Figure 2-4. *Alice's and Bob's gold bars stored in a blockchain*

To give two bars to Bob, Alice takes one gold bar from one box (Box 1 in our example) and one bar from another box (Box 2), marks them as Bob's bars, and puts them into a newly created Box 3. Now Bob has three gold bars – one bar in Box 2 and two bars in Box 3. Alice has only two remaining bars in Box 1 (Figure 2-5).

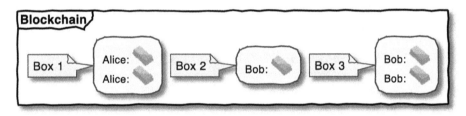

Figure 2-5. *Alice's and Bob's gold bars after blockchain transaction*

Now we can see the first and most obvious difference between the bank and blockchain systems. To get the current balance of a bank user, you just need to check the number of bars in the user box (user account). For the blockchain user, you need to check all the boxes (they are called blocks in the blockchain) and find and summarize all the gold bars belonging to the user.

Neither the bank nor blockchain, of course, would physically move gold bars between the boxes. The bank stores them in a single *vault*, and actual bank transactions used to be done on paper (*ledger*) until computers took over bank operations. The blockchain, however, stores its virtual gold bars in... blockchain.

I hope it's evident that the box is equivalent to a bank account in the bank example, while the gold bar means *dollar*. However, in the blockchain example, the basket is equivalent to the *block*. And guess what the gold bar equivalent is? Right, bitcoin!

In reality, of course, both banking and blockchain systems are more complex. Let's see how both transactions are recorded. From neither Figure 2-2 nor 2-5, we can tell how gold bars were moved between Alice and Bob as they only show the final state of their boxes. So here is another difference between a bank and a blockchain. The bank stores its transaction records and user balances in a centralized database, while Bitcoin stores everything in a decentralized database called a *blockchain*. In both cases, such a place is also called a *ledger*. For our bank transaction, the simplified bank ledger looks like a database record shown in Table 2-3.

Table 2-3. *Bank Transaction Ledger Table*

Sender	Recipient	Amount
Alice	Bob	2

The bank transaction, in addition to adding a new record to the transaction ledger table, also updates two records in another database table, as shown in Table 2-4.

Table 2-4. *Bank User Account Balance Table*

Account	Balance
Alice	2
Bob	3

Simplified Blockchain Transaction

Let's see how Bitcoin records the same transaction on the blockchain. I must admit that while the numbers in Figure 2-4 (the state of the blockchain before our transaction) are correct, I lied about the numbers in Figure 2-5 (the state of the blockchain after our transaction). But I dared to do so only to simplify the explanation because, otherwise, the example with boxes and gold bars wouldn't make sense as they belong to the physical world.

Now, when we are ready to replace boxes with blocks and gold bars with bitcoins, I can tell you that the number of bitcoins in Block 1 (Box 1) remains the same after the transaction is done (i.e., after the Box/Block 3 is created). It makes sense because, unlike bank boxes (account balance records), the blockchain boxes (blocks) can never be changed! The only thing we can do to process a new transaction is add a new block to the existing, unchangeable blockchain.

Then how can we change the user balance? There's only one possible answer: additional information is written to the transaction block that shows where exactly the "new" gold bars (bitcoins) are taken from. So the more realistic (but still not close to the actual ones) blocks before the transaction are shown in Figure 2-6.

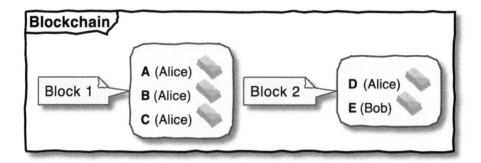

Figure 2-6. *Blockchain transaction outputs before the transaction*

Each capital letter A, B, C, D, E represents a single record associated with a gold bar (bitcoin). Such a record is called output. Each output is labeled with the name of its owner.

As I mentioned before, we can count Alice's and Bob's balances by scanning all the blocks and looking for the outputs that were not used yet in other transactions. So after Alice sent two bitcoins to Bob in Block 3, she only has two remaining unused outputs, C and D, because outputs A and B were used to send two bitcoins to Bob (Figure 2-7).

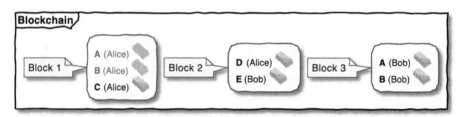

Figure 2-7. *Blockchain transaction outputs after the first transaction*

By counting all unused outputs (while disregarding the used ones A and B), we can get the Alice's new balance = C + D = 2, and Bob's balance = E + A + B = 3. Bob now has his previous output, E, which is still unused, plus new outputs A and B, which are the two bitcoins sent by Alice. I highlighted the *used* outputs in gray color to simplify the counting,

but Block 1 remains exactly the same in reality. We know that outputs A
and B in Block 1 are used only because they are recorded in new Block 3
and reassigned to Bob.

Is it starting to make sense? I am pretty sure it is! Let's move forward
quickly while you have it fresh. But hold on. That's how the Bitcoin
blockchain works! Everything else is technical details – for example, how to
prove that Block 3 was actually approved by Alice (and not forged by Bob)
and how to make sure that Alice cannot spend A and B several times and
send them to herself. But before we get into more details, let's make sure
you really got it.

Let's have Bob now send two bitcoins back to Alice! We are on the
blockchain, so what we need to do is just create a new block, of course. We
can take Bob's output E from Block 2 and output A from Block 3 and put
them into new Block 4, with the label saying that they now belong to Alice
(Figure 2-8).

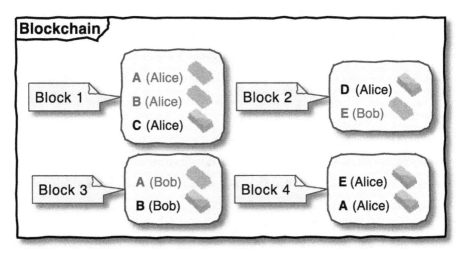

Figure 2-8. *Blockchain transaction outputs after the second*
transaction

Remember that output A, which originally used to belong to Alice? Now it comes back to her in new Block 4! Let's count unused outputs again to get the updated balances. The Alice's new balance is C + D + E + A = 4, and Bob's balance is B = 1.

Note that coin E now belongs to Alice, and therefore it's shown as grayed out in Block 2 in Figure 2-8. But before Block 4 was added to the blockchain, that same coin E belonged to Bob, as shown in Figure 2-7. This fact illustrates the fundamental feature of blockchain: *you must always look at the most recent blockchain copy to get the correct information about balances.* Therefore, if your node is offline, its knowledge about other wallets' balances is outdated.

Dealing with Fractions

Each output represents one bitcoin in our preceding blockchain examples (one gold bar in earlier examples). In reality, however, a single output can contain any amount (within a reasonable range, of course). Moreover, an output almost would never include the whole number of bitcoins. So how will blockchain process a transaction while constantly operating with just fractions of bitcoin? Let's ring another transaction where Alice sends 1.25 bitcoin to Bob to answer this question.

In previous examples, we assumed that each output equals one bitcoin. We will need to raise the level of details and upgrade the diagrams, however, to add a numeric value to each output. We will also introduce another transaction element, which we call *input*.

To send bitcoins to Bob, Alice would need to find unused outputs in previous blocks, mark them with the label saying that Bob is the new owner, and put them into the new block. But Alice does not have an output with a 1.25 value; she only has several outputs of one bitcoin each. Bitcoin resolves this issue by using multiple inputs and outputs in a single transaction and by the ability to send funds back to yourself as a "change."

Input means an unused output from one of the previous transactions. Every transaction has at least one input and one output. In the previous examples, I simplified it by using the same code for both input and output because the inputs and outputs were always equal (one bitcoin). In reality, however, transactions typically have multiple inputs and outputs with different amounts.

There are a couple of rules that regulate input/output processing. They are *hardcoded*, that is, enforced by Bitcoin node software. The first rule is that *the sum of all transaction inputs must be equal to the sum of all outputs* (that's why we can't spend more than we have!). The second rule is that *the same output cannot be used more than once as an input* (that's how double-spending prevention works!).

Going back to our new example – to send 1.25 bitcoin to Bob, Alice needs to find an unused output (or several unused outputs) with a total value equal to or greater than 1.25 bitcoin, use them as an input (or inputs) for the new transaction, and generate a new output of 1.25 bitcoin.

So, Alice takes unused outputs C and D, which gives her two bitcoins and uses them as inputs for a new transaction in Block 5. This transaction generates a new output F which equals 1.25 bitcoin and is labeled for Bob. The remaining balance of 0.25 bitcoin Alice sends to herself as a "change" in new output G (Figure 2-9).

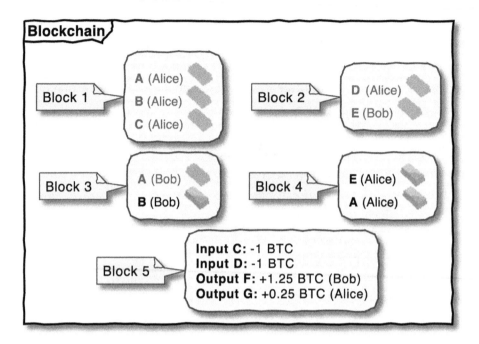

Figure 2-9. *Alice just sent 1.25 bitcoin to Bob*

Alice's new balance: E(1) + A(1) + G(0.25) = 2.25.

Bob's new balance: B(1) + F(1.25) = 2.25.

To simplify the diagram, Blocks 1–4 still only show the outputs, but note that the outputs C and D (Blocks 1 and 2), used as the inputs in a new transaction in Block 5, are grayed out. New Block 5 is shown in a "new format," which records inputs and outputs. Now we are one step closer to how the actual Bitcoin transaction is written into the blockchain.

Transaction Pool

Obviously, Alice or Bob cannot create blocks or generate new outputs – this is something Bitcoin software does for them. Let's see how it works. Alice and Bob use a client software called a *wallet*, which communicates with one of the Bitcoin network nodes we reviewed earlier. The wallet software creates transactions, looks for unused outputs of previous transactions, and generates new transaction outputs. Once this phase is done, the wallet sends a new transaction to the node it is connected to. The node runs some validations to ensure the transaction does not violate any rules (e.g., does not try to spend the same outputs twice). If validation is successful, the node puts the new transaction into the *transaction pool* and broadcasts it to other nodes, which run similar validations before accepting the new transaction. This way, the network prevents rogue nodes from adding invalid transactions.

Even though the Bitcoin network is distributed worldwide and contains thousands of nodes, this process is pretty fast – it typically takes just a fraction of a second to broadcast the transaction and put it into the transaction pool. But the fact that the transaction is validated and accepted by the majority of the nodes does not mean it is complete. To be considered committed, it must be added to a new block. Moreover, several more blocks should be added on top of that block before the transaction is fully confirmed. There is a reason for this long process. To understand it, we need to review the process of generating a new block to the blockchain, which is typically called *mining*.

The Byzantine Generals Problem

After we learned how transactions are recorded on the blockchain, which solves the double-spending problem, it's time to review another critical component of the blockchain tech – *distributed consensus*, which is also associated with mining. Distributed consensus solves the second big problem of decentralized payment systems – the *Byzantine Generals Problem*.[2]

---

[2] Leslie Lamport, Robert Shostak, Marshall Pease. The Byzantine Generals Problem. https://lamport.azurewebsites.net/pubs/byz.pdf

The legend says that several Byzantian armies stood around an enemy city in the siege. The landscape around the city was so difficult that the easiest way to communicate between the armies was by sending couriers through the enemy city. It was also the shortest and fastest path to reach out to most other troops.

In such a situation, the Byzantine generals commanding the armies needed to agree on when to attack the city. So they needed to send the message with the suggested date and time of the attack to each other and get confirmations from other armies. But since they were sending the messengers through the enemy city, they could not know for sure that the recipients received their messages and that the messages they received from other generals were not intercepted and alternated by the enemy. To storm the city, they had to use most of their power. Therefore, if they could not agree on the exact date and time of the attack, they would be defeated (Figure 2-10).

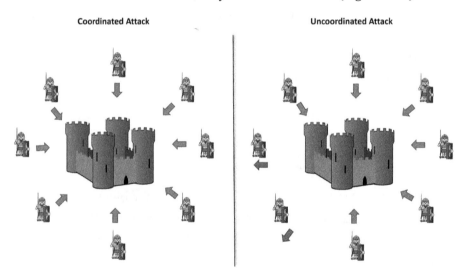

Figure 2-10. *Byzantian armies around the enemy city*

Decentralized payment systems are no exception; they face very similar problems. Bitcoin nodes can communicate with each other, but they do not trust each other. Yet they must agree on a single source of truth – the "right" version of the blockchain.

Proof-of-Work and Mining

The Bitcoin network ensures *Byzantine Fault Tolerance* by implementing a solution to the Byzantine Generals Problem called distributed consensus, or *proof-of-work* (PoW). Byzantine Fault Tolerance means that the network is functional if more than 50% of the participants are loyal. It means two things.

First, the Bitcoin payment system can be trusted even if up to 50% of the participants are rogue players (which is unlikely as the participants have incentives to be loyal). Second, a Bitcoin payment network can be successfully attacked by someone with computing power greater than 50% of the network (or greater than 100% of the loyal participants). This is also an unlikely situation for Bitcoin, given the current number of miners and their enormous total computing power.

The network nodes that actively participate in distributed consensus by employing the proof-of-work algorithm are called miners. I think it is symbolic that the process of creating a new Bitcoin, which is essentially creating new money, is called mining. With the invention of Bitcoin, apparently, we entered a new era of crypto money and thus a new meaning of the old deeds and jobs.

Mining carries two critical functions. First, it creates new bitcoins (hence the name of the process – mining, as the miners mine new bitcoins). Second, it ensures the decentralized nature of the network by providing an opportunity to create a new block for any participant (with enough compute power).

Generating a New Block

When we studied blockchain transactions in the previous section, I intentionally omitted another important detail – once again, to simplify the explanation process and make it gradual as it's pretty difficult to perceive all the blockchain tech concepts and details simultaneously. The fact is that a single Bitcoin block can contain more than one transaction. Moreover, since Bitcoin is very popular and people nowadays use it a lot, Bitcoin blocks always have multiple transactions. It takes about ten minutes on average to generate a new block, which contains most transactions waiting in line while sitting in the transaction pool.

The miner's responsibility is to collect transactions from the pool and compile them into a new block. Then, the miner needs to "solve" the block, that is, find the block hash value that would match the current *network difficulty*. This way, bitcoin ensures a gradual, continuous *emission*. I know there are too many new terms in just a few sentences, so let's rewind and find out what they mean and how they work together.

As I mentioned before, the transaction pool is just a logical area where new transactions are waiting to be picked up for actual processing, which in blockchain means to be added to the new block. The pool is synchronized between multiple Bitcoin nodes.

When a user adds a new transaction to a node, the node validates it to make sure it is formatted properly and doesn't violate the rules, adds it to its local transaction pool, and broadcasts it to several other nodes it's linked to. Those nodes, in turn, also validate, add to their local pool, and broadcast to their "neighbored" nodes – this way, the new transaction is broadcast throughout the entire network of active nodes very fast.

The next step is taking transactions from the pool and generating a new block. This process is called mining, and only a handful of nodes do this (they are called miners). At the very beginning of the Bitcoin network, any node could mine a block (that was the intention). Nowadays, every node can still do it theoretically, but it would be impossible for most of them in practice. The reason is the process of mining which requires a lot of computations that just a single CPU cannot do. Let's see why it is designed this way.

Solving the Block

The miners, who are the owners of the nodes connected through the Internet in a single Bitcoin network, compete with each other trying to "solve" the next block. Here is what the process of solving the block looks like. Each block has a hash associated with it (we learned about hash functions in the previous chapter about cryptography). The hash is calculated using the block header as an input. The block header contains several parameters, such as the previous block's hash (to maintain the blockchain) and the Merkle root of transactions (Table 2-5). The Merkle tree is used to save the computational resources of miners and validating nodes (you learned about it in the previous chapter).

Table 2-5. *Bitcoin Block Header*

Field	Function	Notes
Version	Block Version Number	
Hash of previous block	Hash of the previous block in the blockchain	This is the core of blockchain – that's how the blocks are chained
Time	Current time (block timestamp)	
Network difficulty	Current network target in compact format	Periodically adjusted depending on hash rate (collective computing power of all miners) to ensure an average ten-minute interval between the blocks
Nonce	A number incremented by the miner with each attempt to solve the block	This is how the miner changes the block hash with each iteration while trying to find the hash that is less than the difficulty target

Each block can contain many transactions, and each transaction is hashed. So instead of taking all the transaction hashes as an input of the block hash every time the miner recalculates it, they calculate the Merkle tree once for all transactions and put its value in the header. Now, for validators, it's easy to validate a single transaction – instead of calculating all transaction hashes every time, they only compute a few hashes within the Merkle tree to make sure the particular transaction hash is valid.

Going back to the proof-of-work. The block header also contains *difficulty*, the compact, an encoded version of the *target*, which is the big number that defines how difficult it is to solve the block, that is, how many times the miners need to try to solve it. Another parameter in the block header is called *nonce* – this is the number incremented with each new attempt to *solve* the block. Nonce stands for "number only used once" because it's only used to calculate the hash that matches the target. Otherwise, it's useless. Now let's put all this together.

I am always laughing when I hear a description of the mining process in mass media, something like "solving a very complex mathematical problem" … This is not true! The problem miners are solving is extremely simple – they just try different random numbers in an attempt to match the magic target number, similar to buying and checking numerous lottery tickets to find the winning one. It's simply taking a lot of attempts to guess, which requires a lot of computational power to speed up the process and finish it ahead of competitors.

If you look at any Bitcoin block, you can notice that the block hash has many leading zeros (Figure 2-11). This is not a coincidence. These zeros demonstrate the exact "mathematical problem" that miners are trying to solve. The fact is that the target hash looks like a block hash – it has several leading zeros, like this one: 000000000019d6689c085ae165831e934ff763ae46a2a6c172b3f1b60a8ce26f.

Hash	0000000000000000000201b71233a91239f2800172ea03c0c288d55f03d74c10 🖹
Confirmations	1
Timestamp	2021-09-30 17:26
Height	702937
Miner	ViaBTC
Number of Transactions	1,367
Difficulty	18,997,641,161,758.95
Merkle root	daff0657bcbf31b5d341bd3a4be29c358eec7a542b6230d1f1f3c1e9c95b0f03
Version	0x20600004
Bits	386,846,955
Weight	3,993,494 WU
Size	2,003,492 bytes
Nonce	1,638,802,704
Transaction Volume	3022.02512406 BTC
Block Reward	6.25000000 BTC
Fee Reward	0.04560935 BTC

Figure 2-11. *Bitcoin block 702937. Source: blockchain.com*

The smaller the target number, the more leading zeros it contains, and the more difficult it is to find the hash that would be equal to or less than the target. That's it! That's the problem the miners solve! Every time the miner calculates the block hash trying a new nonce, it compares the resulting hash with the target. If the new block hash value is equal to or less than the target – bingo! The block is solved and can be sent ("broadcast") to the other nodes in the network. The nodes validate the new block and must accept it as a new block in the blockchain if it is valid. Suppose the value of the hash is greater than the target. In that case, the miner tries again by incrementing the nonce value, which "randomly" changes the value of the resulting hash, and repeats this process until they either solve the block or receive the solved block from someone else who was luckier this time.

The network protocol periodically updates the difficulty value to ensure that the average time to solve a new block remains around ten minutes. This way, the network adjusts itself to the constantly changing number of miners. The more miners participate, the higher the difficulty (which means the lower the target number because the lower target value makes finding more difficult).

Temporary Forks and Confirmations

Now, when you know how blockchain and proof-of-work work, you basically understand how Bitcoin works. However, there is at least one important remaining question. What happens if more than one miner solves the block? Which block becomes the permanent part of the blockchain, and how do the nodes know which one is the right one? Here is how it works.

Multiple miners can indeed solve a new block simultaneously, but only one block can be selected as the next block in the blockchain. When such a situation happens, it creates a condition called a temporary fork (Figure 2-12).

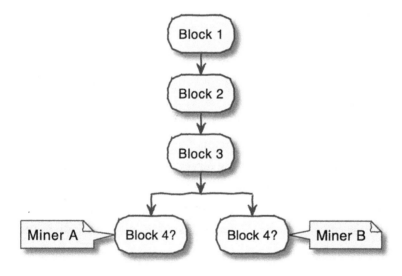

Figure 2-12. *Temporary fork*

The nodes keep track of alternative blockchains created by the temporary fork. Eventually, the longest chain "wins." If there are two parallel chains, the miner, when it solves the next block, must select one of them as the main chain to start solving the next block (remember, there is a previous block hash in the block header, which points to the previous block in the "main" chain). So once one of the miners solves another block, it is added to the "main" chain, making any alternative chains shorter (Figure 2-13).

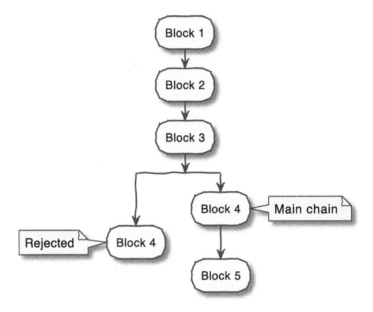

Figure 2-13. *Temporary fork rejected*

The nodes are programmed so that they must automatically accept the longer chain as the main chain. This process also explains that you typically need to wait for several "confirmations" to ensure a particular transaction is fully approved. When your wallet sends a new transaction to the network, it's not considered completed immediately. You need to wait until at least a "first confirmation," which means the transaction is included in one of the new blocks solved by the miners. In large, established networks like Bitcoin, first confirmation is usually enough these days to approve transactions. In some cases, it can happen even earlier (we will review this process with more details in one of the following chapters about crypto payments). However, suppose the transaction amount is large (in other words, the risk of losing funds is significant). In that case, it is customary to wait until four or even six confirmations, which means that there are four or six blocks added on top of the main chain that contains your transaction. In this case, the risk of someone alternating the chain (generating a new chain of several blocks that does not contain your transaction) is almost zero. Note that this is true only for large networks like Bitcoin, with a very high *hash rate* (an overall computing power used to mine the blocks).

A very high hash rate ensures that there is no single miner that can overturn the network. On the other hand, small crypto with a low hash rate is very vulnerable, so you better wait for dozens or even hundreds of confirmations to ensure the main blockchain is stable enough. It cannot be overturned by a rogue miner (we will review this type of attack in a chapter about security).

Mining Rewards

We are getting close to the finish of this chapter. Let's review the miner rewards and how they are earned. The miner reward is generated by a *coinbase* transaction, which is included as a first transaction in the new block generated by the miner. This transaction essentially creates money out of thin air and sends it to the miner's wallet. This is a powerful mechanism to incentivize miners (they pay a lot for their electricity bills!) and ensure continuous, smooth emission.

The rewards are halved (reduced by 50%) periodically – every 210,000 blocks, or about four years – to ensure the finite Bitcoin supply. The emission would never stop without halving, making the Bitcoin supply infinite. Currently, miners receive 6.25 BTC for a new block, which means 6.25 new bitcoins are mined every ten minutes on average. The next halving will occur in the spring of 2024, and the new reward will be reduced to 3.125 BTC.

At the time of this writing, the price fluctuates around $30,000 per one bitcoin, which means that the miner's reward for a new block is around $187,500. This is pretty good money, even after hardware and electricity expenses. But please don't rush to download bitcoin mining software (although it is still free to download, install, and run). You won't be able to mine anything even with a very powerful computer. Yes, the first bitcoins were mined on simple desktop computers with regular CPUs, but it was possible because the number of miners was small, so the network difficulty was low.

These days, it's not even possible to mine Bitcoin with GPU (graphics processing units), which are more powerful than CPU when calculating hash values. The only way to mine Bitcoin today is using ASIC, or application-specific integrated circuit, a chip designed for a single specific purpose – Bitcoin mining. Modern miners use large farms of ASIC devices, which consume a lot of electric power. Bitcoin mining became a unique business niche. It is still open to anyone to join, but you must invest significant money into the hardware, space, and electricity before starting to get revenues.

Bitcoin mining today is not a very democratic and "green" process, which creates many discussions about the future of Bitcoin since there are newer cryptocurrencies that use less power-consuming consensus mechanisms. But at least it ensures the ultimate stability of the Bitcoin payment system, which is not dependent on any single individual, group, government, or region. In the next chapter, we will review alternative crypto technologies, which provide similar characteristics while making the mining process more accessible and "green."

Wallets and Addresses

Let me say a few words about Bitcoin wallets and addresses. We will review the crypto wallets in Chapter 8, but I just want to show you how the Bitcoin addresses are created (using cryptography, which we reviewed in the previous chapter). It's always better to see than to hear, so I recommend you to check out this link which shows how the Bitcoin wallet address is being generated from a *passphrase*.[3]

You can put any passphrase there, and the page will instantly generate the private key and the public address of your Bitcoin wallet! For example, if you enter our favorite `Hello, World!` as the passphrase, it will generate the following private key: `L4j7n8oe3Qr3PcUCVBpqbKDuVdBJHE8ZFGpj4uDNHqHhsN2C44dN` and the following wallet address: `1B6mBn728dVNj3jEo5aKpUkSmXuMHCTD1S`

If you have never used a Bitcoin wallet before, you already have questions about those keys. Or even if you used a Bitcoin wallet, you might have never seen the private key. So why do these keys look like this, and what is their function?

In the previous chapter about cryptography, we learned about public key encryption, elliptic curves, and hash functions. This is how exactly those cryptographic techniques are applied in practice to generate a Bitcoin wallet.

The tools we used to generate the keys will also show you how various cryptographic functions are applied to the initial private key to transform it into the wallet address. Without diving into the details, I just want you to notice that the wallet address is not simply a public key but its obfuscated and shortened version. Whenever you wish to receive bitcoins, you share your wallet address. Your wallet app will use your private key whenever you want to send bitcoins. Don't forget that you should never share

---

[3] Graphical Address Generator. The Royal Fork – A blog about Bitcoin. http://royalforkblog.github.io/2014/08/11/graphical-address-generator/

your private key with anyone! Always store it (or your passphrase) in a secure place!

When you decide to create a new Bitcoin wallet, first, you need to generate the *seed* – a set of words that can be (theoretically) memorized by a human or at least written down on a piece of paper and stored in a secure location (like a bank deposit safe). The seed is also called a *passphrase* or *mnemonic phrase*. In our preceding example, we used the phrase `Hello, World!`, so as you can see, any combination of letters can be used as a seed. Wallets typically use the BIP39 standard, which randomly generates 12 English words. You can experiment with a seed generator using one of the simple online tools.[4] The mnemonic phrase looks like this:

```
patch stand scheme clever emotion mimic
skate mail reward behind tilt charge
```

Security Note   These online tools should be used for learning purposes only. Always use your wallet to generate the seed and the keys. Never use online tools to generate the keys for your wallet! These pages can be monitored by someone who can record the keys and get access to your wallet.

Twelve words are enough to generate a secure pair of public and private keys, and compared to the private key, it is much easier to memorize or write it down on paper. Typically, you don't even see the private and public keys in the wallet. The private key is "hidden" by the wallet user interface, and when you back up the wallet, you are prompted to save the mnemonic phrase. The public key goes through some modifications using SHA-256 and RIPEMD160 hash functions before it is transformed to its shorter version, called the *wallet address*.

---

[4] Mnemonic Code Converter. https://iancoleman.io/bip39/

To make the functions of the mnemonic seed, private key, public key, and address clearer, let's compare the bank account with the Bitcoin wallet (Table 2-6).

Table 2-6. *Comparing Bank Account and Bitcoin Wallet*

Bank Account	Bitcoin Wallet	Description	Visibility
Account number and routing number	Wallet address	Used by others to send funds to you	Public
Account number/ username and password	Public key/private key and wallet password	Used by you to send funds to others	Public/ private
Combination of full name, SSN, DOB, photo ID, email address	Mnemonic seed phrase	Used by bank/wallet to create account/ wallet and/or restore access to your funds	Private

You can see some similarities. There are public and private data elements that are used to transfer funds from and to your account/wallet and restore access to your funds. The bitcoin wallet address is similar to the account number and routing number of your bank account. You can give it to anyone who wants to send you money. But if you're going to send money to someone, you need to access your bank account online with a username and password. You just need to open your wallet app, which is usually protected by a local password to send Bitcoin. The app will use the previously stored pair of keys to create and digitally sign Bitcoin transactions and send it to the network.

When it comes to restoring your access, if you, for example, lost your bank account username and password, or your computer with Bitcoin wallet was stolen, you need a different set of data. For a bank account, you will need to call customer support and provide information about your identity. The downside is that the bank will store your identity information, making it vulnerable to identity theft. On the contrary, the Bitcoin network does not hold the mnemonic phrase or any other information about your identity. Therefore, any customer support would be impossible (welcome to a decentralized world!), and you must take care to keep your mnemonic phrase safe to restore the wallet. If you have lost your mnemonic phrase, your bitcoins are gone forever! So, carefully store your mnemonic phrase as the first thing you do right after creating a new Bitcoin wallet.

What's Next?

There is much more to say about Bitcoin wallets and addresses. For example, multisig wallets allow adding multiple co-owners to the same wallet. Also, there is an option to generate multiple, unique addresses in a single wallet – a new address for each transaction. We will learn about these features in Chapters 5 and 8 while reviewing privacy and wallets' functionality.

That's it; enough about Bitcoin; let's move to the next chapter to learn about other cryptos!

CHAPTER 3

How Other Cryptos Work

There are no rules of architecture for a castle in the clouds.

—G.K. Chesterton

Remember the old saying, "Time is money"? Assuming a clock is a decent representation of time in motion, and a payment system is a way to move money, what is common between a clock and a payment system? The first things that come to my head are consistency and predictability. As much as you expect a particular behavior from your clock – displaying the precise time as long as it has a mechanical or battery power – you also anticipate very specific, preprogrammed conduct from your payment system (as long as it has money injected into it). The most important point is that they both must not err!

Traditional money transfer systems such as SWIFT (Society for Worldwide Interbank Financial Telecommunication) or Visa had enough time and funding to be gradually enhanced and meticulously fine-tuned to very low risk of significant failures. But the new payment systems such as Bitcoin are still a Wild West, especially when it comes to exotic altcoins. Moreover, crypto does not have the luxury of traditional payment systems: they are not centralized, so, theoretically, no one (at least no single entity) is monitoring or maintaining them.

© Slava Gomzin 2022
S. Gomzin, *Crypto Basics*, https://doi.org/10.1007/978-1-4842-8321-9_3

In practice, however, no system can exist and wildly succeed without someone in charge, so radical proponents of decentralization actually lie when they say that no one controls Bitcoin or other cryptos. There are development teams, typically with a financial incentive in the form of a significant stake, in charge of each functioning crypto. Speaking of Bitcoin specifically, there are also miners who watch the developers. And finally, there are communities of investors and traders who keep an eye on both groups. This flimsy looking but, as practice shows, a rather tenacious mechanism of checks and balances works quite well so far.

So why are there so many other cryptos (often called *altcoins* – from alternative coins because they are created as an alternative to Bitcoin), and why are they being created literally every day? There is more than a single answer to this question, as different cryptos were created based on different motivations.

First of all, don't forget that every new crypto is a fundraising opportunity, allowing entrepreneurs to implement their great ideas. And there are two classes of the ideas behind altcoins: "improving the world" (let's call this class *token platforms*) and "improving Bitcoin," which we'll simply call *coins*. The former also often include the latter as they mean to achieve the primary goal. The best example of the "improving the world" group is *Ethereum (ETH)* which offers a concept of the world's decentralized supercomputer. *Monero (XMR)* is a bold example of the second group as it "fixes" Bitcoin flaws related to security and privacy (I have a whole chapter dedicated to Monero later in this book).

Speaking of crypto classification, we must not forget that there is a third, perhaps even bigger, class of crypto: *tokens*. This class piggybacks on token platforms because, unlike token platforms and coins, tokens don't have their own blockchain, drastically reducing the cost and effort associated with their creation and management.

Table 3-1 summarizes some features of the three classes of crypto and lists the examples of each one, so you can better understand the differences.

Table 3-1. *Crypto Classification*

Class	Has Own Blockchain?	Main Feature	Examples
Coin	Yes	Single-purpose cryptocurrency	Bitcoin (BTC) Monero (XMR) Litecoin (LTC) Nano (XNO) GRAFT (GRFT)
Token platform	Yes	Provides the ability to create multiple tokens. Any platform is also a coin	Ethereum (ETH) Solana (SOL) NEM (XEM) Waves (WAVES) Lyra (LYR)
Token	No	Depends on one of the token platforms	Tether (USDT) Chainlink (LINK) USD Coin (USDC) Uniswap (UNI)

Since tokens are based on someone else's blockchain, they are by themselves of no interest from a technological point of view. However, tokens have a tremendous economic value which we will review later. While the platforms sound like the most exciting type of innovation, I would instead focus on the seemingly more modest class of coins. First, because all platforms are coins, after all. Second, we can learn more about the advantages and disadvantages of the original Bitcoin design and how the crypto technology evolved after multiple attempts to fix them.

So, what are the flaws of bitcoin that various altcoins are trying to repair? Unfortunately, there are many. I never tire of repeating that bitcoin is an ingenious invention. But as with every technological innovation, it is not ideal. Remember that Bitcoin is both money and a payment system, like an old ad for "shampoo and conditioner in one," which is both good and bad at the same time because complexity has its price. Another important point is that Bitcoin was created as Internet money (and a payment system accordingly). It is pretty good as such, but not as good outside of the Internet, that is, offline, in the traditional main street world of brick-and-mortar businesses.

And finally, Bitcoin is a fully decentralized system (at least in theory), which means it does not belong to any individual, a group of individuals, a corporation, a national government, or any other organization. But all these extraordinary advantages have a dark side. Table 3-2 helps visualize dependencies between Bitcoin advantages and flaws.

Table 3-2. *Bitcoin Advantages vs. Flaws*

Bitcoin Advantages	Bitcoin Flaws
Decentralization and independence from governments and corporations	Low scalability – cannot compete in transaction volume with payment cards Long transaction processing time (full confirmation time)
Money and payment system in one	Big fluctuations of price
"Native" Internet money	Impossible to process payment offline
Anonymous accounts (wallets) and transactions	Pseudo privacy – the blockchain is public and all transactions can be traced

As you can see, the impressive list of advantages puts Bitcoin into the niche of next-generation payment systems. But it's not surprising that thousands of altcoins have been created in an attempt to enhance Bitcoin technology and fix its flaws that prevent mass adoption by the mainstream.

Perhaps one of the first attempts to enhance bitcoin followed soon after Bitcoin's creation. Litecoin (LTC) blockchain was launched in 2011 by Charlie Lee, two years and nine months after the Bitcoin launch. Litecoin was a *fork* of Bitcoin with a couple of deviations from the original

Bitcoin design (*fork* means that the source code of one crypto is copied from another). One of them was the block generation interval which is four times shorter (2.5 minutes) compared to Bitcoin (10 minutes), which means that, theoretically, Litecoin was four times "faster" than Bitcoin, which probably was a kind of significant breakthrough back then.

Another Litecoin "innovation" was a different hash algorithm used by its proof-of-work mechanism. *Scrypt*, as it was named by its creator Colin Percival, used more memory, making it more challenging to create specialized mining hardware. In addition, the circulating supply was four times bigger than the Bitcoin one (84M vs. 21M).

Even without going deeply into the technical details, I guess you can see the trend discovered by Litecoin and essentially became pandora's box for thousands of developers and entrepreneurs. The simplified formula of the trend: fork and go. Take the existing project (all open source!); tweak some code parameters such as block interval, hash algorithm, and maximum circulating supply; and here you go – the new cryptocurrency is born!

Many projects are still being created by forking, and we will talk about them in one of the following chapters. Many developers, however, went much further as they were not completely dissatisfied with Bitcoin's limitations. They went in multiple directions by creating new platforms or enhancing the blockchain tech and protocols and algorithms around it. Another significant trend was creating new consensus principles, which replaced the original Bitcoin's proof-of-work. There was a new wave of cryptos that declared proof-of-work inefficient and introduced new mechanisms such as *proof of stake (PoS)*, *delegated proof of stake (DPoS)*, and even more different proof-of-"something" models. In addition, there are even more radical design changes in the very core of the crypto tech – blockchain architecture. I talk about things like the *directed acyclic graph* (DAG) and *block lattice*. Not to mention perks like *DeFi* (decentralized finance) and NFT (non-fungible token). All these developments I just listed earlier deserve our attention, but let's look at least at some of them in greater detail.

Proof of Stake

Right after its launch, Bitcoin could be mined on a regular desktop or laptop computer. That was the original vision of the Bitcoin designers: everyone can participate and contribute to the network by validating transactions and mining new coins. But the rising popularity eventually played a cruel joke on Bitcoin: mining on a regular CPU became impossible. Miners started using GPU (graphics processing unit) in the form of gaming video cards and ASIC (application-specific integrated circuit), which is a piece of hardware especially crafted for mining.

Bitcoin mining grew from hobby to business. The proponents of total decentralization say this contradicts the original mission of crypto. Fortunately, inventors and developers didn't sleep and designed a new consensus mechanism called *proof of stake*. The first PoS coin, called Peercoin (PPC), was launched in 2012.[1] Since then, there have been several successful implementations of PoS created, such as Cardano (ADA), Solana (SOL), and Polkadot (DOT).

In PoS, the transaction validation is performed by miners who prove their loyalty to the network by demonstrating that they hold a significant amount (*stake*) of coins. The primary assumption behind it is that if you have a lot of coins, you are motivated to support the network's security and behave as a good player. There is no reason to break the network and do any harm to other participants. There is also a good "by-product" of PoS: energy savings. PoW requires a lot of power to mine the block. PoS does not need such excessive power as the money itself fuels it, and thus PoS coins are "green" compared to their PoW sisters.

Of course, critics of PoS say that it is less secure, more centralized, and prioritizes rich players by giving them significant control over the coin in exchange for their money (rather than the "work" required by PoW).

---

[1] Peercoin. https://coinmarketcap.com/currencies/peercoin/

Although some of these claims are questionable, they are not unfounded and perhaps not devoid of a grain of truth. As usual, I think the truth is somewhere in the middle.

Table 3-3 compares PoW and PoS and shows their advantages and disadvantages.

Table 3-3. *Proof of Stake vs. Proof-of-Work*

	PoW	PoS
Energy savings	Lower	Higher
Security	Higher	Lower
Speed and scalability	Lower	Higher
Accessibility	Higher	Lower
Decentralization	Higher	Lower

Delegated Proof of Stake

Delegated proof of stake, or DPoS, is a further development of PoS. Unlike PoS coins, DPoS coins do not require the stakeholders to validate transactions by themselves but allow them to delegate their voting power to the actual validators. By separating duties between stakeholders and validators, DPoS makes the validation process more accessible, that is, more democratic and less centralized. Virtually anyone can participate in DPoS by voting with their wallets. DPoS stakeholders don't have to be the tech-savvies and run the validation nodes. All they need is to acquire some number of coins and delegate their votes to the validators who do the actual work (run the validator nodes).

Examples of DPoS coins are Tron (TRX), EOS (EOS), and Tezos (XTZ). DPoS is an evolution of PoS; it enhances some PoS features, making it even more efficient than PoW. Table 3-4 compares PoS and DPoS, showing their pros and cons.

Table 3-4. *Proof of Stake vs. Delegated Proof of Stake*

	PoS	DPoS
Security	Lower	Higher
Speed and scalability	Lower	Higher
Accessibility	Lower	Higher
Decentralization	Lower	Higher

Block Lattice

Most coins based on either PoW or PoS (DPoS included) consensus mechanisms use the same type of blockchain initially outlined in the Bitcoin white paper. However, attempts were made to enhance the conventional blockchain design and create a different kind of distributed transaction ledger to "fix" the issues that alternative consensus algorithms could not patch. Block lattice is one of these novel approaches to the distributed transaction ledger design. It is based on a mathematical concept called *directed acyclic graph* (DAG). Without going deeply into the DAG theory (you can easily google it if you want), I must only say that it replaced the original concept of the transaction block, which is defined in traditional blockchain design as a set of transactions. In DAG cryptosystems, each individual transaction typically equals a block. Transactions are still linked to each other using digital signatures (otherwise, it would be impossible to validate), however, in a different way that allows *parallel processing*, enabling enormous scalability and confirmation speed.

There are a few coins based on the DAG concept. One of the most well known is probably IOTA (MIOTA), but I would like to focus on Nano (XNO), whose own interpretation of DAG is called block lattice. Nano and its block lattice are creations of Colin LeMahieu, who launched Nano in 2015. I think block lattice is the most significant and revolutionary invention in crypto after the Bitcoin protocol itself and the privacy CryptoNote protocol (used by Monero) because it opens pandora's box of features that are not achievable with traditional blockchain design. In addition to parallel processing, which enables instant transaction approval and high scalability (the number of transactions that can be processed simultaneously by the crypto network), block lattice enables unique features such as offline transaction processing and wallets that can run on smart cards. I think it's really worth learning in greater detail how block lattice works.

How Block Lattice Works

Block lattice uses the same core cryptographic principles of classic blockchain – transactions are linked to each other using digital signatures, creating a chain that makes them verifiable by the validators and observers. This is a significant difference, however. Unlike blockchain, block lattice links transactions directly, without packaging them into blocks. The word *block* is still in use, but one block contains one transaction, or, more precisely, one half of a transaction. That's another exciting feature of block lattice, which is also the reason to keep the word *block* rather than using the word *transaction* directly.

Each transaction is divided into two parts and represented by a pair of blocks. The first part, called *send block*, is generated by the sender, while the second part, called *receive block*, is initiated by the recipient. But why does block lattice decouple the *send* and *receive* portions of transactions, presumably doubling the size of its ledger? Before answering this question, let's review another exciting feature of block lattice.

Unlike the monolithic structure of traditional blockchain, where blocks are linked to each other, creating a single chain (Figure 3-1), block lattice consists of multiple accounts. Each user account has its own associated blockchain (Figure 3-2).

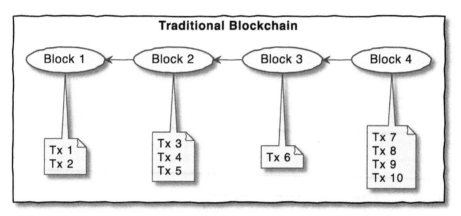

Figure 3-1. *Traditional blockchain*

Note that besides usual links to the previous blocks, the blocks are also linked between the accounts with dotted lines – we will see why shortly.

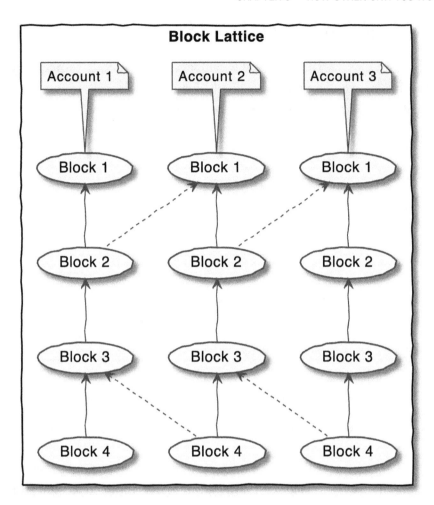

Figure 3-2. *Block lattice*

Now, the word *account* is more appropriate in the case of block lattice than *wallet* because wallet gets a slightly different meaning as a collection of accounts. Each account has an address and the private key associated with it. So only the account owner can write (add blocks) into the account. But every network participant can read all the accounts to be able to validate transactions and prevent double-spending. Now let's see how a simple funds transfer transaction is recorded in a block lattice.

71

How Coins Are Transferred in Block Lattice

Let's say we have two users, A and B, with accounts A and B, respectively. User A has nine coins, while user B only owns two coins, assuming both users previously received these coins from some account X. Those previous receptions are recorded as "*receive*" blocks An and Bn and their initial balances (Figure 3-3).

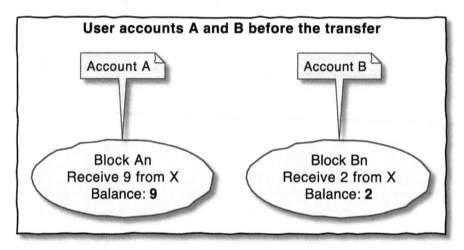

Figure 3-3. *User accounts A and B before the transfer*

Let's say user A wants to send three coins to user B. To do that, user A generates a new "*send*" block A1 and adds it to the "mini blockchain" that represents its account A. Note that the new block contains the information about the new balance of account A after the transfer, which is calculated as 9 – 3 = 6 coins (Figure 3-4).

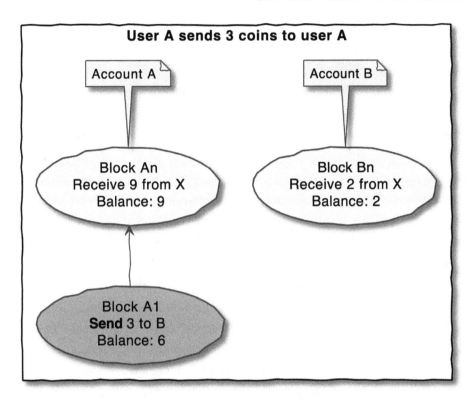

Figure 3-4. User A sends three coins to user B

This is another excellent feature of block lattice: each block of the account contains the account balance, that is, the last block of the account's blockchain always includes the current account balance! It means that a single block is sufficient to provide the most recent information about the state of the user account. In other words, there is no need to scan the entire block lattice and not even the whole account to calculate the available funds (unless you validate the transaction), which in turn enables two unique features.

First, the account (and the entire block lattice) can be *pruned* at some point, reducing the overall size of the ledger. Second, the information about accounts (the latest blocks) can be stored in microdevices, and transfers can be initiated offline. Think about a crypto payment card implemented as a wallet on a smart card, which looks (and behaves) like a traditional plastic payment card but works directly through the crypto network, without the man in the middle!

Now let's go back to our transaction and finish it. As soon as the "*send*" block A1 is validated by the network, the transaction is considered irreversible and completed from the sender (user A) point of view, even though the transfer still did not reach the recipient (user B). Yes, transactions still need to be broadcast to the network as in a traditional blockchain network and validated by the network nodes. However, there is a significant difference: the sender adds this new transaction block to their account chain by themselves instead of waiting for miners to do so. This way, a huge number of transactions can be not only validated but also settled (fully confirmed) simultaneously and almost instantly!

To receive the funds sent by user A and be able to spend them, the recipient (user B) has to generate a new "*receive*" block B1 and add it to their account B. Similar to A1, the new block contains the new balance of the account that includes the received funds and is calculated as $2 + 3 = 5$. Block B1 is linked to two blocks: the previous block of account B (block Bn) and the "*send*" block A1 (Figure 3-5). Such a link creates a structure that resembles a *lattice* rather than a chain *(previously illustrated in Figure 3-2)*, thus the name *block lattice*.

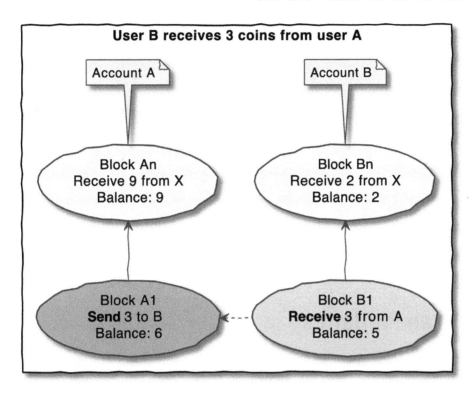

Figure 3-5. *User B receives three coins from user A*

The fact that account blockchains are independent of each other while still linked enough to ensure the validity of the overall ledger is a genius breakthrough in blockchain technology that enables *parallel processing* of transactions. It means that multiple users can simultaneously generate and send many transactions to the network. Those transactions can be validated and, most importantly, settled simultaneously, without waiting for each other. This creates conditions for **real-time, almost instant transaction authorization** and high network throughput (scalability), that is, the **ability to process many *transactions per second (tps)***. Both features are absolutely required for mainstream payment processing. Therefore, **cryptocurrencies based on block lattice can easily compete with traditional plastic card payments without the man in the middle – a centralized payment processor**.

Table 3-5 summarizes the block lattice features compared to traditional blockchain.

Table 3-5. *Blockchain vs. Block Lattice*

	Blockchain	**Block Lattice**
Scalability (tps)	Low	High
Transaction approval (confirmation) speed	Low	High
Ability to process offline transactions	No	Yes
Ability to prune the ledger	Limited	Yes
Offline transfers and wallet on microdevice (smart card)	No	Yes

Token Platforms

Finally, let's talk about token platforms. First, crypto Bitcoin provides a minimum set of features required to implement both Internet money and the payment system. But right after its launch, inventors around the world were inspired by Bitcoin's success and started working on more sophisticated applications of blockchain technology. The most well-known and successful platform to date is Ethereum, created by Vitalik Buterin in 2013. Ethereum was designed as a distributed computer that can execute distributed apps such as smart contracts.

At first glance, Ethereum has the main design similar to Bitcoin: a distributed network of nodes, with blockchain as the distributed transaction ledger and proof-of-work as a distributed consensus algorithm (but now they are moving toward "Ethereum 2.0" with proof of stake). However, in addition to simple transactions, Ethereum can execute a programming code, also known as a *smart contract*, which runs on Ethereum Virtual Machine (EVM). The smart contract code (EVM code) can be written in high-level programming languages such as Solidity.

There are many applications of smart contracts, such as *multisignature wallets* (we will review them in the chapter about wallets), financial agreements, trading, loans, etc. Let's examine one of the simple scenarios for smart contracts to understand the concept.

Let's say you want to send someone money, but you don't want it to be collected before a specific date. This can be (relatively) quickly done by writing a (somewhat) simple smart contract.

Another huge application of smart contracts is creating custom tokens such as ERC-20 (fungible tokens) and ERC-721 (non-fungible tokens, or NFTs). These are essential features in today's crypto economy. Many crypto projects were launched by simply creating an ERC-20 token, which can become a new cryptocurrency. In Lyra, for example, we used to have an ERC-20 token that was tethered to the LYR token. This way, LYR could be traded on Ethereum using Uniswap, an Ethereum-based decentralized exchange and trading platform for ERC-20 tokens.[2] However, it turned out to be very expensive because of the high Ethereum transaction fees and practically useless for average traders.

It's worth mentioning that these days Ethereum is not the only token platform that can be used to create custom fungible tokens or NFTs. There are other platforms such as Waves (WAVES),[3] NEM (XEM),[4] and others that allow you to create custom tokens without programming (no need to be a programmer and write the smart contract code). When we started the GRAFT project, we used the NEM blockchain to create a Mosaic token that represented the GRFT coin even before the launch of the GRAFT mainnet.

---

[2] Uniswap. https://uniswap.org/

[3] Waves. How to create and manage your own token. https://docs.waves.tech/en/building-apps/how-to/assets/issue

[4] Namespaces and Mosaics. https://rb2nem.github.io/nem-dev-guide/09-mosaics/

What's Next?

The diversity of crypto technologies allows creative developers to choose the ideas for their future creations from the long menu of existing techniques and use them as the foundation of their next big crypto. But those who prefer not to write the code and quietly piggyback on the existing, well-tested tech also have an option to launch their token on one of the existing platforms.

In Chapter 12, I will show you how to create your own ERC-20 token on Ethereum without programming. In addition, you will learn how to create NFT without a single line of code.

But now, let's continue studying the crypto theory. In the next chapter, we will talk about one of my favorite topics: security. But not just cybersecurity, but cryptosecurity, that is, security of blockchain networks.

CHAPTER 4

Cryptosecurity

If you obey all the rules, you miss all the fun.

—Katharine Hepburn

Strictly speaking, *cryptosecurity* is a discipline that covers communications security using cryptography. Recently, however, this word received a different meaning: *security of cryptocurrencies*. I think there is a good chance that the new definition will eventually replace the original one because more and more people are worried about the security of their crypto, while very few scholars (at least compared to the global army of crypto users) are dealing with cryptography applied to communication.

Cryptosecurity covers three main areas:

- **Security of centralized "backend" environments** built for crypto exchanges, crypto payment processors, online crypto wallets, and other "overhead" structures built on top of decentralized "bare" blockchains. These companies, unfortunately, are still absolutely required for the day-to-day functioning of crypto. The problem is that they are susceptible to all traditional security vulnerabilities as any other conventional FinTech organizations like plastic card payment processors, banks, etc. This situation is illustrated by the following "Inauguration Day" story, which I hope will give you

© Slava Gomzin 2022
S. Gomzin, *Crypto Basics*, https://doi.org/10.1007/978-1-4842-8321-9_4

enough material to get an initial food for thought.
Hundreds of books cover this more "traditional" area of
cybersecurity if you want to research it further.

- **Security of the end-user environments** (like crypto
wallets) – We will talk about it in a chapter about crypto
wallets.

- **Security of the core crypto technologies** – Mainly
blockchain protocols and crypto node networks. That's
probably the most exciting and uncharted territory, so
it's also worth spending some time reviewing it.

Cryptosecurity, as cybersecurity in general, is a cat and mouse game.
"Good guys" (developers) invent new technologies such as multiple
variants of blockchain protocols and distributed consensus algorithms.
"Bad guys" (*black hat* hackers) try to break those technologies and
algorithms, mainly with one goal: to steal money. Because crypto's
precisely like that – it's all about tech and money! There are also "good bad
guys" in the middle – *white hat* hackers (one will even call them *security
researchers*) – who play (with great pleasure!) the role of bad guys while
trying to prevent them from winning this game. Let's look at cryptosecurity
from the "neutral" point of view of white hats, trying to understand and
explain both sides of the game.

Inauguration Day

It was an important day for Americans and many other people around the
world: the inauguration day of President Barack Obama. The attention
of all the US media was focused on the American capital. News feeds
were dominated by various stories on one topic: how the historical event
unfolds in Washington, DC. Here is President George W. Bush, now
already ex-president, leaving Washington, DC, in a presidential helicopter,

making a farewell circle over the capitol, and heading to the Andrews Air Force Base to board the plane to go back to his home in Texas. Here is President Obama, now 44th US President, taking the oath (which, by the way, later had to be repeated due to an error) ... Events are broadcast live on TV, and online publications are not far behind, publishing comments in real time.

If someone wanted to surprise the world with unexpected news, it would be impossible to think of a more unfortunate day. After all, any high-profile news would have passed entirely unnoticed in the shadow of the main event that determined the life of the whole country, and the entire world, for at least four years in advance, and as it turned out later, for eight whole years, since Obama was re-elected for a second term. But the same would be true in the exact opposite direction. If someone wanted to hide an announcement and make it go as unnoticed as possible, they could not find any better day to make their disclosure.

Perhaps, that is why the executives, lawyers, and public relations advisors of Heartland Payment Systems (HPS), one of the largest payment processors, chose this day to break the news to the world: 130 million credit and debit card numbers have been stolen and put up for sale on the darknet marketplace. It was the largest payment card data breach in history.

The strangeness and surprise of this breach were not that the card numbers were stolen, and not only in their record number. Such thefts happened quite regularly by that time, and, besides, there were also significant breaches – take, for example, the TJX breach in 2006–2007 with 48 million accounts. The uniqueness of the HPS breach consisted of two things.

Firstly, the cards were stolen for the first time not from cash registers in stores but from a reliable (as everyone thought before the incident) data center. Unlike merchants who don't have many security resources, payment processors operate in "sterile" data centers with everything they need to solve most security problems. In addition, retailers must secure thousands and thousands of cash registers, which is by itself an almost impossible task because the payment technology was not originally designed with security in mind. Protecting a limited number of servers concentrated in a couple of data centers is a much more technologically practical and financially feasible task.

The second feature of the HPS breach that was unexpected for that time was the way of collecting information – using a network sniffer – a special program that "sits down" on the network and listens to all messages between participants in this network. Thus, data in transit, which stands for communication between servers, was attacked, not the servers themselves. Before this, the primary method was a simple download from a hard drive. The reason was most likely that by that time, many retailers and processors were already certified according to PCI DSS (Payment Card Industry Data Security Standard), which was created through the efforts of five major credit brands – Visa, Mastercard, American Express, Discover, and JCB – and by that time had already gained some strength.

The first version of the PCI DSS was published in December 2004, four years before the breach. One of the main requirements was (and still is) encryption of data at rest (on hard drives). The creators of the standard naively believed that this was a panacea for all ills. The history of subsequent breaches showed and still demonstrates how wrong they were. But were they that naive? Maybe not. In the absence of even minimal security at all stages of the payment process, all the way from the magnetic card reader and the cash register to the payment processors and banks, the creators of the first PCI just had to patch the most giant hole through which hundreds of thousands of dollars were siphoning away with a loud whistle almost daily. This hole was the credit card data in clear text sitting on hard drives. Millions of transaction records rested peacefully on the disks of hundreds of thousands of cash registers and servers in the form of log files and databases. Unencrypted. Just come and take.

Plastics or Crypto: No Difference

At the time of the HPS breach, many servers and even cash registers were already encrypted, but PCI did not require encryption of internal communications. Hackers successfully exploited this "vulnerability" of the security standard. PCI compliance did not save HPS, just as any security standard did not save and will never save many others. Security must not be built based on compliance with any standard but on the basis of taking into account all threats, risks, vulnerabilities, and infiltration scenarios.

Speaking of infiltration, as I said, the data was extracted using a network sniffer, but how did this sniffer get into the closed network of the "secure" data center? This is probably the time to talk about how the data breach works in general. And here is the most important thing: *data breach equally works for payment processors and crypto exchanges.* SQL injection, which was used to penetrate the HPS network, was, in fact, among other techniques used to hack crypto exchanges.[1] Even though crypto technology is very different from payment card tech, crypto companies use the same data centers and security software as their competitors from the traditional FinTech. The only difference is targeted data. In the case of the payment processor, it is an enormous number of database records containing magnetic tracks. It can be even simpler for crypto exchange: just a single private key to unlock the crypto wallet.

The history of security breaches associated with crypto exchanges, despite its young age, is not inferior in its richness and diversity to the longer and infamous security record of the payment card industry. The first major crypto breach happened in 2011 with Japanese crypto exchange

---

[1] Kris Oosthoek, Christian Doerr. Cyber Security Threats to Bitcoin Exchanges: Adversary Exploitation and Laundering Techniques. www.cyber-threat-intelligence.com/publications/TNSM-2020-bitcoinexchangehacks.pdf

Mt. Gox, when hackers stole $8.74m worth of bitcoin.[2] According to the same source, approximately $12.1 billion in cryptocurrencies was stolen between Jan 2011 and Dec 2021. The most popular method of crypto theft has been the infiltration of the crypto-exchange security system.

The Great Infiltration

Infiltrating the data center is not trivial but, at the same time, not an impossible task. You don't need to break the physical walls. There are more elegant ways, thanks to application software. There are two main phases in any breach, and both are equally difficult (from a hacker's point of view). By the way, the defense is also built on the same two-phase principle. There are at least two possibilities (in reality, more) to stop the breach using completely different means of protection.

First, the hacker needs to get into the victim's network or server. This is the first phase of infiltration. You can do this in many ways, such as hacking a web application, phishing email, or simply using your credentials if you are hacking your own company (insider threat). But here is a very important point: it is impossible to jump directly to the second phase of the breach without completing the first. There are no exceptions to this rule. Thus, the hacker should always have the right tools in his arsenal for both phases, and the security guys should always have at least two lines of defense.

In the case of the infamous HPS breach, the infiltration was carried out using SQL injection. Unfortunately, various penetration methods are outside of this book's scope, but I will talk about SQL injection in greater detail as an example.

---

[2] The 10 Biggest Crypto Exchange Hacks In History. https://crystalblockchain.com/articles/the-10-biggest-crypto-exchange-hacks-in-history/

The second phase is collecting data and sending it home. As a rule, this phase is entirely independent of the first one and requires different knowledge and toolset. The mere fact that a hacker has penetrated a network or a computer does not guarantee the successful completion of the breach (although it is probably still the most critical phase). In fact, many breach attempts end in the first phase if the second line of defense is strong enough to keep the hacker at bay until the intrusion is discovered and eliminated. In the case of the HPS breach, the second line of defense was weak, and the hackers were able to install a sniffer in the right place and silently upload a massive amount of data to their command center.

How SQL Injection Works

Now back to SQL injection. What is it? Jeff Forristal, also known by the alias Rain Forest Puppy, was one of the first people to document SQL injection. Forristal wrote the first public discussion about it back in 1998.[3] Even if you are not a security guy, you have probably heard the name, but you hardly understand what it means. And if you are a security guy, you may not fully understand how it works and, most importantly, how to deal with it. Since SQL injection has long been one of the most common penetration methods, let's see how it works.

SQL stands for *Structured Query Language*, which most database management systems such as Microsoft SQL Server, Oracle, or MySQL employ to provide the application developers with the ability to manipulate the data stored in the database. By executing a *SQL statement*, a privileged user can do pretty much everything with the data elements or entire databases: create, read, modify, or delete. The web application often impersonates such a privileged database user because it needs to manipulate data on behalf of its users.

---

[3] How SQLi was discovered. http://mobile.esecurityplanet.com/network-security/how-was-sql-injection-discovered.html

SQL injection is an attack in which malicious SQL code is inserted or appended into user input parameters passed by the web application to the SQL server for execution. Even if you are not a programmer, the SQL language is very self-explanatory. Here is a simple example of an SQL query that returns the status of the application user with a given username and password from the database table that contains information about all application users:

```
select count(*) from users where username = 'john.smith' and
password = '123456'
```

If a user with such a username and password exists, the result of this query will be 1. If the user does not exist (i.e., the specified username or password is wrong), the result will be 0.

Let's assume that web application login logic checks if the user exists and grants access to the application based on the result of such a query. Our vulnerable web application takes the username and password as HTTP request parameters and passes them directly to the backend SQL server:

```
http://www.mycompany.com/login?username=john.
smith&password=123456
```

An attacker, who does not know the correct username and password, can try to manipulate the URL parameters and inject the SQL code through the password parameter by simply entering the following text as the password:

```
unknown' or '1'='1
```

The resulting URL will look like this (%20 is equivalent to space and %27 to '):

```
http://www.mycompany.com/login?username=john.smith
&password=unknown%27%20or%20%271%27=%271
```

After the web application constructs the query and passes those parameters to the SQL server, the resulting SQL statement will be

```
select count(*) from users where username = 'john. smith' and
password = 'unknown' or '1' = '1'
```

Since '1' = '1' is always true, the result of the executed query will always be at least 1 regardless of the actual value of the user password. Thus, an attacker will be logged in to the web application as a legitimate user.

Although this simple example illustrates the idea of how SQL injection works, in practice, the SQLi attacks are much more complex. A successful SQL injection attack would require a good understanding of the SQL language and its dialects (each SQL server has slightly different syntax) and multiple trial attempts. But there is good news for hackers and bad news for the rest: there are various tools that automate SQLi attacks. Those tools simplify and speed up the attacks and make them affordable for average hackers. Like many other things, you can buy it from darknet marketplaces for a few bucks (more precisely, for a fraction of Bitcoin or Monero), or you can find and download a free version if you don't mind the risk of getting a free add-on in the form of some Trojan or keystroke logger.

There are two main protection measures against SQLi attacks which complement each other but are not necessarily interchangeable: input validation and WAF (web application firewall). While the former may require significant changes in the application code, the latter can be implemented in virtually any environment running any legacy code without the need to modify the applications. Ideally, those two protection measures should be used together to form two layers of protection. Such multilayer protection against the same threat is called *defense-in-depth*, the best practice approach applied in many security areas.

Ransomware Attacks

To finalize this topic of "traditional" cybersecurity, I must mention the ransomware attacks that are so popular nowadays. A ransomware attack means that an attacker gains access to your data, makes it useless (by encrypting it), and tries to sell you the decryption key in exchange for some amount of crypto. I took a couple of slides from the research conducted by Ken Westin,[4] a security researcher and my friend, who kindly allowed me to use his work to help explain the mechanics of ransomware attacks.

The ransomware attack is typically a product of multiple hackers who have different specializations and provide services to each other, doing business like mainstream software and cybersecurity industries. Some of them steal credentials and sell them to others. Others conduct an actual attack by finding and destroying offsite backups and encrypting all the valuable data on the victim's servers (Figure 4-1).

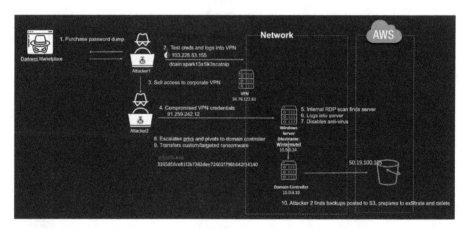

Figure 4-1. *Ransomware attack flow*

---

[4] Ken Westin. www.linkedin.com/in/kwestin/

The result of ransomware attacks often looks like the one shown in Figure 4-2. The victim receives the message that the data and backups are gone (encrypted), with detailed instructions on paying to get their data back.

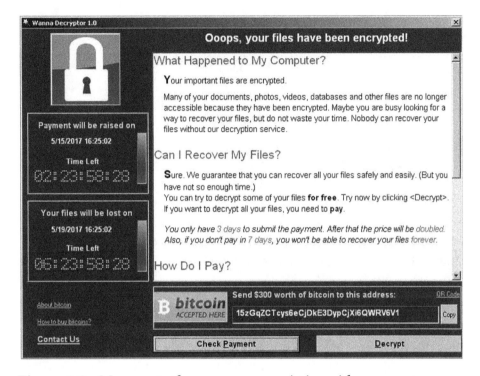

Figure 4-2. *Message to the ransomware victim with payment instructions*

Despite the popularity of ransomware attacks, the primary connection between crypto and ransomware is that hackers ask for payment in Bitcoin (stupid) or Monero (wise choice). Many hackers are still using Bitcoin, despite its transactions being publicly visible on the blockchain and therefore traceable. Ken Westin traced proceeds from multiple ransomware attacks to several crypto exchanges (Table 4-1). The names of the exchanges are hidden as he did not want to compromise their reputation.

Table 4-1. *Exchanges That Received Ransomware Proceeds. Source: Ken Westin*

Crypto Exchange	Total Proceeds (USD)
XXXXX	19,000,476
XXXX	18,856,173
XXXXXXXXX	8.834,355
XXXXXX	5,279,807
BTC-e.com	1,324,429
All Others	10,809,385

Note that if hackers used Monero for payments, no one could ever trace their transactions (more about Monero in Chapter 6). Apparently, they are not too worried about the traceability of their transactions, which hints at their physical location in one of the hacker-haven countries such as Russia or China.

Ironically, the risk of ransomware attacks for the crypto exchanges themselves is relatively low compared to other types of attacks. Think about it – if you are hacking a crypto exchange and you managed to penetrate their perimeter – wouldn't you try to steal the private keys to their wallets and wipe out their accounts altogether? In any case, those hackers who can't steal the keys may still decide to conduct a ransomware attack. So, the most important thing any company or individual can do to protect their assets from ransomware attacks is a good backup strategy. It's been true for decades, and it's still true today.[5] Create offsite backups, that is, those not located in your network and won't be accessible even if your network is breached. By the way, this is relevant to any sensitive data storage from your personal Google Drive to corporate databases.

---

[5] Ransomware. Schneier on Security. www.schneier.com/blog/archives/2008/06/ransomware_1.html

Attacks on Blockchain Protocols

Now let's finally talk about the most exciting part – attacks invented specially to hack the crypto tech. There are many of them, but the following are probably the most noticeable. Most attacks on blockchain exploit the double-spending problem. We already know that blockchain technology is designed to prevent double-spending by using digital signatures and other measures. This is correct, but only when the system works under "normal conditions." However, if the blockchain system is abused, it may lead to catastrophic results.

So let me remind you what the double-spending problem is first (we briefly reviewed it in Chapter 2). Double-spending is simply a situation when the payer is trying to spend the same money twice. Such a scenario is possible not only in the crypto world. Imagine you come to the store, buy some stuff, and proceed to check out. You want to pay with a credit card, and then the power suddenly goes down. Suppose the store manager decides to continue store operation without power. In that case, they may start accepting credit cards manually (that's how they were handled initially, by the way, before the electronic payment systems were introduced). They will write down your card account number, your name, etc., on a piece of paper, retain this info for further processing, and let you go. Now, instead of going home and enjoying your purchase, you go to the next-door store and pay with the same credit card, which brings you over the credit card limit. When both stores settle your payments at the end of the business day, one of them (most probably the first one) will get a *chargeback* – that's the special term for the payment processor to refuse the payment.

This is the classic example of double-spending! And it is not a theoretical one – there are stories about people blocking satellite antennas of remote stores to prevent them from getting online authorizations for stolen cards.[6] Cryptocurrencies seem to be in a better position by definition as they are not supposed to function without Internet access. That's true, but at the same time, there is another huge "vulnerability" in blockchain tech that can cause double-spending: decentralization. Unlike credit card processors who control the authorization processes by their centralized servers, crypto consists of thousands of stand-alone "authorizers" – network nodes – who must get consensus on every single transaction. Attacks on blockchain disturb such consensus by tricking the rules of the game.

51% Attack

A 51% attack can be performed on proof-of-work by malicious miners when they have the majority of the hash power. It can also be conducted on proof-of-stake blockchains. In general, the 51% attack can be performed when malicious stakeholders gain the majority of the loyal network participants to alternate the blockchain. Here is how it works:

1. The attackers create a "parallel" (alternative) chain of blocks where they record transactions sending funds to themselves. They do not publish the alternative chain yet.

2. They record a similar transaction in the main chain that instead sends funds to a crypto exchange.

3. The attackers then use the deposited funds for trading to another crypto.

---

[6] Gas thieves block satellite with foil to use stolen credit cards in Macomb Township. https://www.clickondetroit.com/news/2012/09/20/gas-thieves-block-satellite-with-foil-to-use-stolen-credit-cards-in-macomb-township/

4. Once trading is done, they withdraw the revenue in another cryptocurrency, making their transaction irreversible (the exchange cannot block it anymore).

5. The attackers release the alternative chain, which is longer than the current "main" chain. Since the network nodes must accept the longer chain (that's how blockchain networks are supposed to work!), they convert the alternative malicious chain into the main chain, which effectively cancels all transfers made in that chain, including deposit transfers to the exchange.

The 51% attack probably is the most practical one – I can tell you with 100% confidence because yours truly witnessed such an attack while it was unfolding in real time. It was an attack on GRAFT (GRFT), the crypto I co-created, with one of the crypto exchanges involved. I don't know (and wouldn't say even if I knew) how significant the loss was, hopefully not that big. I can only say that our team worked with the exchanges to mitigate future attacks by increasing the number of confirmations required for deposit acceptance. The increased number of confirmations makes it more difficult (expensive) for the attackers to generate an alternative chain. Eventually, it becomes more costly than their financial gain from the attack.

Now you know why crypto exchanges require different numbers of confirmations for different cryptocurrencies for their deposit acceptance. These numbers depend on the hash rate (for proof-of-work currencies) or, in other words, on how many people are involved in the process of transaction approval (i.e., how widespread the cryptocurrency is). For proof-of-stake cryptos, this dependency is more complicated. Still, it generally follows the same logic: the more supporters the crypto has, the less the risk of the successful 51% attack (and many other attacks as well!).

While this number can be in the low single digits for popular crypto like Bitcoin, less popular crypto must compensate for the low hash rate by dozens or even hundreds of required confirmations.

Figures 4-3 to 4-5 show the number of confirmations required by the LAToken crypto exchange for BTC, USDT, and DOGE. Note that these numbers are not universal and can vary from exchange to exchange. You can see that LAToken considered BTC to be the safest one (which is difficult to argue with) with only two confirmations required, while USDT is the least reliable one in this group, in their opinion. USDT is based on the Ethereum network, and I am not sure why, but they think that 12 blocks need to be added on top of the block containing your transaction to consider it finalized. Maybe they have their reasons (bad experiences with Ethereum?). We don't know, and they probably won't tell us.

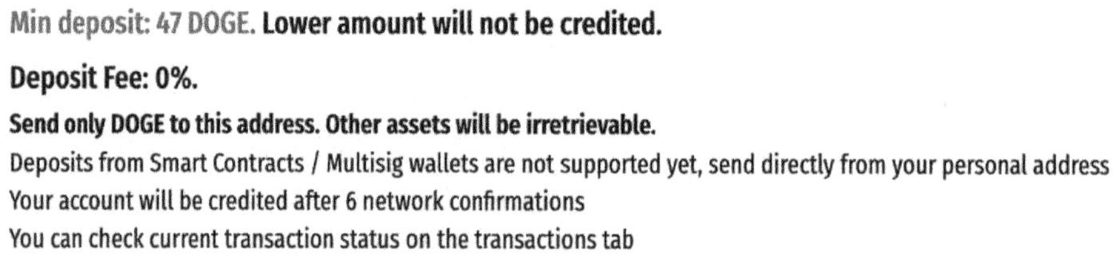

Min deposit: 47 DOGE. **Lower amount will not be credited.**

Deposit Fee: 0%.

Send only DOGE to this address. Other assets will be irretrievable.

Deposits from Smart Contracts / Multisig wallets are not supported yet, send directly from your personal address

Your account will be credited after 6 network confirmations

You can check current transaction status on the transactions tab

Figure 4-3. *DOGE requires six network confirmations*

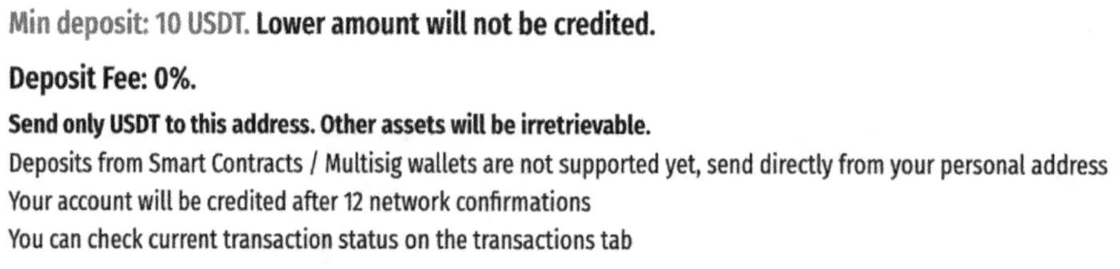

Min deposit: 10 USDT. **Lower amount will not be credited.**

Deposit Fee: 0%.

Send only USDT to this address. Other assets will be irretrievable.

Deposits from Smart Contracts / Multisig wallets are not supported yet, send directly from your personal address

Your account will be credited after 12 network confirmations

You can check current transaction status on the transactions tab

Figure 4-4. *USDT requires 12 network confirmations*

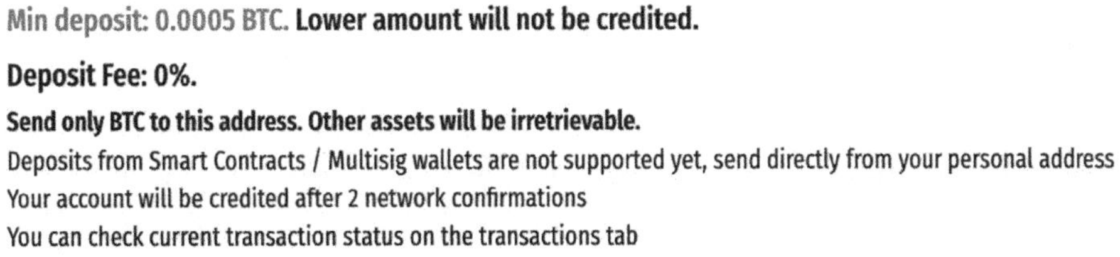

Min deposit: 0.0005 BTC. **Lower amount will not be credited.**

Deposit Fee: 0%.

Send only BTC to this address. Other assets will be irretrievable.

Deposits from Smart Contracts / Multisig wallets are not supported yet, send directly from your personal address

Your account will be credited after 2 network confirmations

You can check current transaction status on the transactions tab

Figure 4-5. *BTC requires two network confirmations*

More Attacks on Blockchain

Other attacks are more exotic and so more challenging to conduct. Still, they are mainly based on the same principle of exploiting the blockchain double-spending vulnerability in one way or another. The **Finney attack**, for example, is the "mini-version" of a 51% attack. The attacker premines the block with a transaction that transfers funds back to their wallet and sends a "parallel" fraudulent transaction to the recipient, such as the merchant. The fraudulent transaction uses the same inputs as the premined transaction but sends them to the merchant. Once fraudulent payment is accepted by the recipient (before it is added to the blockchain, the attacker broadcasts the premined block, which effectively reverses the fraudulent transaction.

The original transaction is "ousted" by the new one because we know that two transactions using the same inputs cannot be recorded in a blockchain. The premined transaction is already added to the block accepted by the network, so it takes preference over the original payment transaction, which is not recorded in the blockchain. Therefore, it is dangerous to accept crypto payments without full confirmation, that is, before the payment transaction is recorded in the blockchain.

What's Next?

The common vector for most attacks on crypto is the attackers trying to double-spend their funds, and the way they do it is through accumulation and concentration of excessive hash power (for proof-of-work cryptos) or funds (for proof-of-stake coins). The more participants are in the crypto network, and the better the distribution of the hash power or stake funds, the fewer chances the blockchain is prone to be hacked. That's why cryptocurrencies with the highest market capitalization are paradoxically safer despite being the most desirable targets for hackers.

The next chapter will discuss an even more exciting aspect of the crypto ecosystem: privacy. One might ask, why is it more interesting than security? Even despite its complexity, cryptosecurity is more obvious, no matter how paradoxical it may sound. We know about multiple blockchain vulnerabilities; we understand the threats and can build protections accordingly.

On the contrary, crypto privacy is a huge invisible threat. Most people don't even realize how dangerous crypto is when you touch it. You start playing with it assuming you are incognito while, in fact, you are not at all.

CHAPTER 5

Crypto Privacy

When you see something that is technically sweet, you go ahead and do it and you argue about what to do about it only after you have had your technical success. That is the way it was with the atomic bomb.

—J. Robert Oppenheimer

Did you know that the US government can legally seize your cash without any court order and charges against you? I didn't until I read an article[1] in *The Washington Post* about a former Marine pulled over by police when traveling from Texas to California to see his daughters. The police searched his car and found $87,000 in cash in the trunk. The ex-Marine was not arrested or charged with any crime. However, the police still decided to seize the money using a legal procedure called "adoption," which allows federal authorities to take cash or property they suspect is connected to criminal activity without levying criminal charges. His only "crime" was that he did not trust banks and wanted to carry cash with him. I wouldn't believe that this is a truthful story, but *The Washington Post* is one of the sources I still trust.

This story shows that our money is not safe from criminals and governments (the government representatives behaved like criminals in this case), even in the form of cash. Since many people call crypto "cash for

---

[1] A former Marine was pulled over for following a truck too closely. Police took nearly $87,000 of his cash. The Washington Post. https://apple.news/ AJSIclIvXRbu3s_OTOOU3HA

© Slava Gomzin 2022
S. Gomzin, *Crypto Basics*, https://doi.org/10.1007/978-1-4842-8321-9_5

the Internet," what are the perils of using crypto compared to traditional money? Would a similar story be possible with Bitcoin or other cryptos? Of course not. Does it mean crypto is much more secure than cash or electronic payments like plastic cards? Yes and no. Although crypto is a significant step up in security and privacy, it has privacy threats. These are new, often unknown, and poorly studied vulnerabilities, and therefore crypto can be even more dangerous for unsophisticated users than cash or cards. Let's see how to avoid them.

While working on the GRAFT white paper,[2] my first crypto project, I spent a lot of time researching privacy coins. Such coins provide their users with adequate security and protect their identities beyond the "Bitcoin standard." When people first dive into the exciting world of crypto, they don't pay much attention to the downsides of blockchain technology. However, start comparing Bitcoin with plastic payment cards, famous for their huge number of security holes. You will be surprised to find that crypto does not withstand the criticism, disproving its much-advertised privacy features. There is a simple explanation for this perception discrepancy.

Bitcoin Is Pseudonymous!

The inventors and first adopters of Bitcoin assumed that the very fact of the decentralized nature of the Bitcoin network and anonymous access to the blockchain would fully protect the user's privacy. They underestimated the ingenuity of people around crypto, who are not necessarily against the crypto philosophy but maybe just want to make it better by hacking it. That's the original hackers' philosophy, by the way –

---

[2] Slava Gomzin, Dan Itkis. Graft: Decentralized, Real-time Credit, Debit, and Crypto Payment Processing Network. `https://github.com/graft-project/graft-white-paper/blob/master/graft-white-paper-1.02/graft-white-paper-1.02.md`

they don't want to break anything, but they are rather convinced that by exposing vulnerabilities, they will eventually make the product more robust. Yours truly is not an exception, and my books reveal some facts that help make this world a little better.

The main problem with privacy was an assumption that anonymous access to the blockchain would protect the user's privacy. That was wrong. The issue is hidden in the very nature of the blockchain – its public availability. **Anyone** can access and track **all** transactions on a blockchain. Compare it to your credit card, and you get the opposite picture. Your transactions are private (to some degree, which we will discuss later), but access is not private (you must fully disclose your identity to get a payment card issued to you). Table 5-1 compares the privacy of plastic payment cards and pseudonymous cryptocurrencies.

Table 5-1. *Comparing Bitcoin and Plastic Payment Card Privacy*

	Bitcoin	**Plastic Payment Cards**
Access	Pseudo-anonymous, i.e., does not require identity disclosure, but the link can be established through blockchain analysis and online surveillance	Requires full identity disclosure
Transaction traceability	Transaction data is publicly visible, but there is no direct link to user identity available out of the box	Transaction data is not visible to public, but readily available to selected corporations, governments, and hackers
Ability to enhance privacy	Available through using special tools	Not available
Absolute privacy	Available through converting funds to privacy-centric coin	Not available

Making Your Bitcoin Transactions Private

So which technology – Bitcoin or plastic payment cards – provides better privacy? Although there is no simple answer to this question, I still vote for Bitcoin for multiple reasons. First of all, it is decentralized, and no one can stop me from using it! I admit a fundamental flaw in "traditional" crypto like Bitcoin or Ethereum: they make all your money movements public. And it's possible to establish the link between your wallet and your identity; it's just a matter of time and effort.

However, it should be noted that there are special tools that allow users to significantly improve their privacy even if they use pseudo-anonymous coins like Bitcoin. There are ways to hide your transactions – from simple methods like generating a new, unique wallet address for each transaction to more sophisticated ways like coin mixers. If you are still in love with Bitcoin, Ethereum, or any other pseudonymous coin (this is not sarcasm, no worries, I get it) and not ready to switch to privacy-centric coins but want to get closer to the real freedom from the big brother, let's review these relatively simple tools.

Unique Wallet Address per Transaction

Using a unique wallet address for each transaction is very simple as most wallets support this feature out of the box. Typically, you just need to make an extra click. The Bitcoin protocol supports a crypto standard that allows a single private key to generate an unlimited number of wallet addresses. Most importantly, it is impossible to link those addresses to each other. As shown in Figure 5-1 for Electrum wallet 3, every time you receive bitcoins, click the "New Address" button to generate a new, unique address.

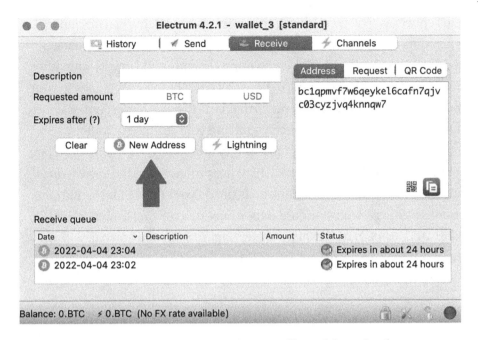

Figure 5-1. *Generating a new, unique wallet address in the Electrum wallet*

What happens if you use unique addresses? It helps keep your incoming transactions unlinked, making establishing your identity a more difficult task. The problem, however, is outgoing transactions. When you send bitcoin, your wallet combines the transaction from multiple inputs, which effectively links those transactions that previously looked unlinked. You can reduce this effect by using multiple wallets, but only to a certain degree. To completely hide your transactions, you need to use other, more powerful methods.

Coin Mixers (Tumblers)

Although the legal status of *coin mixing* services, or *tumblers*, is questionable, you should know about them. For some people like journalists or political dissidents, privacy is vital and even more important than any legal concerns. The concept of a coin mixer is simple: instead of sending your coins directly to the recipient, you send them through the mixing service. The mixer "grinds" them to mix the inputs and outputs with other people's coins and, after some delay, sends the "brand-new" coins to your recipient. The result of such a performance is that it is almost impossible to reliably establish the link between your and your recipient's wallets.

One tumbler service that I find pretty interesting is *ChipMixer*.[3] They set their own rules of the game, which are probably not the easiest ones, but most make sense. What they do is divide your deposit into multiple chunks ("chips") with standard denominations starting from 0.001 BTC: 0.001 BTC, 0.002 BTC, 0.004 BTC, etc. (Figure 5-2), and you can withdraw these "chips" as private keys (Figure 5-3).

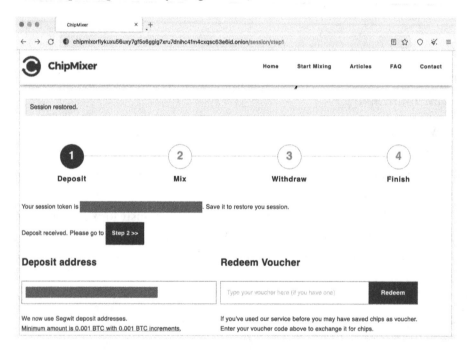

Figure 5-2. *ChipMixer deposit screen*

---

[3] https://chipmixer.com

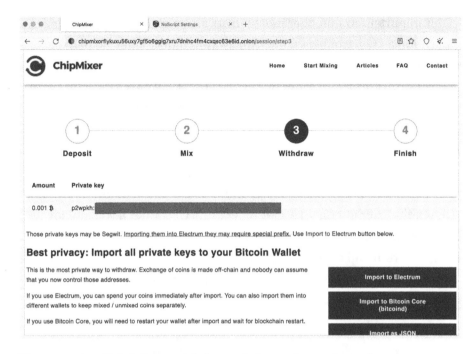

Figure 5-3. *ChipMixer withdrawal through a private key*

This way, it works like a "time machine" as you withdraw your funds using transactions that haven't been done yet but will be done in the future because a private key is not a transaction; it's just a piece of information that allows you to process transactions. So, at the time of "withdrawal," you do not withdraw anything until you use this private key to send funds to someone else. In fact, ChipMixer says that *"this is the most private way to withdraw. Exchange of coins is made off-chain, and nobody can assume that you now control those addresses."*

Sounds too good to be true! Well, that's because it's not exactly too good. The problem is that if someone (ChipMixer in this case) knows your private key, they can still use your funds. So, suppose you don't send the funds associated with the withdrawal private key immediately to your other wallet. In that case, you should come to terms with the idea that you completely trust ChipMixer (which is highly not recommended).

It's important to note that most mixers are proprietary, centralized applications. They can be a scam, run away and disappear, go bankrupt, or the government can shut them down. Please think twice before you trust your private keys to them or anyone else! It's like sharing your bank account credentials. Do it only if you really need it. There is always a risk of losing. At least reduce the risk by dividing large amounts into several transactions.

Another caveat is that not many wallets support an easy private key import out of the box. In fact, they provide import instructions for only one GUI (graphic user interface) wallet – Electrum. Of course, if you already use this wallet, it's okay. If you don't, it's not a big deal either. What you can do is install Electrum and create a wallet just for the purpose of ChipMixer private key imports (Figure 5-4). From there, you can transfer the entire balance immediately to your permanent secret wallet or directly to your recipient.

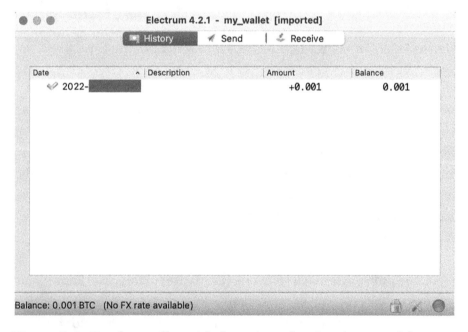

Figure 5-4. *Exodus wallet with the private key just imported from ChipMixer*

With that said, this mixer works fine. Note that they don't charge any fees! They accept donations, though, in the form of excessive amounts of deposits. For example, if you send 0.0015 BTC, you get a 0.001 BTC chip, and 0.0005 goes to ChipMixer. Another good feature is that they support *SegWit* (not all wallets have it), which means that withdrawals can be made with lower fees. We will talk about SegWit in a chapter about wallets.

The Onion Router (TOR)

As you noticed in the previous section about coin mixer, there was a strange address in the browser's address bar pointing to the ChipMixer website (Figure 5-3):

`chipmixorflykuxu56uxy7gf5o6ggig7xru7dnihc4fm4cxqsc63e6id.onion`

It starts with the prefix `chipmix`, which hints that it may be related to the ChipMixer website. And it ends with the suffix `.onion`. Don't try to google the `.onion` Internet domain – it does not exist in the regular World Wide Web as you know it. Onion is the suffix of the *darknet* (a.k.a. *dark web* or *deep web*) address. And that address is pointing to the same site as the `https://chipmixer.com/` website but located in the darknet and accessed through the *onion cloud* or *TOR network*.

TOR (The Onion Router) is another powerful privacy tool that can complement the previous methods we reviewed. TOR allows fully secure, anonymous, untraceable access to the Internet, especially if you use onion addresses. The onion cloud is the network of servers called *relays* or *nodes* located all over the world that ensures anonymity and untraceability of your Internet connection. When you access a website through a *TOR browser*,[4] your computer's IP address is hidden and cannot be linked to the destination site's server. Instead, the data between your computer and the website hops through *TOR nodes* (at least 3) which obfuscates your Internet traffic.

---

[4] `www.torproject.org/download/`

Not all websites are connected to the onion cloud directly, but you can still access regular websites with their standard URL using the TOR browser. For example, if you type `https://chipmixer.com/`, it will bring you to the same ChipMixer website. The connection will be through the onion cloud, with an *exit point* at some random TOR node located anywhere in the world. From that *exit node*, all the way until the website, the "last mile" will be through the regular "open" Internet. Such a connection is more secure and private than a standard browser like Chrome, but it can still be intercepted and traced. So, to use the full power of the onion cloud, you better use the onion addresses (if they are available).

VPN (Virtual Private Network)

Is there anything more secure and private than TOR? A VPN (virtual private network) is not more secure than TOR, but it complements its security and privacy and provides a much higher connection speed.

What Is VPN?

Its function is basically similar to TOR: hide your location and Internet identity (IP address). The difference is that a VPN is a centralized service, so your data can be hacked or seized by the government. All VPN operators, of course, state that they don't retain or disclose any information about your activities, but how can you verify that? Let's hope nothing like this ever happens, but the first cybersecurity principle is "zero trust," so don't assume anyone cares about your privacy more than you do.

How Does VPN work?

It's straightforward. When you install a VPN client app on your computer or phone, it will route all your Internet connections to the closest VPN server (instead of sending them directly to the websites you are browsing). From there, your connection goes to another server, which can be located in a different part of the world (which you can usually choose). It's called an *exit server*, similar to a TOR exit node. What it also does is it is replacing your original IP address with its IP address, making your call efficiently anonymous.

There are three important effects of the Internet connection protected by VPN:

- The website you browse does not know who you are and where you are from. They cannot track your activities and cannot establish any link with your other activities on the Internet.

- Your ISP – the company such as AT&T that provides you with the Internet access, records all your Internet traffic, sells this data to other companies, and reports it to the government (yes, don't be surprised!) – won't be able to know anything about your Internet activities anymore. The only activity they will ever record is your connection to the VPN entry server; that's it.

- Another interesting "side effect" of VPN is that you can pretend to be in a different place by selecting an exit point in a specific country (Figure 5-5). Hackers widely use this to trick websites that track user geolocation and regulate access based on it.

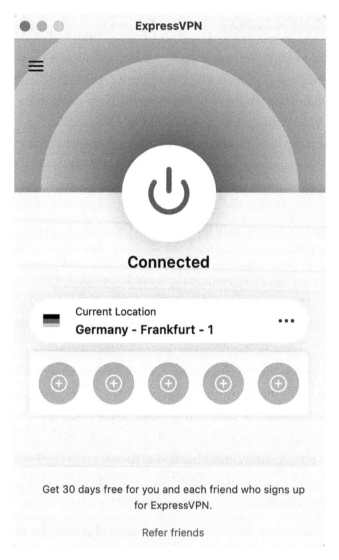

Figure 5-5. *VPN connection with an exit point in Germany*

Note that if you use a standard browser like Chrome, it's important
to enable private browsing (Incognito Browsing in Chrome). Otherwise,
your identity can still be established, and your activities can be tracked
using metadata submitted by your standard browser. Using a TOR browser,
however, is the better option.

If I Use TOR, Should I Use VPN As Well?

The answer is yes. When you use a VPN and TOR, you increase your chance of surviving the surveillance and avoid some hacking attacks. No one even knows that you ever connect to the TOR cloud because VPN hides this fact. If your data leaks from the VPN, you are still protected by TOR and vice versa.

Some good examples of VPN services are *ExpressVPN*[5] and *NordVPN*,[6] but there are many others. Even though there are some free VPN services theoretically, I have never managed to find one that reliably works. So come to terms with the fact that privacy is not free and find the service that fits your needs and wallet (your regular wallet, not necessarily crypto).

Besides the Case with the Coin Mixer, Should I Use TOR and VPN?

If you want to keep your transactions fully private, you should use your crypto wallet with both a VPN and TOR, or at least a VPN, as this is the easiest one, and it provides additional privacy benefits beyond just crypto.

Using crypto wallets with TOR can be a nontrivial task and may require running a node because not all "light" wallets support TOR. But a VPN is typically a straightforward, one-click user-friendly app that can be installed on any computer and phone. It is transparent for the wallet app, meaning there is nothing you need to configure specifically in the wallet app to use a VPN – just launch the VPN app.

---

[5] www.expressvpn.com/support/troubleshooting/download-vpn-app/
[6] https://nordvpn.com/download/

Choose the Right Wallet

There are different types of wallets, such as *thin wallets* and *full node wallets*. Crypto wallets rely on external services, either decentralized (including the crypto networks themselves) or centralized (app servers). The very fact that your wallet communicates with a third-party service is a privacy concern because that service can record your IP address and your activity and therefore establish a link between your identity and your financial transactions.

So, the first step toward the privacy of your wallet is making sure it does not depend on third-party centralized services. Full node wallets such as Bitcoin Core provide better privacy as they rely only on the full node running on your local computer or network (Figure 5-6).

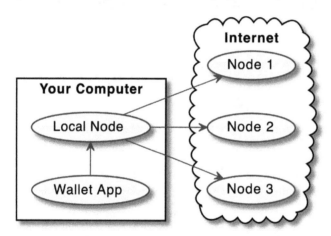

Figure 5-6. *Full node wallet like Bitcoin Core*

But Electrum, for example, relies on a special wallet server, which can be run by anyone, including people who want to watch and analyze your transaction activity (Figure 5-7).

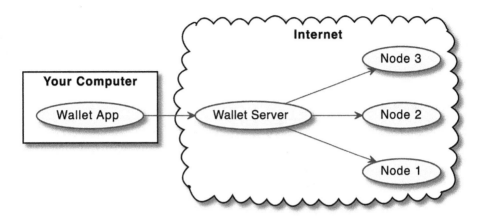

Figure 5-7. *Thin wallet like Electrum requires a centralized "man in the middle"*

The good news is that this "man in the middle" can be you. Electrum provides an option to run such a wallet server on your local machine and connect it to the full Bitcoin node, which you also run locally.[7] Such configuration can be helpful if you want to use ChipMixer and other features offered by the Electrum wallet. But if you use a different mixer service and don't need all these features like hardware wallet support, there is another, less complicated (but less featured) option: *Bitcoin Core GUI wallet.*[8] It contains the full Bitcoin node, so the only thing it depends on is the decentralized Bitcoin network itself. In addition, it is developed as a community project and does not belong to any corporation.

Run Your Wallet with TOR

The next step toward better privacy of your wallet is making sure its communication with the Bitcoin network is private, that is, no one can

---

[7] https://driftwoodpalace.github.io/Hodl-Guide/hodl-guide_64_
eps-mac.html

[8] https://bitcoin.org/en/download

see your IP address and establish the link between your identity and your transaction activities. The Electrum wallet can be easily configured to communicate through TOR. Even though it communicates to the third-party server, it still makes sense to route it through TOR because TOR hides your IP (Figure 5-8).

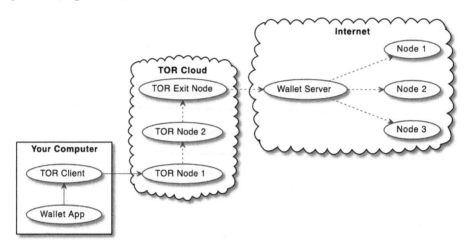

Figure 5-8. *Thin wallet like Electrum on the TOR cloud*

Note that if you decide to run your local Electrum server, you don't have to set up the wallet app to communicate through TOR, as it will talk to the server locally. Instead, you will need to set up your local Bitcoin Core node to communicate through TOR. Such TOR configuration will also work for the Bitcoin Core GUI wallet (Figure 5-9).

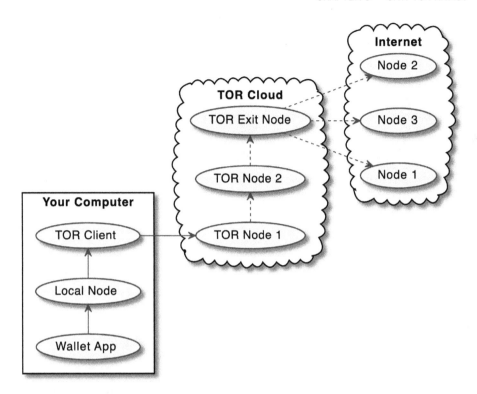

Figure 5-9. *Full node wallet like Bitcoin Core on the TOR cloud*

In addition to Bitcoin Core installation, which is pretty straightforward, there are only a couple of simple steps that are required to set up Bitcoin Core to work with TOR:

- Install a TOR browser (this is simple; just click download and follow the instructions).

- Launch the Bitcoin Core wallet, go to Preferences ➤ Network, and check "Connect through SOCKS5 proxy," as shown in Figure 5-10. Then restart Bitcoin Core, and make sure that the TOR browser is running.

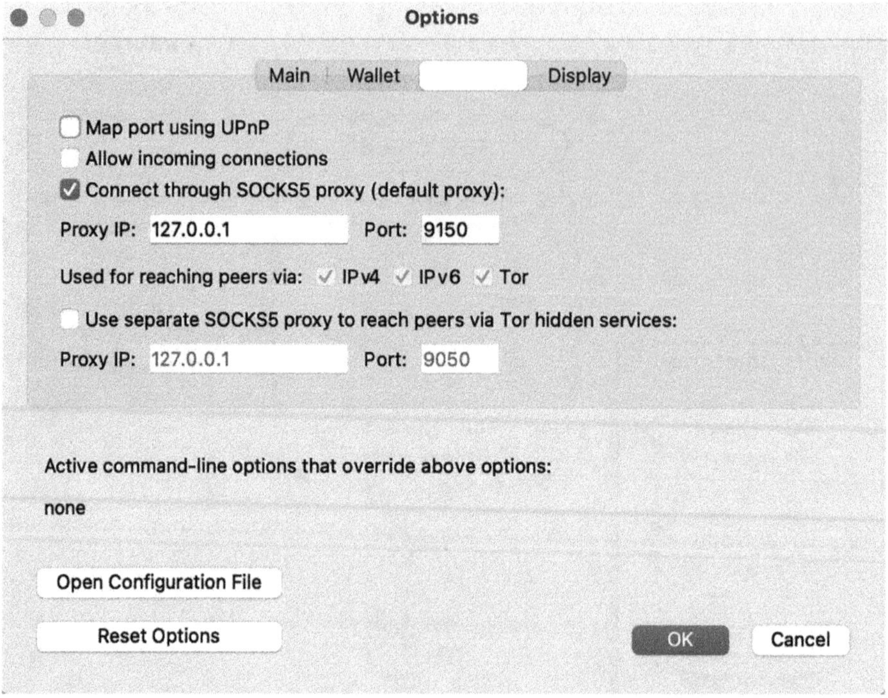

Figure 5-10. *Bitcoin Core wallet configured for the TOR network*

Note that the default port number is 9050. If your wallet does not communicate with the network (shows 0 active connections when you tap over the network icon in the bottom right corner), change the port to 9150 and restart the wallet again.

Bitcoin TOR Nodes

With the TOR network enabled, your Bitcoin Core now communicates with Bitcoin nodes through TOR, which hides your IP address from anyone and your activities from your ISP. Your communication, however, can still be traced from the TOR exit node all the way to the Bitcoin nodes, so there is another small step you can take with the privacy of your wallet.

You can tell your Bitcoin Core to connect only to the Bitcoin nodes connected through the TOR cloud. And you already know what it means: these nodes must have onion addresses instead of regular IP addresses.[9] When you are connected to Bitcoin nodes through TOR addresses, it closes the loop: your connection is fully "TORified."

Now you need to tell your wallet to use only TOR. Unfortunately, Bitcoin Core GUI does not support this configuration yet, so you will have to do it manually. You will need to find the *bitcoin.config* file, open it with text editor, and add the following lines:

```
onlynet=onion
dnsseed=0
dns=0
addnode=kpgvmscirrdqpekbqjsvw5teanhatztpp2gl6eee4zkowvwfxwenq
aid.onion
addnode=bnx4povtqynvwnui5oqm5xcxqvat3j7yzgn6mqciuyszqawhuayvy
aid.onion
addnode=wyg7twmf7t3pfvfpdcfd64wvjj2pkccuui7ew34ovnqung5f623b4
yyd.onion
addnode=nqb5q6d4nhp54ziahhm2oxopqwyyulg7nrqwrcmfvwhj7y7xasae
g7ad.onion
addnode=glm52zywiqrcxuwswvgjsxr5pfeggil7uci4z5tbpvb4rjyu5hwjh
tid.onion
addnode=hhnh56qcpr5menru2u6zsvuox4qnymsmyl67rwihatuliexim64kj
sqd.onion
addnode=vp4qo7u74cpckygkfoeu4vle2yqmxh7zuxqvtkazp4nbvjnxl2s3
e6id.onion
addnode=ew7x2hv76f7w7irfyektnbhd42eut27ttbfgggu7lbpxsyrlfvsuj
uqd.onion
```

---

[9] www.reddit.com/r/Bitcoin/comments/kzhhgk/bitcoin_core_0210_tor_v3/

```
addnode=qxkgr5u4rmwme5jticjuuqrecw5vfc5thcqdxvbffwbqgqkdin7s7
vid.onion
addnode=wn3ffvfxdnhsgpw4oxhv4bhwhyylzqx72ndtdy4sucueoa7awdmw3
nid.onion
addnode=zn7ruedj5mbrlncprwqigin5x2knqjkkw2oh4xzeba4lnlrjvenc
t5yd.onion
addnode=h5k7h7pakm5yiqxdmljqrbpeg4qmg5lpepw7qzg2cwfawxnzwczf5
qqd.onion
addnode=I7ppfrklg4pkqmlgkx23qgrgh4xqm7ssvhdafe6xo5dueilwz5pts
uad.onion
addnode=yeb55drehnp22i2qsmv2tpszwzu3avgl2bas44u7srw267kovoyff
jad.onion
```

onlynet=onion tells the wallet to communicate exclusively using
TOR. dnsseed=0 and dns=0 tell the wallet to stop looking for non-TOR seed
nodes. You can check to make sure you're connected to TOR by going to
Debug window ➤ *Peers*. You should see several nodes with only onion
addresses, like in Figure 5-11.

NodeId ▼	Node/Service	Ping
0	↑ kpgvmscirrdqpekbqjsvw5teanhatztpp2gl6eee4zkowvwfxwenqaid.onion	523 ms
1	↑ bnx4povtqynvwnui5oqm5xcxqvat3j7yzgn6mqciuyszqawhuayvyaid.onion	453 ms
2	↑ qxkgr5u4rmwme5jticjuuqrecw5vfc5thcqdxvbffwbqgqkdin7s7vid.onion	532 ms
3	↑ zn7ruedj5mbrlncprwqigin5x2knqjkkw2oh4xzeba4lnlrjvenct5yd.onion	620 ms
4	↑ I7ppfrklg4pkqmlgkx23qgrgh4xqm7ssvhdafe6xo5dueilwz5ptsuad.onion	1046 ms

Figure 5-11. *Bitcoin seed nodes with TOR "onion" addresses instead
of IP addresses*

What's Next?

Although there is a common perception of crypto as a stronghold of privacy, you can see that this is not true for most coins and tokens. Pseudonymity provided by Bitcoin and others only creates an appearance of safety, masking the actual state of the crypto privacy. This is dangerous because we have not yet developed instincts that would intuitively protect ourselves in the crypto world, similar to how we manage to navigate the physical realm of cash and plastic cards.

Fortunately, however, there is a solution already: privacy-centric coins. We will see how Monero, the best privacy-centric technology, works in the next chapter. Looking ahead, I'll just say that if you start using Monero, you can forget most of the tricks you just learned about in this chapter.

CHAPTER 6

How Monero Works

There was a reviewer a while back who wrote that my pictures didn't have any beginning or any end. He didn't mean it as a compliment, but it was. It was a fine compliment.

—Jackson Pollock

Disruptive technology means that we keep the benefits of the existing things and enjoy the new tech's advantages. Let's take electric cars as an example. They provide all the benefits of traditional gasoline cars – they can drive, have a somewhat comparable price, and are still as safe and convenient as the best "dirty" cars. But on top of that, electric cars are "green" and less noisy. If we follow this logic, which can be observed with any other innovative technology, the new payment systems based on crypto must provide all the benefits of the traditional banking system and plastic cards, even before we get decentralization, universal access, and other new features.

If we want cryptocurrencies to go mainstream as a new payment system, we must ensure some degree of privacy currently provided by corporate systems such as Visa or PayPal. The last thing we want is to publish our credit card statements for anyone to study, but this is precisely what public ledgers of most cryptocurrencies do!

© Slava Gomzin 2022
S. Gomzin, *Crypto Basics*, https://doi.org/10.1007/978-1-4842-8321-9_6

Fortunately, there is a solution to this problem: privacy coins based on unique privacy-centric blockchain technologies. There are three most bold designs and implementations of privacy coins: Zcash (ZEC),[1] Dash (DASH),[2] and Monero (XMR).[3] Perhaps, Monero is the most outstanding one as it has a stunning design.

Why Monero Is Important

In my opinion, Monero is the second most important crypto innovation since Bitcoin. Some experts can argue, of course, because there are other inventions such as Ethereum's "supercomputer." They are also right since those inventions are very important for the evolution of crypto. However, let's remember the original purpose of Bitcoin, the very first cryptocurrency. I will cite the Bitcoin white paper once again: "electronic payment system based on cryptographic proof instead of trust, allowing any two willing parties to transact directly with each other without a trusted third party."[4] The keyword here is the *payment system*. That's the original purpose of Bitcoin and all other cryptocurrencies – replacing traditional centralized payment technologies with the decentralized alternative.

Bitcoin or Ethereum transaction records are available publicly, in clear text. Despite some degree of anonymity, it is not impossible to establish a link between a wallet and the identity of its owner. That's why Monero, as the most successful privacy-centric cryptocurrency, is a considerable step toward broad consumer and business acceptance. Since buyers and merchants will never agree to "publish" their day-to-day transaction records, perhaps privacy-centric crypto is the only way to go mainstream.

---

[1] https://coinmarketcap.com/currencies/zcash/

[2] https://coinmarketcap.com/currencies/dash/

[3] https://coinmarketcap.com/currencies/monero/

[4] Annotated version of Bitcoin white paper. https://genius.com/2683791

In a chapter about cryptography, I told you that explaining cryptography without math is very difficult. I was afraid of even thinking about explaining Monero. It sounds like it's impossible to talk about Monero without higher math, tough cryptography, and, finally, some source code fragments. And yet I will try at least because I believe that everyone who wants to use crypto in any way needs to know and understand privacy coins, especially Monero.

CryptoNote

Not surprisingly, Monero is not the only and not the first privacy-centric cryptocurrency. iPhone wasn't the first smartphone. Tesla wasn't the first electric car. And so in crypto, there were and still are other attempts to create privacy coins, even before Monero. Like how we count the era of blockchain and cryptocurrencies from Satoshi Nakamoto's white paper, we can measure the age of privacy coins from the *CryptoNote* white paper.[5] Like the legendary Bitcoin proposal, the CryptoNote manuscript was authored by an incognito person, with the pseudonym Nicolas van Saberhagen, and published on October 17, 2013. While we don't know who this person (or group?) is, no one can stop us from speculating. Maybe Satoshi and Nicolas are the same people?

There are several versions of the CryptoNote and Monero origins, but I must tell you the unique one. It is an unusual story because it's not published anywhere but was told to me in person by one of the developers working on the GRAFT project. This guy – let's name him Sergei (it's not his real name) – was based in Moscow, Russia, and has demonstrated himself as a very talented programmer right after he started his work on

---

[5] Annotated version of CryptoNote white paper. `https://web.getmonero.org/resources/research-lab/pubs/whitepaper_annotated.pdf`

the project. GRAFT is a fork of Monero, which means it's using a cloned Monero source code as a base for its new features. And Monero, in turn, was forked from Bytecoin (BCN),[6] which was based on the CryptoNote protocol (Figure 6-1).

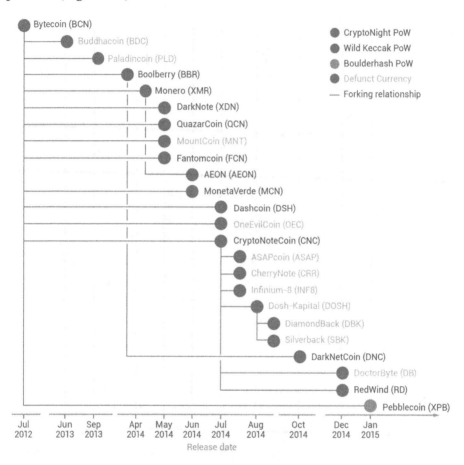

Figure 6-1.   *The forking tree of CryptoNote-based coins. Source: ihodl.com[7]*

---

[6] https://coinmarketcap.com/currencies/bytecoin-bcn/
[7] https://ihodl.com/infographics/2018-05-08/chart-day/

So, when Sergei started to immerse himself into the jungle of the original source code, he found something he did not like. According to Sergei, his findings pointed out that Russian secret intelligence services had created the Monero source code. He refused to provide the proof and almost immediately aborted his participation in the project. Sergei said he does not want to be involved as he fears for his life. Maybe it was simply paranoia, which is a "side effect" of many talented people. I don't know. I am just transmitting the story to you as it is. What I know for sure is that Monero reliably keeps all its secrets!

Now let's go back to the CryptoNote white paper. The document defines several principles of a new cryptocurrency that was supposed to fix Bitcoin's flaws. While it's mainly focused on privacy features like "untraceable transactions" and "unlikeable payments," it's also proposed other exciting innovations such as a new proof-of-work mining algorithm and a different emission schedule. Let's review the privacy features as those are things we mainly like Monero for.

Untraceability and Unlinkability

To understand what untraceability and unlinkability are, let's look at the Bitcoin blockchain one more time. On a very high level, as we reviewed previously, Bitcoin transactions consist of inputs, which are outputs of the sender's previous transactions, and outputs, which the recipient can spend in the future. The sender wallet's private key digitally signs the inputs and outputs, so the funds' movements can be traced throughout the blockchain. The outputs are sent to a specific recipient address (derived from the recipient wallet's public key), so they can be linked to the recipient's wallet.

The transaction can be more complex because a single bitcoin wallet can generate multiple addresses. A recipient who wants to hide his identity can generate a new wallet address for each new incoming transaction.

Those addresses can only be linked if you know the wallet's private key, which means the outside observer won't be able to link those multiple transaction outputs to a single recipient's wallet. At a glance, this feature looks like an excellent security and privacy mechanism, but the idyll breaks quickly when it comes to the need to spend those outputs.

When such a user, who received bitcoins through multiple transactions using unique addresses, wants to spend, they need to create a new transaction that includes these various outputs as new inputs signed by the same private key. This fact explicitly points to the ownership, linking previously unlinked transactions to the user wallet.

Cryptographic Monero Technologies

A single magic technology does not provide Monero privacy, but it is instead built out of several cryptographic techniques, with each of them ensuring a different aspect of privacy or security (Table 6-1).

Table 6-1. *Cryptographic Techniques Used in Monero*

Cryptographic Technique	Type	Privacy or Security Feature	What It Does
Stealth addresses	Privacy	Protecting identity of recipient	Hiding (encrypting) the recipient's address[8]
Ring signatures	Privacy	Protecting identity of the sender	Hiding the sender's address by adding multiple "fake" senders[9]

(continued)

---

[8] https://steemit.com/monero/@luigi1111/understanding-monero-cryptography-privacy-part-2-stealth-addresses

[9] https://medium.com/asecuritysite-when-bob-met-alice/ring-signatures-and-anonymisation-c9640f08a193

Table 6-1. (*continued*)

Cryptographic Technique	Type	Privacy or Security Feature	What It Does
Pedersen commitments	Privacy	Protecting transaction amount from public view	Hiding transaction amount by replacing it with equations that can be still publicly validated without knowing the exact amount[10]
Range proofs (recently replaced by bulletproofs)	Security	Protecting transaction amount from public view; preventing fraudulent transactions that generate funds	Allows the validator to make sure that transaction amount is not reversed (no new funds are generated)[11]
Key images	Security	Preventing double-spending	This technique allows users to spend their funds only once, although no one still can see the details of transactions[12]
Diffie-Hellman key exchange	Security and privacy	Used in encoding and decoding of the stealth address	Used to secretly communicate a shared secret between anonymous sender and recipient to secretly transmit the output that can be spent only by the recipient[13]

---

[10] https://monero.stackexchange.com/questions/3035/in-ringct-how-are-the-range-proofs-kept-separate-from-the-pedersen-commitments/3040#3040

[11] https://masteringmonero.com/book/Mastering%20Monero%20First%20Edition%20by%20SerHack%20and%20Monero%20Community.pdf

[12] https://monero.stackexchange.com/questions/9958/what-keys-are-being-used-to-create-the-key-image-and-how-is-it-verified?noredirect=1&lq=1

[13] https://monero.stackexchange.com/questions/6283/what-is-meant-by-diffie-hellman-exchange-in-the-official-cryptonote-paper

While the main three techniques – stealth addresses, ring signatures, and Pedersen commitments – ensure privacy, there are additional techniques, range proofs and key images, that are required to secure the transactions in addition to standard blockchain security measures such as digital signatures. These extra security controls are necessary because, unlike pseudonymous crypto such as Bitcoin, Monero hides important transaction details from observers, making it impossible to validate transactions using just digital signatures. Let's review these techniques and see how they work together to create amazing technology.

View and Spend Keys

Before we move to privacy and security techniques, let's see how Monero wallet addresses are different from Bitcoin and other cryptos. When you see a Monero address for the first time, you can immediately notice it is longer than a Bitcoin one.

Bitcoin Address:

19dENFt4wVwos6xtgwStA6n8bbA57WCS58

Monero Address:

48W5ysjzTcUcBHtqHxURm56fLr6cSBCcyWfRMuaPfCwZGx7nGdx9Q3tHFxoG7n
MW6A1HnEohN2xwvRErXezdjcicCtFTTg4

This is because it consists of two public keys: the *public view key* and the *public spend key*. The senders use both these public keys when they create a transaction. The wallet owner uses the *private view key* to see the transactions. The *private spend key* is used to make transfers (spend).

Since transactions on the Monero blockchain are invisible to anyone besides their senders and recipients, the wallet owners can provide the private view key to someone if they want them to see their transactions, but without any risk of spending their funds. This feature, for example, can be used for audit purposes. But if you want to spend Monero coins, you have to have the private spend key.

Similar to Bitcoin, Monero keys and address can be generated from the mnemonic seed, so you can store your wallet offline (write it to a piece of paper) as a sequence of 25 English words, like this: *gels adhesive corrode hawk iguana husband kitchens inmate geyser video sapling taunts razor essential abyss jewels sabotage aunt bifocals boyfriend knee hornet superior together adhesive.* So, you can always restore your Monero wallet (both keys, the address, and all the transactions) as long as you keep those words.

Here is one feature that illustrates how Monero is different from Bitcoin. If you type a Bitcoin address into one of the Bitcoin blockchain explorers, it will show you all transactions associated with this address and the current balance! Not exactly a good privacy feature, right? When you do the same with the Monero address, you will only get the sarcastic notification shown in Figure 6-2.

Search by block height / block hash / transaction hash /	🔍

Explorer   Stats   Rich List   API

Uh-oh

For a moment there it seemed that you were trying to peek into this Monero address:

48W5ysjzTcUcBHtqHxURm56fLr6cSBCcyWfRMuaPfCwZGx7nGdx9Q3tHFxoG7nMW6A1HnEohN2xwvRErXezdjcicCtFTTg4

No?

Hmmm... it really looks like you were, like, trying to check out this dude's balance.

Well,

Monero says 'No'!

Figure 6-2. *This happens if you try to check the transaction history associated with the Monero address*

Stealth Addresses

Not every Monero user today knows that the first versions of Monero, which were based mainly on the CryptoNote protocol, did not provide complete privacy. For example, transaction amounts were still visible. But protecting the recipient's identity was the first, most obvious, and perhaps the easiest-to-understand privacy feature, allowing me to review it more thoroughly.

In Bitcoin and most other cryptos, the recipient's address is an integral part of the transaction. It's really difficult to imagine: How can you send money to someone while keeping the recipient's address a secret? As with many other genius inventions, the solution is simple: the recipient's address is hidden from anyone... besides the recipient (and, of course, the sender, but that's obvious). This logic uses the fact that no one actually cares about the transaction besides the recipient. The blockchain, in this case, is just a colossal mailbox, with the sender dropping their package into it and the sender checking the entire content and looking for their package (Figure 6-3).

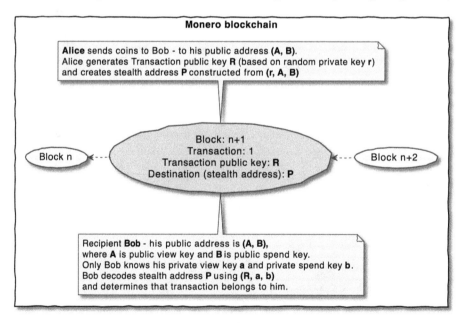

Figure 6-3. *Alice sends coins to Bob using a stealth address*

To be more specific, what the sender Alice does when creating a transaction is encrypt the actual address of the recipient (A, B) with the one-time private key of the transaction r. There are two public keys, A and B (both taken from the actual recipient's wallet address), and one private key, r (randomly generated by Alice), used to create the *stealth address* P. The public key from the randomly generated pair is added to the transaction as a *transaction key* R, in addition to the destination stealth address P.

Now, here is the very important part. To find the incoming transaction, the "invisible" recipient Bob needs to scan the entire blockchain and decipher the stealth addresses of each transaction using his private keys (a, b) and the public key of the transaction R. Bob uses his address (or more precisely, the two private keys that comprise his address – the *view key* a and the *spend key* b), the stealth address P, and the transaction key R to check whether the transaction belongs to him. Yes, this can be a very long and CPU power–consuming process, and that's why the Monero wallet is very different from other cryptos.

But fortunately, there are techniques that are used to optimize the finding of transactions. For example, the Monero wallet does not scan the entire blockchain every time you launch it. Instead, it examines the recent transaction only and remembers where it stopped the scanning last time.

Ring Signatures

Ring signature is a cryptographic function that creates a digital signature that can be performed by any member of a group of signers. In fact, only one key is actually used to sign the message, but it is impossible to say which key from the group was used. In Monero, it means that in each transaction, in addition to the actual sender, there is information about the group of ten "fake" senders (Figure 6-4).

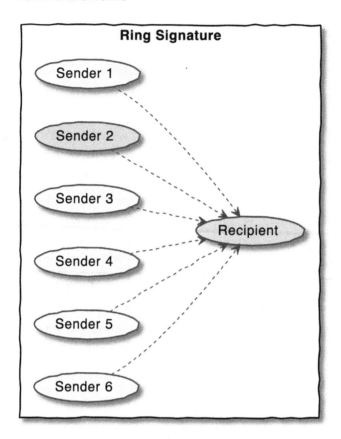

Figure 6-4. *Ring signature – all senders look valid, but only one of them is real*

These senders are not fake as they are taken from various previous transaction outputs throughout the blockchain, and every one of them could be potentially included in the transaction. Figure 6-5 shows 11 public keys, which are the outputs of different transactions included in the ring signature.

Amount	Key Image
— 0.000000000000	9f18cac64317300333b8f3cff1e89996f3906428e961d22d2c26a3c03d1bdf70

From Block	Public Key
2095178	aa1bb5f2362ce147c62f590c73fee56356f20a17f61e6f1d7462c900e420c168
2097082	9ac947727d28d2336a0dc7032156ebb4e64c7327a6f47565dd583b0a4f6f54ae
2097831	9474d8497666bb6a33ec043f94291fb3bfd45704198cfc5f2c50ccae51b91f49
2098566	260a04e2497ead9652411c8061fadf880e1e583d997d1526429d7292b3bf6e9a
2098744	b379145a40fb680616b8ca238236a9fee6ecd17e51bcfdc9b9f958047cfed6b0
2098748	0b137ce7f1650db6c115caef8aa5edda9cb2960ccda6a72d18a6bb1e14525055
2099013	1be623d224c5e5a39aaf6d3aa17f6c3c08cac8c5f2a6314a94d6f8ea55ee559c
2099345	7de4eed7ad5052c4de0744a078f53928f7b11622992e8d93aeba5ae6d8369bc0
2099463	ad4939c130bb2d8ff40b9af8f7882e778a86d30b2ee7eb6da499f32371ac0d18
2099560	8c1692cbed853f55cea2d83551f72a76b3da167125cf480da68abad454ec1752
2099576	c5fd16a055d77ca638a86a8cbab68ec13512a5352cff97188867cbed5785663c

Figure 6-5. *Eleven outputs are included in the ring signature; only one of them is the real input*

Only one of these public keys comes from the actual sender and is used as an input for the transaction. Remember that amounts are also confidential, so it doesn't matter how much previous transactions contain.

You may say that since the actual sender is in the group, there is still an indirect reference to the sender's identity. That's true, but don't forget that the recipient is also unknown. So, if we translate your Monero transaction to plain English, it will look like "*someone, maybe it's you, maybe not, send some unknown amount to someone unknown. Even if I suspect you are the sender, I cannot prove it because it can also be anyone from the group of eleven people.*" Using this transaction's output as an input, the next

transaction will make this "knowledge" even more miserable. Another
11 senders will be added to the list of potential sources, which eventually
wholly removes any traces of the authentic original sender.

Churning

So, in conjunction with stealth addresses, ring signatures provide solid
privacy to both the sender and the recipient. Want to get it even stronger?
Use the technique that is called churning – send your funds to yourself.[14]
This way, you increase the "distance" between the original sender and
your current spendable output, adding more "fake" senders and stealth
recipient addresses in the middle.

Pedersen Commitments and Range Proofs

Amount commitments, or *Pedersen commitments*, or simply *commitments*,
is the cryptographic mechanism used by Monero to hide transaction
amounts. Not everyone knows about it, but in the original version of
Monero, transaction amounts were not hidden. You can see an example of
the transaction from block 200,000[15] shown in Figure 6-6.

---

[14] https://monero.stackexchange.com/questions/4565/what-is-churning?
noredirect=1&lq=1
[15] https://localmonero.co/blocks/tx/9b68d1dc65030ad37c543a139b556f7488
ac20f1d2d651f357c0f8fd505ec99b

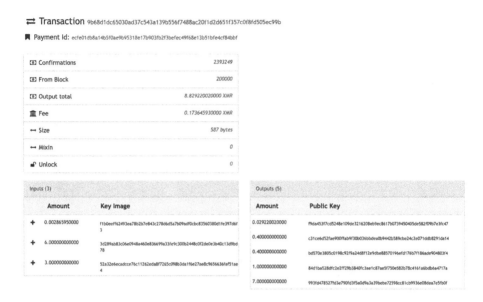

⇄ **Transaction** 9b68d1dc65030ad37c543a139b556f7488ac20f1d2d651f357c0f8fd505ec99b

🔖 Payment Id: ecfe01db8a14b5f0ae9b95318e17b903fb2f3befec49f68e13b51bfe4cf84bbf

🔢 Confirmations	2393249
🔢 From Block	200000
🔢 Output total	8.829220020000 XMR
🏦 Fee	0.173645930000 XMR
↔ Size	587 bytes
↔ Mixin	0
🔓 Unlock	0

Inputs (3)

Amount	Key Image
✚ 0.002865950000	f1b0eeff62493ea78b2b7e843c278d6d5a7b09adf0cbc83560380d1fe397d6f3
✚ 6.000000000000	3d289ab83c06e0948a460e836699a33fe9c300b2448c0f2de0e3b40c13d9bd78
✚ 3.000000000000	52a32e6ecadcce76c11262eda8f7265c098b3da1f6e27ae8c9656636faf51ae4

Outputs (5)

Amount	Public Key
0.029220020000	f9da453f7cd5248e109de321620b8eb9ec8617b0739450405de582f09b7e3fc47
0.400000000000	c31ce6d52fae900ffab9f30b036bbdea0b9442b589cbe24c2e071ddb8291da14
0.400000000000	bd570e3805c0198c92f9a24d8f12e9dbe8857019e6efd176b7f186ade904803f4
1.000000000000	84d1ba528dfc2e2ff29b3840fc3ae1c87ae5f750e582b78c4161a6bdb6a4717a
7.000000000000	993fd478527fd3e790fd3f5a0d9a3a39bebe72598cc81cb9936e08dea7e5fb0f

Figure 6-6. *Monero transaction before RingCT with visible amounts*

Pedersen commitments were part of Ring Confidential Transactions, or RingCT, a cryptographic mechanism introduced in a white paper authored by Shen Noether.[16] RingCT was first used in Monero in 2017. It is based on *ring signatures* described earlier.

A Pedersen commitment is a cryptographic algorithm that proves that the sum of transaction inputs equals the sum of outputs without revealing the actual amounts. It is used to obfuscate the Monero transaction amount. An example of a Monero transaction from block 2,500,000[17] with an obfuscated amount is shown in Figure 6-7.

---

[16] https://eprint.iacr.org/2015/1098
[17] https://localmonero.co/blocks/tx/c39652b79beb888464525fee06c3d078463 af5b76d493785f8903cae93405603

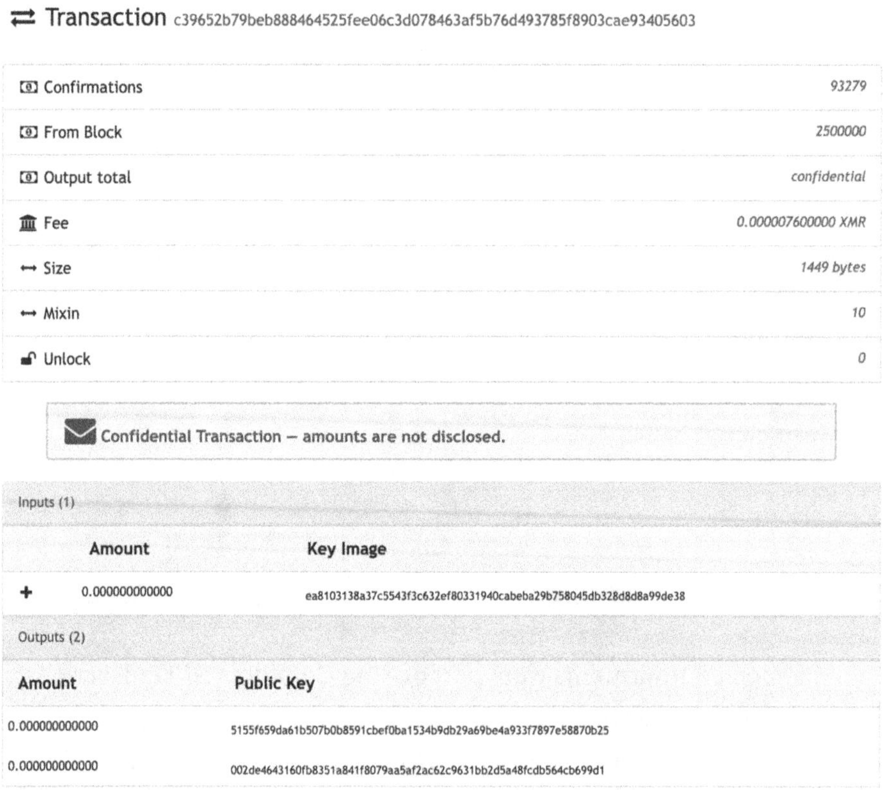

⇄ **Transaction** c39652b79beb888464525fee06c3d078463af5b76d493785f8903cae93405603

⊡ Confirmations	93279
⊡ From Block	2500000
⊡ Output total	*confidential*
🏛 Fee	*0.000007600000 XMR*
↔ Size	*1449 bytes*
↔ Mixin	*10*
🔓 Unlock	*0*

✉ Confidential Transaction — amounts are not disclosed.

Inputs (1)

Amount	Key Image
✚ 0.000000000000	ea8103138a37c5543f3c632ef80331940cabeba29b758045db328d8d8a99de38

Outputs (2)

Amount	Public Key
0.000000000000	5155f659da61b507b0b8591cbef0ba1534b9db29a69be4a933f7897e58870b25
0.000000000000	002de4643160fb8351a841f8079aa5af2ac62c9631bb2d5a48fcdb564cb699d1

Figure 6-7. *Monero transaction from block 2,500,000 with the hidden amount*

Range proofs are needed to ensure that the committed amount is greater than zero and less than the limit to prevent fraudulent manipulations and create free money. Range proofs were recently replaced by more efficient *bulletproofs*, which do the same by doing it faster and using less transaction space, which is so valuable in blockchains.

Key Images

All these privacy and secrecy features are great, but if Monero transactions are so hidden, how does it protect itself from double-spending? The sender, the recipient, and the transaction amount are hidden. Yet, the network (i.e., essentially anyone who has a copy of the blockchain) should be able to validate the transaction and make sure the funds are not double-spent. The former is done through RingCT, which validates the sender and the amount without public disclosure. But the latter is done using an additional mechanism called *key images.*

Each Monero transaction includes a key image for each input used in the transaction (you can see the key image in Figure 6-7). The key image is generated using the one-time public key of the corresponding input and the secret shared between the sender and the recipient.

The key image is part of the ring signature and uniquely represents the public key associated with the output of the previous transaction that is being spent. If the input public key owner tries to spend the associated funds again, the resulting key image will be the same. Otherwise, the ring signature won't be valid. So, before adding a new transaction to the blockchain, the validators (miner nodes) scan the entire blockchain to ensure the same key image was not present in previous transactions.

Learn More About Monero

I should say that I realize that understanding Monero is a challenging task that deserves a separate book. After reading this short chapter, I cannot imagine that you fully understand it, but at least I hope it gives you some starting point. If you want to learn more about Monero, you can find the list of references that I believe will save you some time you would otherwise spend googling.

Understanding Monero Cryptography, Privacy is an excellent description of Monero math which consists of two blog articles: *Introduction (which talks about ECC, the particular curve, private and public "keys," and a bonus section on how Monero addresses are generated)*[18] *and Part 2 – Stealth Addresses.*[19] Despite it being short, this is one of the best descriptions of Monero basics. Unfortunately, the author apparently lost interest in writing and discontinued the series, so the other essential elements of Monero's design remained without his coverage.

Zero to Monero: A technical guide to a private digital currency for beginners, amateurs, and experts:[20] This is a free book, which is the complete Monero reference, but I warn you: it has a lot of heavy math... If you are not afraid of math, this book is for you. Otherwise, the following one will be more useful to you.

Mastering Monero: The future of private transactions:[21] This is also a free book, very detailed, but unlike Zero to Monero, it has a minimum amount of math required for understanding. Thus, it is more suitable for nonmathematician readers.

Finally, Table 6-1, which contains the list of cryptographic techniques used in Monero, has references for each entry that best describes the corresponding technology.

---

[18] https://steemit.com/monero/@luigi1111/understanding-monero-cryptography-privacy-introduction

[19] https://steemit.com/monero/@luigi1111/understanding-monero-cryptography-privacy-part-2-stealth-addresses

[20] www.getmonero.org/library/Zero-to-Monero-2-0-0.pdf

[21] https://masteringmonero.com/book/Mastering%20Monero%20First%20Edition%20by%20SerHack%20and%20Monero%20Community.pdf

What's Next?

I think the emergence of Monero in its importance is not inferior to the invention of Bitcoin. This becomes especially obvious when you look at crypto as a payment system that must compete with plastic cards, which have no intention to give up their positions anytime soon. After all, if we seriously consider cryptocurrencies as an alternative to plastic cards, it is clear that no one will use a coin that exposes all our financial operations to the public. To continue this discussion, the next chapter is all about the primary purpose of crypto: processing payments.

Crypto payments are very different from cash and plastic cards that most people still use these days. If crypto technology is so wonderful, why haven't we abandoned our leather wallets and switched to paying with crypto yet? I will answer this question in the next chapter, which will help transition to the next part of this book: Using Crypto. You will also learn how to spend Bitcoin and other coins and tokens in places that would not seem to accept crypto at first glance.

CHAPTER 7

Crypto Payments

If a man is wise, he gets rich, an' if he gets rich, he gets foolish, or his wife does. That's what keeps the money movin' around.

—Finley Peter Dunne

I decided to designate the entire and separate chapter for crypto payments even though other chapters in this book are condensed, and their material could also be stretched to several chapters. This is because payments are a very special topic for me. For many years, I have been dealing with electronic payments as a software developer first, then as a security guy, and later even as an entrepreneur. In 1999, I started working for an Israeli startup called Retalix,[1] which created one of the first mainstream touch screen point-of-sale suites for supermarkets, convenience stores, gas stations, and fast-food restaurants. An additional key differentiator of their checkout solutions was integrated payment processing – another innovation back then.

Suppose you have ever seen a c-store at the travel center that serves truckers or even at your regular neighborhood gas station. If you are old enough, you may recall what the checkout counter looked like 20–25 years ago: it had multiple terminals for various types of magnetic payment cards

---

[1] TechCrunch. NCR Acquires Retail Point Of Sale Software Company Retalix For $650 Million Cash. https://techcrunch.com/2012/11/28/ncr-acquires-retail-point-of-sale-software-company-retalix-for-650-million-cash/

© Slava Gomzin 2022
S. Gomzin, *Crypto Basics*, https://doi.org/10.1007/978-1-4842-8321-9_7

that had already become very popular. Each device had a single purpose of accepting payment with a particular card type. For example, credit cards were processed separately from debit cards, gift cards, and fleet cards (special payment cards used mainly by truckers).

New-generation integrated point-of-sale systems resolved this issue by using a single payment terminal, also known as a *pinpad* or *POI* (point of interaction), with special software running on the in-store server that routes payment transactions to a specific authorizer (*payment processor*) based on the card *BIN (bank identification number) range* – the six-digit prefix of the *PAN* (primary account number).

Each payment card type and brand have a unique BIN prefix assigned by the issuing bank. For example, all Visa card account numbers start with 4, all Mastercards with 5, etc. Additional "flags" – special numbers located at predefined positions within the magnetic tracks – can also affect the routing. Integrated payment processing was a significant change for the retail industry because it simplifies the checkout process, which means faster checkout and lower expenses.

I'm talking about this topic not because I'm writing a memoir. The then state of the payment card industry resembles the current state of the crypto payment business. There are dozens of high-profile cryptocurrencies that are popular and widespread enough to be accepted as payment. There are even hundreds more that potentially could also be taken if there was a standard way to do so. But many cryptos have technology unique enough to make their acceptance different from others, requiring individual processing.

Why Pay with Crypto?

Apple Pay was introduced in 2014 and slowly but surely became a popular alternative to traditional plastic cards (in part because it is based on the same plastic cards). Apple Pay and its sister (or brother?) Google

Pay are very convenient, especially in restaurants with new payment terminals placed on every table. I hope Google Pay provides a similar user experience, although I have never tried it. I am an Apple fan, but I am not paid (unfortunately) by Apple to advertise their products (but they usually speak for themselves).

Anyway, with Apple Pay or Google Pay, the only thing you need is your smartphone, no need to carry your physical wallet full of plastic cards. Not to mention it's very secure compared to plastic cards, with their magnetic stripes and account numbers written all over the face of those cards...

If there is any issue with payment, app, or card, you have Apple or bank support ready to help 24/7. If you lose your phone, your card is still safe and can be reattached to a new device. Even if you lose your card or it is stolen, you can still get a replacement and even a refund for the stolen money.

So why would I use anything else for payment? Why Bitcoin, for example? It isn't easy to understand and use. Its value isn't stable. If something happens with the payment or your wallet, no one is there to help you! Well, maybe a payment processor if the payment is facilitated through one, but then your payment is not private anymore, which defeats the primary purpose of crypto. But if your wallet is lost with the private key, and there is no backup, it's gone forever, and nobody will be able to recover your money.

So, there should be something to motivate users to start paying with less convenient and more risky things. Something that traditional plastic cards and even mobile phone payments cannot provide. Maybe Bitcoin will magically change to provide all the convenience and user experience of traditional payments, in addition to unique things such as freedom from governments and corporations?

What can Bitcoin do that those plastic cards can't? The most important difference, in my opinion, is accessibility. People living in developed countries enjoy easy access to banking. But almost one-third of the global population is still unbanked.[2] If you don't have a bank account, you cannot get a debit or credit card. If you don't have a plastic card, you cannot use Apple Pay.

There is another thing that we just discussed in the previous two chapters: privacy. Only crypto can keep you free from the dictate of big corporations and surveillance of authoritarian governments. But different crypto networks and payment implementations can strengthen or weaken those obvious advantages of crypto over plastic.

Why Crypto Payments Are Difficult

There is an essential factor that makes crypto payment processing difficult. The first cryptocurrency – Bitcoin – was designed as the "Internet money," and most subsequent "altcoins" followed suit. The unknown inventor of Bitcoin did not think about "offline" payments in regular brick-and-mortar stores. It's somewhat opposite to what's happened to a magnetic payment card, which was initially designed for transactions in a traditional store. When online shopping started getting traction, there were many technical and security issues. In fact, the *EMV* ("Europay, Mastercard, and Visa," also known as *chip-and-pin*) card still doesn't have a worthy security solution for ecommerce. That's why your modern chip-and-pin cards are still coming with account numbers printed on them, which is definitely not the best security feature.

So, when crypto became popular enough just a few years after Bitcoin's invention, naturally, the question arose of adoption by the mainstream brick-and-mortar businesses. But it turned out that most cryptos are not suitable for being accepted in retail environments out of the box. Confirmation time, which is the time required to write a transaction into the blockchain "deep" enough so it would be impossible to reverse

---

[2] https://globalfindex.worldbank.org/

the payment, is so long that the cashier won't be able to wait in most cases. High-volume retailers are fighting for each millisecond (literally) required for payment authorization because it saves them a lot of money. Milliseconds are multiplied by hundreds of their stores with thousands of checkout lanes. Shorter approval time allows them to serve more customers with fewer cashiers and saves on their payroll.

Most advanced merchants process payment card authorization in less than one second. For comparison, the average time of first confirmation for a Bitcoin transfer is ten minutes. It is not uncommon to require at least three and up to six confirmations for a Bitcoin transaction to be considered irreversible. With less popular blockchains, where the cost of a significant attack on the blockchain is much lower and manageable even for an average person, the number of confirmations would rise to dozens or even hundreds. The number of confirmations means the number of blocks added to the blockchain on top of the block that contains a given transaction. The deeper the blocks are "buried" into the blockchain, the more difficult it is for an attacker to mine a valid alternative chain that does not contain the original transaction.

In the software world, of course, almost every problem eventually gets resolved. The problem with multiple confirmations has been solved as well. At least, there is resolution available for top cryptocurrencies. Any solution, however, has a price tag. In the case of crypto, this price tag is quite heavy not just because of the financial cost, which is also significant and adds to the cost of each transaction. The main cost is rather ideological.

Crypto was created as a decentralized, anonymous money and payment system, which simply means that anyone can use it, and no state government or corporation should be able to control it. But crypto payment processing in mainstream retail, especially "offline" brick-and-mortar stores, requires a centralized entity, a "man in the middle" between the buyer and the merchant. There should be someone – we call them a *payment processor* – who uses additional tools to allow merchants to process the transaction within a reasonable time.

In addition, most merchants are not ready to deal with hundreds of cryptocurrencies. Even handling one or two cryptos can be a big deal for them as it will create an accounting nightmare. Retailers do their accounting in local fiat currency, and they are not in the currency exchange business. So, payment processors resolve this problem by making payouts in their local fiat currency, with the crypto exchange going behind the scenes. Now let's see how technically retail crypto payment processing is made possible.

Custodial Payment Processing

There are two typical ways crypto payment processors implement payments. The first method – let's call it *custodial* or *account-based payment processing* – is faster and safer (for the merchant). Still, it somewhat limits the adoption and decreases the freedom and privacy of the buyer to the minimum because it requires the buyer to create and maintain an account with the payment processor. The payment processor becomes a custodial crypto wallet in this case. Custodial means that someone else owns the private keys for your account (wallet).

To process payment, the buyer first needs to create an account and deposit some amount of crypto. Since deposit can be done in advance and not at the time of the purchase, there are no time constraints for the transaction approval time. When it comes to the actual purchase in the store, the processor does not move the actual crypto on the blockchain. Instead, they just transfer the virtual amount from the buyer's account to the merchant account, which can be done instantly. The merchant can then withdraw crypto later or get a payout in fiat if the processor provides such a service. This type of payment processing is shown in Figure 7-1.

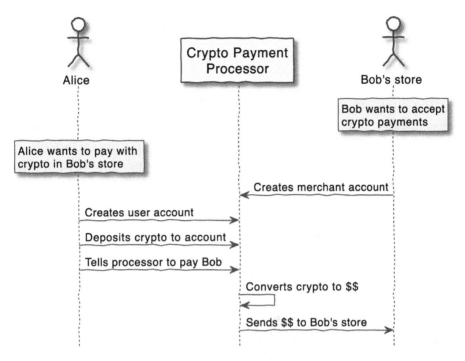

Figure 7-1. *Custodial payment processing*

The advantage of this method is that it can be applied to virtually any cryptocurrency, regardless of the type of technology it's using, or the time it requires to confirm its transaction. Perhaps the most well-known example of account-based payment processing outside of crypto is PayPal. They also recently started doing crypto transactions using the same old good approach. To use PayPal, you must create a user account and identify yourself each time you transfer money.

Note that the merchant itself can become the crypto payment processor for itself. Unlike plastic cards that belong to payment brands like Visa and Mastercard, crypto does not belong to anyone, and anyone can use it without buying any license. For merchants, it's much easier than becoming a plastic card payment processor, which is almost impossible.

Non-custodial Payment Processing

Another type of payment processing by third-party processors is using information collected from a particular crypto network to analyze the risk of transaction reversal and generating preliminary authorization when the risk is low enough to be acceptable by the merchant. This method is slower and less safe than custodial because it takes time to wait until the risk becomes acceptable, even though some risk is still there. To minimize the probability of chargeback or eliminate it, you would need to wait until several confirmations, which, as we already know, can take minutes or even hours. Let's take Bitcoin as an example to understand how this method works.

When you pay with Bitcoin, your wallet app generates a transaction record broadcast to the distributed network of Bitcoin nodes. Despite a large number of nodes and their vast spread throughout the world, Bitcoin transactions will reach many of the nodes surprisingly fast – within a fraction of a second. Once the transaction reaches the node, it's validated and placed into the transaction pool. Typically, once it's in the transaction pool, it has only one way from there to the blockchain in one of the subsequent mined blocks. It may take time (depending on the fee amount and other factors) for one of the miner's nodes to put it to the new block. Still, it will eventually happen, sooner or later, if the transaction is valid, that is, if there is no double-spending attempt associated with the transaction inputs (Figure 7-2).

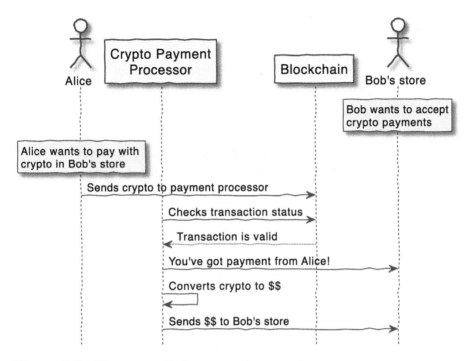

Figure 7-2. *Non-custodial payment processing*

So why can't we consider a transaction completed once it's in the transaction pool? The answer is network latency and possible network fragmentation. The fact that the transaction reached one node and has been placed in its transaction pool does not necessarily mean that other nodes did the same. Theoretically, another node or cluster of nodes might receive a similar transaction that contains inputs constructed from the same outputs but addressed to a different recipient. Suppose there is a problem with broadcasting – for example, a widespread Internet outage. In that case, two groups of nodes may end up containing two different transactions and consider both of them valid simultaneously. Eventually, however, one of these transactions will be invalidated by the majority of the nodes because only one can make it into the blockchain.

All this means for the payment processor is that it cannot rely on a single node to consider transactions valid. However, if the processor has access to (or, even better, owns) several always-on, trusted nodes distributed geographically, and those nodes all confirm the transaction's validity, it's fair to assume that such a transaction has a good chance of being eventually added to the blockchain.

Such a preliminary confirmation is very realistic with robust blockchains such as Bitcoin or Ethereum because attacks on those blockchains are costly and unlikely. In addition, the amount of average retail transaction is so low that the risk of losing such a transaction is acceptable for the merchant or payment processor with large daily sales volumes.

This method is more convenient and safer for the buyer because it does not require them to create an account, disclose their identity, and trust the processor to store their money. So this method probably has better chances of being accepted by a broad audience. The disadvantage, however, is that this does not work for all crypto but only for the top blockchains where the risk of attack is minimal.

The bottom line is that crypto payment processing is possible and accessible today. Still, we should not forget that it pulls us back from an idealistic decentralized, free world to a more conventional and convenient but limited world of corporate dictate and government control.

Two-Tier Crypto Networks

All methods are suitable, and the result justifies the means in the race to create a perfect crypto payment system, which requires correcting some flaws of the original Bitcoin design. One of the ways to do that was the invention of so-called two-tier networks. In such a two-tier architecture, the first tier is the blockchain network itself, taken as it is in its original design, while the second tier, which is also called *layer 2*, is running on top of the first layer while complementing it by the features such as instant confirmations, private transfers, and low transaction fees.

One of the first implementations of the two-tier crypto network was Dash (DASH) which introduced the concept of *masternodes*. While Dash is a PoW blockchain, its layer 2 network of masternodes uses PoS to facilitate instant approvals and private transactions (for an additional fee).

Even though two-step transaction processing seems to be a novel idea in crypto, the concept is borrowed from the traditional plastic card processing mechanism, which divides transactions into two phases: *authorization* and *settlement*. While authorization is processed fast (within milliseconds), which allows using plastic cards for real-time payments in a brick-and-mortar business environment, the settlement takes hours and even days (Figure 7-3).

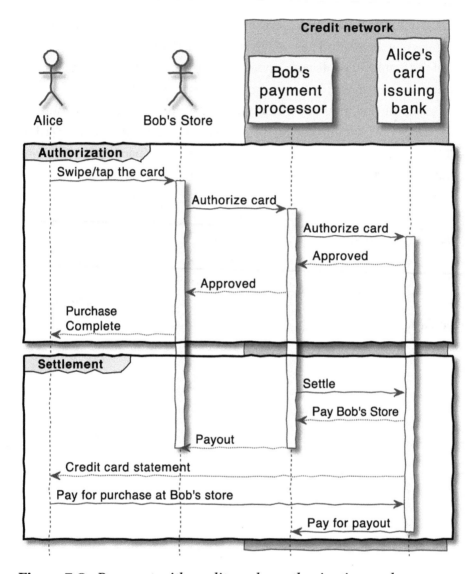

Figure 7-3. *Payment with credit card – authorization and settlement process*

Authorization gives the payee somewhat high-degree assurance that the payment can be accepted, but only the actual settlement makes the transaction 100% paid (make the actual money movement). There are certain things that can go wrong in the period between authorization and settlement, which may create a chargeback – a situation when the payee is refused to get the payout for the transaction.

Two-tier crypto networks work based on similar principles (Figure 7-4). The blockchain itself (layer 1) is the settlement system, which provides slow but complete confirmation for the transactions. The network of masternodes (layer 2) provides instant authorizations, which are later settled at the blockchain. The masternode cannot guarantee 100% that a transaction will be settled on the blockchain simply because the transaction is not finalized until it is recorded in a block by the miners, and this block remains in the main chain buried under several more recent blocks. But masternodes use several techniques that allow them to make authorization safe and reliable.

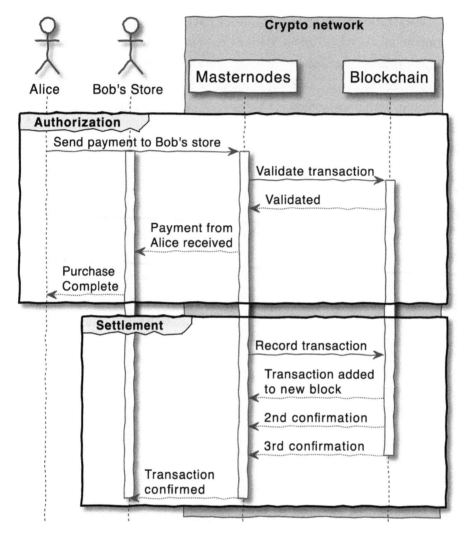

Figure 7-4. *Crypto payment using a two-tier network*

Many crypto projects followed the two-tier trend in an attempt to "repair" the basic blockchain tech and allow crypto payments to enter the mainstream. Yours truly has designed a two-tier GRAFT network which was supposed to enhance a private Monero-based blockchain to enable instant, private retail payments. But everything has its time. If you start too late, there is always someone else who's already done it and has the advantage. If you start too early, the businesses and consumers are simply not ready for adoption. Determining the right time for your project is one of the keys to success.

Lightning Network

A chapter about crypto payment would not be complete without mentioning the *lightning network*. What is a lightning network?[3] It is a layer 2 "superstructure" on top of the Bitcoin blockchain that allows processing payments *off-chain*, that is, without recording each transaction in the Bitcoin blockchain, which in turn enables payment processing with greater speed and lower fees. Sounds fantastic, isn't it? It is an exciting technology, and what's most important is that it actually works. However, as with any crypto tech, it has its downsides. First, let's see how lightning works and discuss its advantages and main drawbacks.

How Lightning Works

Let's take our favorite Alice and Bob scenario when Alice wants to send one bitcoin to Bob. According to lightning design, the pair needs to open a channel between them to make transactions, making a deposit from both sides using a smart contract. But opening a channel requires recording transactions on the Bitcoin blockchain, which defeats the purpose of lightning – avoiding on-chain recording as much as possible to save on transaction fees and speed up the authorization process. Fortunately, lightning allows reusing existing channels to route transactions through them.

---

[3] https://lightning.network

Let's say both Alice and Bob already have channels previously opened with Carol. Lightning knows about it and automatically sends one bitcoin from Alice to Carol and then from Carol to Bob (Figure 7-5).

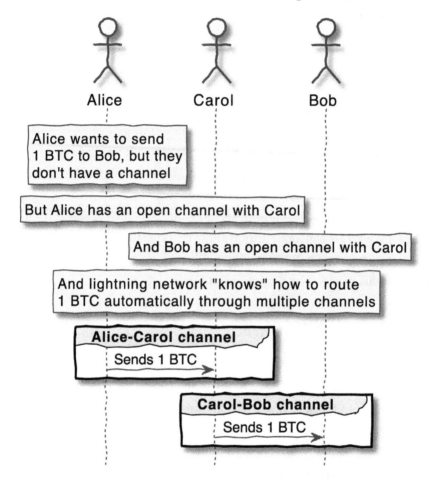

Figure 7-5. Lightning transaction between Alice and Bob

In reality, the routing can be much more complex, and there are special super nodes – hubs – that maintain a lot of open channels with multiple participants and between the hubs themselves.

A channel is basically a smart contract between two participants. Any side can cancel the contract anytime, creating an on-chain transaction to get the channel deposit back. At the same time, the other party does not lose its contribution and automatically receives it back.

Lightning Cons

The apparent pros of lightning are **transaction speed** (instant confirmations), **high scalability** (it can process much more transactions per second than the Bitcoin blockchain), and **low transaction fees**. But there are also significant cons:

- Lightning nodes must always be online to make the network functional. If a large hub goes down, the contracts need to be closed on-chain and re-created (also on-chain) with different hubs. Not very decentralized!

- Transaction fees must be higher to make the lightning network profitable. Node operators need to get paid to keep the nodes "always-on."

- Large hubs make the network less decentralized, defeating the original idea of crypto and reducing participants' privacy.

- The special wallet is required for lightning transactions, and not all wallets support lightning.

- Participants must open channels, that is, make deposits as you do with prepaid cards, which means they declare their balances and cannot keep them offline.

Prepaid Cards Loaded with Crypto

Crypto prepaid cards are an interesting symbiosis of traditional plastic cards and cryptocurrencies, which allows you to spend crypto in every place that accepts traditional plastic card payments. It works simply by loading your prepaid card, issued by one of the payment brands such as Visa or Mastercard, from your crypto wallet. At the time of "load," your crypto is exchanged for dollars, so the card is functioning as a regular debit card accepted in most retail locations. One example of such a prepaid crypto card is BitPay[4] (Figure 7-6).

---

[4] https://bitpay.com/card

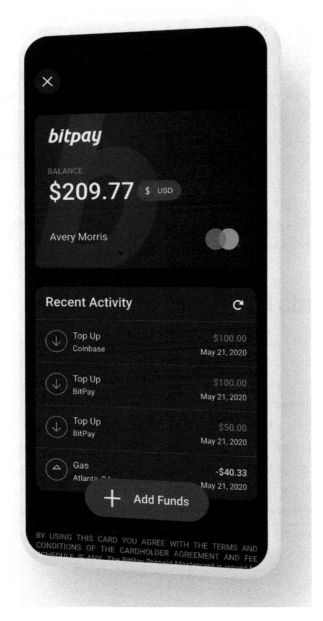

Figure 7-6. *BitPay prepaid debit card linked to the crypto wallet.*
Source: bitpay.com

The card has both a virtual version (available in the BitPay wallet app) and a physical plastic card with a chip, which can be used as a regular payment card.

Of course, a prepaid card defeats the original purpose of crypto as it makes you dependent on a centralized, corporate world because there is a company that facilitates loading funds from your crypto wallet to the card (like BitPay), a payment brand that provides the payment network (like Mastercard in the case of the BitPay card), and a bank that actually issues the card (like Metropolitan Commercial Bank which issues BitPay cards and maintains the associated dollar accounts). But on the other hand, it makes your crypto assets very liquid and eliminates the need to use exchange when you want to spend your coins.

Gift Cards Purchased with Crypto

Another rather ingenious way to use crypto as a payment method is gift cards. Most retailers still don't accept cryptocurrencies as a tender (payment method accepted at the checkout). However, they all have one thing in common: they sell (and accept as tender) their own branded gift cards. So, if you could buy a gift card with crypto, you would be implicitly allowed to pay with crypto for many goods and services. Good news: You can do it today! Several websites sell multiple branded gift cards for crypto. *Bitrefill*[5] is one of the biggest, available in several countries and selling gift cards for various chains. They currently sell gift cards issued by 383 brands representing different business areas, from Amazon and Walmart to American Airlines to The Cheesecake Factory.

---

[5] https://bitrefill.com

Bitrefill accepts Bitcoin, Ether, USDT, and some other coins. How does it work? You select the gift card and the amount and go to the checkout, where you are offered to pay with one of the cryptocurrencies. To minimize the transaction fee, you can select the lightning option. In the case of lightning, the transaction fee can be just around 1 cent.

During the checkout, the website will display a payment QR code ("quick response code") and the buttons, which you can use to start the payment in the wallet. The payment can be processed using a wallet that supports lightning, for example, Electrum. Assuming you already have a lightning channel previously open with a deposit large enough to cover the price of the gift card (Figure 7-7), you can copy/paste the lightning invoice address into the Send tab or select the Electrum wallet and click the Pay in Wallet button (Figure 7-8).

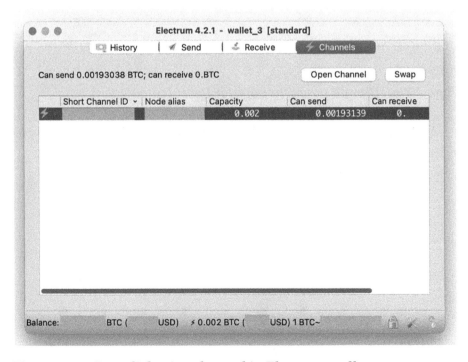

Figure 7-7. *Open lightning channel in Electrum wallet*

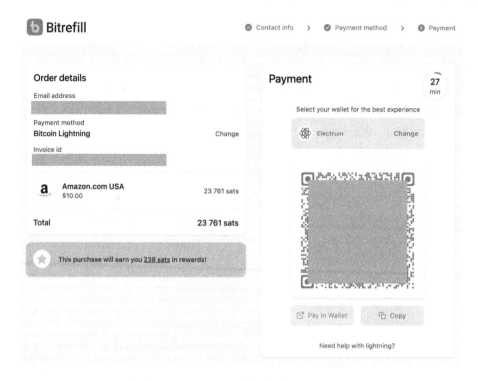

Figure 7-8. *Bitrefill payment page for lightning payment*

After the payment is processed, you will get a special code that you can redeem immediately in the virtual or physical store (Figure 7-9).

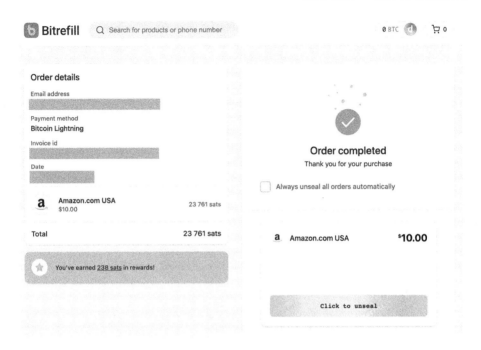

Figure 7-9. *Gift card codes can be instantly redeemed at the retailer's website*

What's Next?

Despite the variety of crypto payment technologies, crypto payments are still kept on the outskirts of mainstream business. There are many reasons for it, and I hope you know more about these reasons now after finishing this chapter. I still believe that the future belongs to crypto payments. Perhaps, not in the same form as we know them today.

Our current monetary and payment systems are insecure and too heavily dependent on governments and corporations that are not always honest, to say the least. There are, and there will be, new crypto technologies. Eventually, one of them will find that unique combination of business necessity and consumer satisfaction – the right wow factor to break through and push it into the mainstream.

This chapter concludes the first part of the book. I believe you have got enough theory now and are eager to go to the field. Any encounter with crypto begins with the topic reviewed in the next chapter, so it's easy to guess its content. I will start the second part of the book, which talks about the practical side of crypto, discussing crypto wallets.

PART II

Using Crypto

CHAPTER 8

How to Choose the Wallet

> *The task of helping the drowning people is in the hands of the drowning people themselves.*
>
> —Ilya Ilf, Yevgeny Petrov. *The Twelve Chairs*

To tell the truth, this chapter should be the first one in this book. So, if you skipped it all the way to this chapter, I totally get that. But if you didn't and already read previous chapters, I hope it will be easier for you to understand how different wallets work and what pros and cons each type of wallet has.

When it comes to selecting a wallet, it's all about two things: private key storage and usability. Let's talk about the keys first. Private keys can be stored in the cloud, software, or hardware. The cloud option means that you don't own the keys, and they are managed by someone else for you. Even if you can "see" and download the keys, it still doesn't mean you own them. This approach is similar to traditional banking, and therefore it is pretty convenient.

The bank manages an account for you and stores your money. You get credentials (username and password), so only you, the owner, can access your account and transfer your funds. The only problem is that if the bank decides to freeze your account, they can do it anytime. Even if it's

© Slava Gomzin 2022
S. Gomzin, *Crypto Basics*, https://doi.org/10.1007/978-1-4842-8321-9_8

done by mistake, it doesn't matter – you still lose access to your money. Also, the bank can go bankrupt. And here come the differences between a traditional bank and a *custodial* crypto wallet, that is, the wallet that stores and manages the private keys for you outside of your device, the same way your bank stores your fiat money and manages your accounts for you.

First, with most big banks, the chance of them going bankrupt is low. Remember the great recession of 2008 and how the government bailed out the major banks?[1] Second, deposits in most banks are insured by FDIC[2] (Federal Deposit Insurance Corporation) for up to $250,000. Both these lifebuoys do not apply to crypto, however.

Typical crypto-financial companies won't be bailed out by the government (unless they also belong to a big bank). There is no FDIC insurance to recover your lost crypto if the wallet provider goes bankrupt or disappears. The bottom line: Think twice before deciding to trust your crypto money to someone else.

If I managed to convince you already not to use custodial wallets, let's see what the other choices look like. The alternative is *non-custodial* wallets, which can be divided into different categories. The first and most popular category is *hot*, or *software* wallets. The fact that hot wallets are the most popular is no coincidence since they represent the best balance between decent security, privacy, and usability.

Another category is *cold* or *hardware* wallets, which would be helpful for you if you are looking for maximum security. Note that the privacy of hot and cold wallets is about the same because when it comes to transactions, they all communicate with the network and write transactions into the blockchain in the same way (basically, through a hot

---

[1] www.forbes.com/sites/mikecollins/2015/07/14/the-big-bank-bailout
[2] www.forbes.com/advisor/banking/4-key-facts-about-the-fdic

wallet). Thus, you really should go down the cold (hardware) wallet path if security (not privacy) is your highest priority – for example, if you store huge amounts of assets or operate in an insecure environment.

One more important wallet characteristic is what coins and tokens it supports. There are single- and multicurrency wallets. Suppose you are an entrepreneur or developer who needs to receive and send payments in crypto. In that case, you will probably focus on a single coin such as Bitcoin or Ether and shop for the best in the single-currency category. You will have many choices because besides "Bitcoin-only" and Ether-only," almost all multicurrency wallets support Bitcoin and Ether. Therefore, for Bitcoin- or Ether-like coins, you can choose a wallet using the decision tree shown in Figure 8-1.

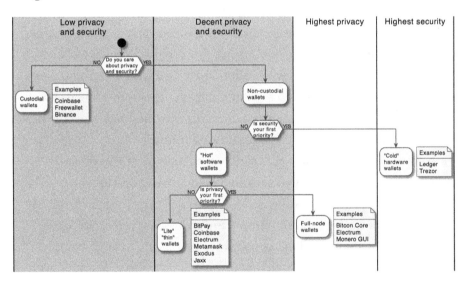

Figure 8-1. *Wallet selection decision tree*

But if you are a trader or investor, you don't have too many choices because you will probably have to deal with more "exotic" coins and tokens. In this case, one of the lite, multicoin wallets probably would be your best and only choice. But it would help if you understood what all these epithets mean first.

Custodial Wallets

This is the most simple and obvious category. The wallet provider stores private keys in their cloud, and they manage everything for you. Although I don't think using custodial wallets is a good idea for security and privacy reasons, I realize that this can be a good option for some people. After all, we trust banks to manage our fiat accounts. And here, I must mention a couple of advantages of custodian wallets. First, if you lose your credentials (username and password required to access your account), the custodial wallet provider should be able to help you restore your access, so your money won't be lost forever. This is an obvious advantage over a non-custodial wallet where you only rely on yourself.

Another advantage over non-custodial wallets is the ability of custodial providers to transfer funds between user accounts instantly and for free. This is possible because they don't move any crypto between wallets. They store all crypto in one large wallet and only transfer funds between accounts by updating the data in their database. This is precisely what banks do with your bank accounts, and that's why they also typically move funds between your accounts instantly and for free.

If you are unsure about your readiness to manage the keys (and backups!) by yourself, and you see other clear advantages for you, go ahead and start from a custodial wallet. Some examples of custodial wallets are Coinbase,[3] Freewallet,[4] and Binance.[5] However, all crypto exchanges, basically, are custodial wallets as you can store crypto in your account managed by the exchange. Note that Coinbase provides a custodial web wallet as an exchange, but it also has a non-custodial wallet under the same name,[6] which is confusing if you don't know the difference.

---

[3] www.coinbase.com/
[4] https://freewallet.org/
[5] www.binance.com/
[6] https://wallet.coinbase.com

Custodial wallets are usually straightforward in use and have an intuitive interface, so there is no need to provide additional instructions. You just go to the website and create an account, as with most other websites.

Caution   Always use MFA (multifactor authentication), even if it is optional. Most crypto trading platforms (exchanges), which are also custodial wallets, these days provide MFA. If you find one that doesn't have MFA, just avoid using it. Without MFA, it's just a matter of time – not if but when – your account will be hacked, and your crypto assets will be gone…

Non-custodial Wallets

The word "non-custodial" is not widely used because it is a technical term, and there are more chances to hear descriptions like "lite" or "thin client" (they are the same); "cold," "hardware," or "offline" (all these three mean the same thing); or "full node" wallet. There are also more exotic types like CLI (command-line interface) and paper wallets.

All the above are subcategories of the "non-custodial" category of crypto wallets because they provide their users with complete control over the private key. You should use these wallets if you want to leverage the full power of decentralized crypto technology.

Caution   It is very important for all types of non-custodial wallets described as follows to back up the private keys and/or mnemonic seed (mnemonic phrase)! With a non-custodial wallet, you are the only custodian of your money and responsible for wallet recovery if something happens with your device. If your computer is burned, your mobile phone is stolen, and you don't have a backup of your private keys or mnemonic phrase, your coins and tokens are gone forever!

Hot vs. Cold Wallets

Hot (also known as *software*) wallets are the online ones. They run on a device connected to the Internet, and the device owner can make transfers. Most crypto wallets are hot. The rest are called *cold* (or *offline*), like *hardware* and *paper* wallets.

Theoretically, you can also transform a hot wallet into a cold one by disconnecting your device from the network. This way, you can ensure it's impossible to hack remotely. Note that it's still possible to steal the device and recover information from there if it's not encrypted or if the password is not stored correctly.

Lite (Thin Client) Wallets

Lite, or *thin client,* wallets are the biggest category of crypto wallets for two reasons: they are very convenient for users and relatively easy to implement and maintain for developers. There are many good wallets, and it's up to you which one you want to use. Don't stay stuck with a wallet if you feel something is not working for you – you have a choice. Try several wallets and see which one works best for you.

Lite wallets consist of a client (the app running on your desktop computer or mobile phone) and a server (the brains running somewhere in the cloud). Hence, the name "thin client" or "lite" is because the part that runs on your device is just an interface to the wallet provider's server. Even though this scheme does not precisely fit the decentralized concept of crypto, it does its job for average and less sophisticated users. Most importantly, a lite wallet is the only option if you want to keep multiple coins and tokens in one wallet. More privacy-centric wallets like full node or CLI typically support only a single coin.

Desktop vs. Mobile Wallets

Many wallets provide both *desktop* and *mobile* versions. This is almost a rule for lite wallets as it's easy to implement. Lite, or thin client wallet, has client and server apps, which is the standard pattern for implementing mobile apps. Desktop follows the same principle. One of the interesting examples is the BitPay[7] wallet. Their desktop and mobile versions have very similar user interfaces (Figure 8-2), making it easy to switch if you use desktop (laptop) computers and mobile phones, which many people do these days. But for some reason, the mobile version has more features such as buy, exchange, and prepaid card management.

---

[7] https://bitpay.com/wallet

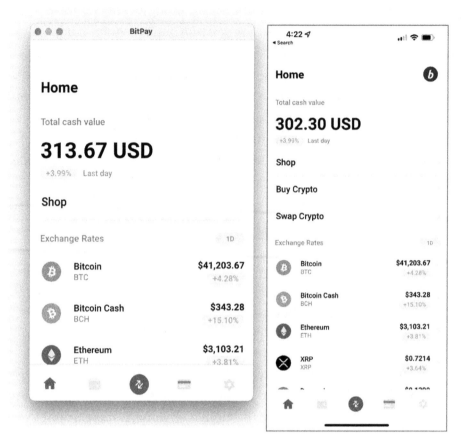

Figure 8-2. *BitPay desktop (left) and mobile (right) wallets*

Note that mobile wallets can be non-custodial, that is, you can still retain ownership over your private keys. This is the case for BitPay, Coinbase, and other mobile wallets. In any case, for a non-custodial wallet, it is very important to back up your private keys and/or mnemonic phrase.

Multisig Wallets

A *multisig* (*multisignature*) wallet allows more than one owner to manage the account. Spending (generating, signing, and sending transactions to the network) requires multiple users to give their "approval." There are various multisig schemes with multiple numbers of signers and different types of involvement.

The simplest and probably most popular multisig scheme is "1-of-2," where there are two owners with equal rights. It's like two users with access to the same bank account. Both owners can spend independently. They can be, for example, spouses or co-founders. Another popular scheme is "2-of-2," which requires both owners to sign the transaction and implements a "dual control" security principle. More complex x-of-y schemes can also be used for a more sophisticated organizational structure.

Not all the coins support multisig, but "main" coins such as Bitcoin, Ethereum, and Monero do. The same for wallets – not all of them support multisig, but most do.

Full Node Wallets

Full node is an important category because it provides maximum privacy, and privacy is an essential factor for many people who deal with crypto for either ideological or personal safety reasons. Full node is a self-explaining name – the wallet is connected to the full network node running on a local computer or network. A typical crypto network node exposes a special API (application programming interface) that full node wallets can use to make a local call and get necessary data. These calls usually are not exposed for remote access because, otherwise, your node could end up serving an enormous number of wallets. Therefore, it is necessary to run the node on your computer.

Running a node is not as difficult as it might seem at first glance, but it requires a set of minimum resources available on your machine. For example, the size of the Bitcoin blockchain at the time of writing this text is 324 GB, which is growing every ten minutes.

I don't want to go into the details of the node setup – there are excellent instructions you can find online.[8] I just want to mention that you don't have to store the entire blockchain. There are some advantages of storing blockchain, but for many users, it's unnecessary unless you want to fully support the Bitcoin network by holding the full copy of the ledger. If this is not your primary goal, you can reduce storage consumption and enable *Prune block storage* in Preferences (Figure 8-3).

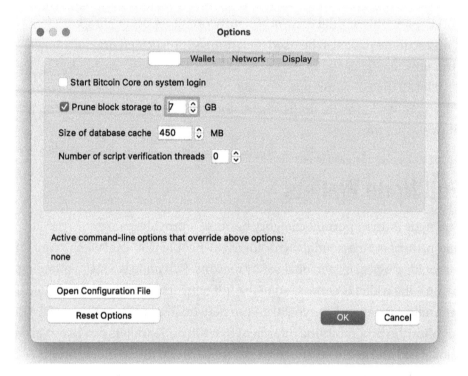

Figure 8-3. *Check Prune to limit the size of local blockchain storage*

---

[8] https://bitcoin.org/en/full-node#what-is-a-full-node

Another tip: You don't have to run the wallet continuously. If you use your wallet occasionally, uncheck *Start Bitcoin Core on system login* (Figure 8-3) and just run it before you need to do something. But note that it will take time to sync up with the network if you haven't run it for a long time.

Hardware Wallets

Hardware wallets (also called offline or cold) are the most secure because they store private keys in a secure chip isolated from your desktop computer or mobile phone and are therefore difficult to hack. It is also protected by physical security controls such as physical buttons. Thus, it is impossible to move your funds if someone, for example, hacked into your computer without your explicit approval.

When your hot (software) wallet is connected to a hardware wallet, it enables MFA (multifactor authentication) for your overall wallet solution, where the hardware becomes a second authentication factor ("something you have"). This effectively creates a hot wallet with an elevated level of security. Your primary authentication factor is the password to your wallet and the private key – "something you know."

Now a brief digression into cybersecurity. To make MFA fully functional, there should be at least two factors present from three possible categories: "something you know," "something you have," or "something you are." That's why MFA sometimes is also called 2FA (two-factor authentication). "Something you know" is simple: this can be a password, a private key, or any other piece of secret information. "Something you have" should be something physical – like your phone or, even better, a dedicated piece of hardware like a hardware wallet. And finally, "something you are" is biometric like your fingerprint, face, etc.

It's important to note that if you have two or even more authentication factors of the same category, it is not considered MFA. For example, if you have a password as a first factor and a one-time code sent to your email, this is not MFA if access to your email is protected only by a password. Your password and one-time code (also protected by the email's password) belong to the same authentication factor unless your email account requires MFA – in this case, you can rely on the email's MFA as a second factor. But in general, even if you need to enter ten different passwords to access the wallet, it is still considered a single factor – "something you know."

The idea behind MFA is that it's easy for hackers to break a single factor, for example, steal all your passwords stored in one file. But it's much more challenging to simultaneously get hold of your second factor (like hardware wallet).

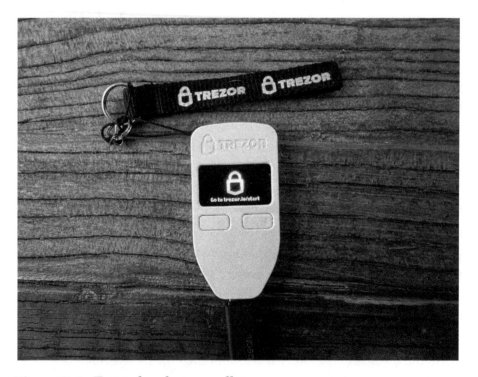

Figure 8-4. *Trezor hardware wallet*

Figure 8-5. *Ledger hardware wallet*

Trezor[9] (shown in Figure 8-4) and Ledger[10] (shown in Figure 8-5) are the two most popular hardware wallets and, therefore, probably the most reliable. This is how it works, unfortunately for software and hardware startups, in security: the more the product is used and abused, the higher the chances that someone finds vulnerabilities earlier, and so the vendor already has fixed them.

---

[9] https://trezor.io/
[10] www.ledger.com/

Caution   Avoid using unknown, unpopular, homegrown, and newly developed products related to security, whatever it is – a piece of hardware, software library, or encryption algorithm. It's not like fine art or music when you just follow your taste. In security tech, follow the crowd! Also, avoid buying security stuff on the secondhand market. Who knows what you get in there in addition to what you are supposed to get! Buy only directly from the vendor.

Paper Wallets

Paper wallets are also a subcategory of cold (offline) wallets because they exist only on paper. A paper wallet is basically a private key and sometimes a public key (address) printed or handwritten on a piece of paper. The excellent news about paper wallets is that they cannot be hacked because they do not exist in electronic form (if they are created properly, without leaving traces on your computer!). But paper can be destroyed or stolen as any other physical property, so it's better to keep it in a safe place like a bank deposit.

CLI Wallets

All the wallets described earlier, both custodial and non-custodial, have GUI (graphic user interface), that is, they present the user with the interface containing screens with buttons and other visual controls. But you will be surprised to know that the *CLI* (*command-line interface*) wallet is the biggest category of crypto wallets because of every cryptocurrency coin. That is, any crypto with its own transaction ledger has a command-line wallet that developers create as part of the project's core code.

CLI is the easiest (for developers!) and probably the safest (for everyone) wallet because it usually comes with the full node running locally. While GUI wallets can support only selected features of a coin, CLI wallets always support all the features that the coin provides because the development team uses them during coding and testing. Although CLI might look scary for inexperienced users, it's not that different from GUI. You just type commands instead of clicking a button; that's it! With that said, you can use a CLI wallet only if you really need it – for example, if you participate in developing a crypto project.

Not Sure Yet Where to Start?

It depends on what you are going to do. Table 8-1 shows some non-custodial wallets and their most essential features.

Table 8-1. *Some Non-custodial Wallets and Their Features*

Wallet	Supported Crypto	Category	Hardware Wallet Support	Multisig Support
Bitcoin Core GUI	BTC	Full node	No	No
MetaMask	ETH and ERC-20 tokens	Lite	Trezor and Ledger	No
Electrum	BTC	Lite	Trezor	Yes
Electrum with/server	BTC	Full node	Trezor	Yes
Coinbase	BTC, BCH, LTC, ETH, ETC, XRP, XLM, DOGE, and all ERC-20 tokens	Lite	Ledger	Yes
Monero GUI	XMR	Full node	Trezor and Ledger	No
Exodus	181 coins and tokens[11]	Lite	Trezor	No
BitPay	BTC, BCH, ETH, WBTC, LTC, DOGE, SHIB, GUSD, USDC, USDP, DAI, and BUSD	Lite	No	Yes

---

[11] www.exodus.com/status/#supported-assets

Here are some additional tips:

- Suppose you are just starting with crypto and want to experiment with a small amount of Bitcoin or Ether. In that case, you can try BitPay or Coinbase as they have a straightforward, intuitive interface, run on any desktop and mobile OS, and yet are secure enough (both are non-custodial wallets).

- If you plan to invest a significant amount in Bitcoin for a long time, use Bitcoin Core, which can be configured for super privacy, or Exodus[12] with a hardware wallet (very secure).

- If you are going to do much trading with multiple coins and tokens, you can go for something like Exodus or MetaMask.[13]

- If you decide to go extreme and achieve maximum security and privacy, you can combine full node and hardware wallets. For example, for Bitcoin, set up an Electrum wallet with a personal server[14] and full node running locally and connected through TOR, with keys stored in the Trezor hardware wallet.[15]

- For Monero, you can use a Monero GUI wallet connected to a local full node with Ledger Nano or Trezor hardware wallets.[16]

---

[12] www.exodus.com/

[13] https://metamask.io/

[14] https://driftwoodpalace.github.io/Hodl-Guide/hodl-guide_64_eps-mac.html

[15] https://blog.trezor.io/using-trezor-with-electrum-v3-a0b9bcffe26e

[16] https://github.com/monero-ecosystem/monero-GUI-guide/blob/master/monero-GUI-guide.md#how-hardware-wallets-work-with-monero-gui

- It's very normal to use several wallets simultaneously if you need them for different purposes described earlier.

What's Next?

There is a variety of crypto wallets available for you on the market. Most of them are free for various reasons. Some wallets are maintained and financed by the crypto project teams, making them an add-on that comes as part of the crypto ecosystem. Others monetize their products by providing additional services to the wallet users, such as a built-in exchange.

If you don't care much about privacy and security, you can start with a simple custodial wallet. However, beginning with a non-custodial wallet would be wiser if you understand all the implications. With a non-custodial wallet, you must remember that your funds are gone forever if you lose your wallet and don't have a backup of the private key or mnemonic seed!

Now, when you are equipped with a suitable wallet, we can discuss getting your first crypto. Even though crypto equals money in most cases, you might be surprised that there are still multiple ways to get crypto for free. In the next chapter, I will show you how to get some small amounts just to get started and play with crypto or even earn a more significant number of coins or tokens in exchange for performing all kinds of strange activities. You will also learn how to mine Monero!

CHAPTER 9

Getting Crypto for Free

We haven't the money, so we've got to think.

—Ernest Rutherford

Almost 100 years ago, in 1923, American engineer Vladimir Zworykin submitted a patent application for a complete television system, which included descriptions of camera, transmitter, receiver, and screen (which he named kinescope).[1] Dr. Zworykin eventually was credited with the invention of television, which heavily influenced our lives. I don't think he could have imagined that his creation would become the primary tool of the powerful propaganda machine that helped create the most aggressive autocratic regime of the 21st century on the territory of his country of birth.

On the TV development road map scale, however, crypto is still in 1936. Is it going to influence our lives eventually as strongly as TV did? I think it is, but hopefully not in the wrong ways as it happened with television. Nevertheless, TV and crypto have at least a couple of common characteristics.

---

[1] www.bairdtelevision.com/zworykin.html

© Slava Gomzin 2022
S. Gomzin, *Crypto Basics*, https://doi.org/10.1007/978-1-4842-8321-9_9

First, and probably most obvious, is that both technologies are very difficult to comprehend, especially for an average, nontechnical person, and initially perceived as a kind of miracle. These days, perhaps, every engineer, not even directly connected to electronics, or even tech-savvy high schoolers understand how television works. But a century ago, TV was like crypto today, on the cutting edge of technical progress, with many competing ideas and solutions and violent patent battles around them.

At least, crypto does not have a patent problem, as most crypto tech is open source, that is, the code that anyone can use free of charge. We learned something during these hundred years. It's not just about the idea. The idea by itself does not cost much. The ability to implement and deliver is what is most important for success.

But I would like to focus on another, quite paradoxical thing that is common between TV and crypto: they both bring in a lot of money to people who wisely manipulate them while coming to the end user for free. Both have "exceptions" or "extensions," like paid cable subscriptions and purchasing crypto through the exchange. But at its core, the original idea is that you can get them for free. In fact, you can still get TV channels on the air open to everyone, and that is how TV started and attracted billions of viewers. And you can still receive crypto free of charge from various sources, and that's how it started as well, by a group of enthusiasts mining Bitcoin on their laptops and now already engaging hundreds of thousands or even millions of people around the globe.

Can we still leverage the original mission and get some crypto for free? The answer is yes and no. It's probably no if you are a professional trader or serious investor because you simply don't have time to spend on this. Your time might be allocated more effectively and bring better returns if you pay. But if you are a newbie in crypto, and you are just curious to understand what it is and just want to "touch and feel" it, or maybe you have no financial ability to invest significant cash, the answer is definitely yes.

Faucets

Perhaps, faucets are the easiest way to get the smallest amount of crypto. Faucet is a public wallet funded by crypto project developers, enthusiasts, patrons, or marketing departments that can send you a micronumber of coins or tokens. Who are the owners of the faucet wallet, and why do they do it? As in most cases with free crypto, the answer is the same: promotion.

The mission of the first faucets (let's call them "type 1" faucets for convenience) was to convert you to the user of that coin or token by giving you a small amount of specific crypto to play with. You start learning more about the project, download and install the compatible wallet, and begin monitoring the exchange rate; in other words, you become a crypto community member. The idea is that when you collect enough knowledge and get some initial "trial" amount to play, like with traditional marketing, your next step will be *buying*.

Nowadays, another type of faucet (let's name it "type 2") is more common, and it is even more driven by marketing motives. People are attracted by free stuff to the website; the website gets paid by advertisers for the number of clicks on their ads. Users are forced to do various tasks, from clicking links to playing games. To prevent users from abusing the faucets by automating the process and downloading significant amounts, there are multiple tricks like asking to solve CAPTCHA (Completely Automated Public Turing test to tell Computers and Humans Apart).[2]

Since Bitcoin price is very high these days, it's impossible to find a classic Bitcoin faucet anymore, that is, the faucet of type 1, which simply dispenses a small number of coins without forcing you to play some idiotic games or bombarding you with suspicious ad pages. But there are still traditional faucets available for less "commercialized" crypto. For example, Free Nano Faucet[3] is very simple – you enter your Nano (XNO) address

---

[2] www.imperva.com/learn/application-security/what-is-captcha
[3] https://freenanofaucet.com/faucet

(you can use an Exodus wallet or any other wallet supporting Nano to generate one quickly), and you receive a small amount of Nano within seconds. It does not require you to do any registration or perform any task. That's how the first faucets used to work for Bitcoin. Unfortunately, not anymore.

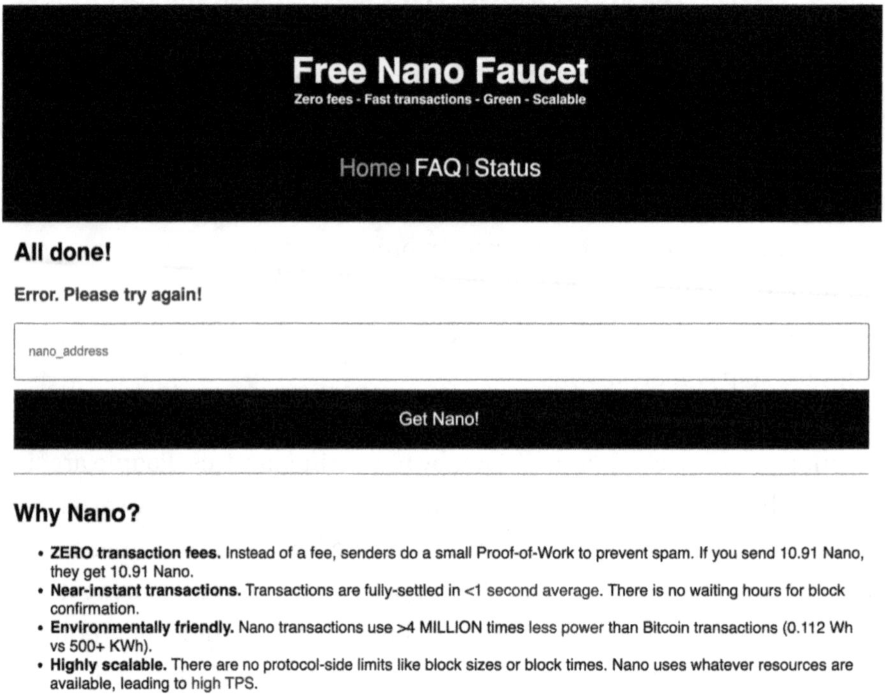

Figure 9-1. *Free Nano Faucet*

Looking at the simplistic website of Free Nano Faucet, you can see the properties of the "type 1" faucet. On one page, it tells you the story of Nano and explains its core principles (Figure 9-1). The amount of Nano this faucet dispenses is scanty – about $0.00006 at today's prices (Figure 9-2).

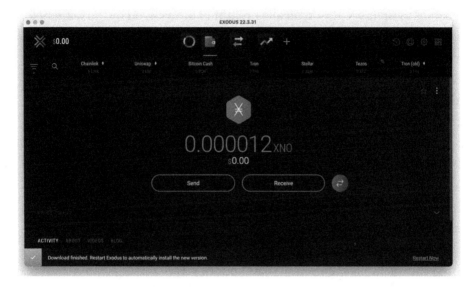

Figure 9-2. *Nano balance received from a faucet in the Exodus wallet*

But given that Nano is one of the few cryptos that do not charge transaction fees, you can use these fractions of the coin for testing transfers between your wallets virtually indefinitely. Just note that to prevent DoS attacks on its network, Nano requires wallets to do some amount of PoW before sending funds. In my opinion, this is one of the downsides of the Nano system because it limits its usability. For example, it would be difficult, if not impossible, to implement a Nano wallet on microdevices such as smart cards as they wouldn't have enough computing power to perform PoW.

Airdrops and Bounties

Sometimes, it's difficult to distinguish between *airdrop* and *bounty*. However, there is supposed to be a clear boundary between them. Airdrop is free crypto that (almost) literally drops from the skies on you. Airdrop does not require you to do anything in exchange for some amount of crypto. Why? Promotion, of course. New crypto projects have extensive reserves of their crypto – typically premined or reserved by the team before the project launch. These reserves are usually generously spent on various marketing activities, including airdrops.

In fact, an airdrop is similar to a faucet but in the reverse direction. Instead of you finding the coin, it finds you. Crypto exchanges often conduct airdrops as part of the promotion campaigns for newly listed coins or tokens. If you are an existing exchange user, you are automatically a potential candidate to become an investor in new crypto. So, one day, you can notice that in your exchange wallet suddenly appears a small amount of new crypto you have never heard about before. It's not a bug in exchange software; it's an airdrop!

Since typical "pure" airdrops are entirely free, their amounts are insignificant and less common than bounties. If you compare airdrops and bounties to faucets, it's like reverse type 1 and type 2 faucets, respectively. Type 2 (bounties) are more common and can bring larger, sometimes significant, payouts because they require you to do something. For example, share and like posts about crypto projects on social media, write articles, make translations of project white papers to different languages, write an essay about the project, and much more.

Bitcointalk

You can find info about bounties and airdrops on the Bitcointalk forum at bitcointalk.com, which historically became the de facto standard for posting announcements of new crypto projects, as well as alerts about airdrops and bounty campaigns. The Bitcointalk forum is both attractive and annoying. It is an interesting media because the most known cryptos have started their journey from an announcement on Bitcointalk. For example, Figure 9-3 shows the Ethereum project announcement in 2014: "Ethereum: Welcome to the New Beginning."[4]

---

[4] https://bitcointalk.org/index.php?topic=428589.0

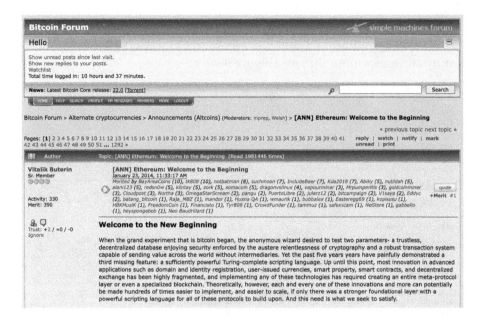

Figure 9-3. *Ethereum project announcement on the Bitcointalk forum*

Bitcointalk can also be disturbing at the same time as any social media that allows anonymous accounts. Some people tend to say (and do!) bad things when they feel impunity. With that said, if you decide to become a professional crypto bounty hunter, you probably cannot avoid using Bitcointalk.

How to Find Bounties

As I said, airdrops often find you without your will, but it does not work the same way with bounties, so you need to search for them. There is a de facto standard in the Bitcointalk forum for message subject prefixes in square brackets. For example, new project announcements have the prefix [ANN] (see Figure 9-3 again). Special messages, typically marked by the [Bounty] prefix in the subject, announce bounty campaigns for new and existing crypto projects. You can use the Bitcointalk search engine to search for bounty announcement threads (Figure 9-4).

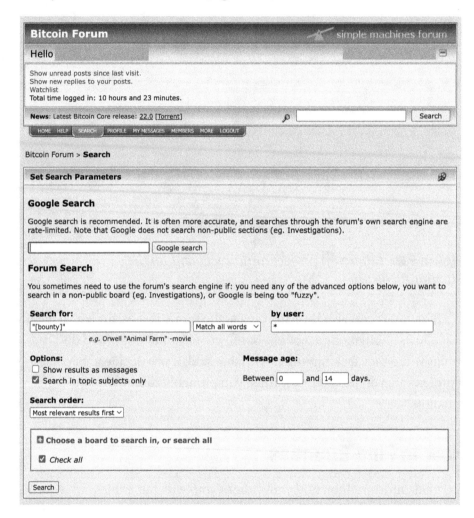

Figure 9-4. *Search for bounty announcements on Bitcointalk*

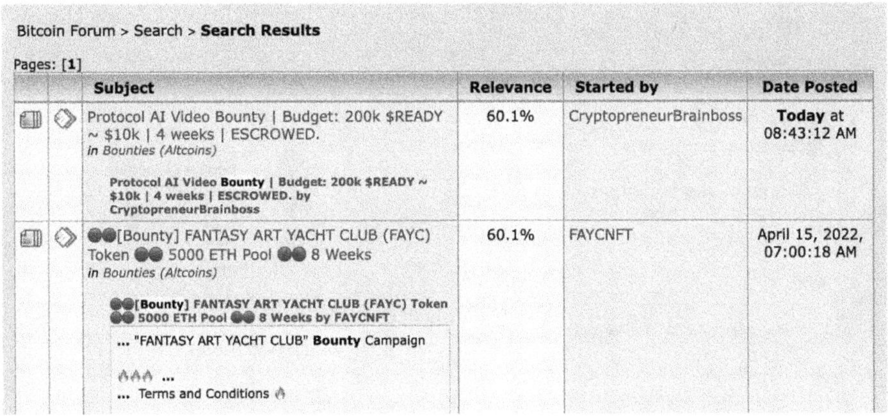

Bitcoin Forum > Search > **Search Results**

Pages: [1]

	Subject	Relevance	Started by	Date Posted
	Protocol AI Video Bounty | Budget: 200k $READY ~ $10k | 4 weeks | ESCROWED. *in Bounties (Altcoins)* **Protocol AI Video Bounty | Budget: 200k $READY ~ $10k | 4 weeks | ESCROWED. by CryptopreneurBrainboss**	60.1%	CryptopreneurBrainboss	**Today** at 08:43:12 AM
	●●[Bounty] FANTASY ART YACHT CLUB (FAYC) Token ●● 5000 ETH Pool ●● 8 Weeks *in Bounties (Altcoins)* **●●[Bounty] FANTASY ART YACHT CLUB (FAYC) Token ●● 5000 ETH Pool ●● 8 Weeks by FAYCNFT** ... "FANTASY ART YACHT CLUB" **Bounty** Campaign ⚘⚘ ... ... Terms and Conditions ⚘	60.1%	FAYCNFT	April 15, 2022, 07:00:18 AM

Figure 9-5. *Search results with bounty threads on Bitcointalk*

The result of such a search will look like the one shown in Figure 9-5. When you click one of the messages in the search result, you will usually see a bunch of details about the bounty campaign, including the rules, the camping fund, the reward amounts, etc.

In addition to Bitcointalk, many Telegram groups are dedicated to bounties like the one shown in Figure 9-6.[5] In that group, you can see more than 48,600 users! These are 46,000 bounty hunters watching for new campaigns and looking for the latest crypto projects.

---

[5] https://t.me/s/Bounty

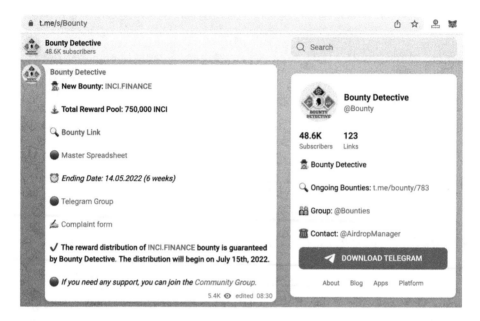

Figure 9-6. *Telegram group that advertises various bounty campaigns*

If you played in the stock market and found a company like Tesla or Apple in the very early stages and got enough shares for pennies, you could become a millionaire. The same with crypto: find another future Ethereum, get some bounty coins, and wait. It's even better than the stock market because you can earn coins or tokens either entirely for free (airdrop) or in exchange for a simple work (bounty). The only problem is – with both stock and crypto markets – that you need to find and select that unique project from thousands of others. That's why many bounty hunters just plow the new crypto market by participating in all available bounty campaigns in the hope that at least one of them will become *the* one.

AMA Rewards

AMA stands for *Ask Me Anything*. This is a prevalent form of promotion, especially for new crypto projects. AMA allows the investors to learn more about the project technology, financials, the team, and the founders. For the project team, it is an excellent way to spend their crypto funds on promotion in the form of bounty.

Special investment communities such as Telegram groups organize AMA sessions for a fee (paid by the crypto projects that are being promoted). Some venues require payments in "hard" currency such as Bitcoin or Ether, but some accept new crypto being promoted. Active participants (people who ask questions) receive bounty rewards, usually paid out in crypto that is being promoted.

Besides Telegram, AMA can be conducted on YouTube and other social media platforms. You can find AMA session schedules on the famous *CryptoMarketCap* website, on their events page.[6] In addition, you can look for the #AMA tag on Twitter.[7]

Bitcointalk Signature Campaigns

Signature campaigns on the Bitcointalk forum are an attractive marketing technique that is probably unique to crypto, so it's worth mentioning. Suppose you already visited Bitcointalk in relation to the previous section about bounty campaigns. In that case, you might have noticed that almost every post on that forum has a signature associated with the poster. Bitcointalk signatures are similar to your automated email signature, which you can set up in Microsoft Outlook, Gmail, or any other mail management system. When you post something on the Bitcointalk forum,

---

[6] https://coinmarketcap.com/events
[7] https://twitter.com/search?q=%23AMA

your post is automatically followed by the signature you previously defined in your account settings. However, there is a difference between those signatures and those you are familiar with.

Smart owners of the Bitcointalk forum, which is a commercial enterprise like everything that surrounds crypto, came up with the idea of ranking the user accounts based on their *activity* (number of posts or comments) and *merit* (this one is similar to social media likes but they are transferred from one user to another). The rank of your account, in turn, defines the size and the quality of the signature you can attach to your posts and comments. Table 9-1 shows how Bitcointalk account ranks are related to the signature limitations.

Table 9-1. *Bitcointalk Account Rank Requirements and Signature Limitations*

Account Rank	Minimum Activity	Minimum Merit	Signature Limitations
Brand new	0	0	No signature allowed
Newbie	1	0	No styling. No links
			No colors. No personal images. No font size. No background color. No tables Max 50 characters
Jr. member	30	0	No styling. No links
			No colors. No personal images. No font size. No background color
			No tables
			Max 150 characters
Member	60	10	No colors. No personal images. No font size. No background color
			No tables
Full member	120	100	No font size. No background color
			No tables
Sr. member	240	250	No background color
Hero member	480	500	No limitations
Legendary	775	1000	No limitations

I am describing the signatures in great detail because numerous crypto-related projects use them as a powerful marketing tool. Bitcointalk signature campaign involves multiple users who replace their signatures with those specifically designed for the campaign and advertise a particular crypto project. When users participating in the campaign post on the forum or comment on other users' posts in various threads, their signatures are displayed along with the text they post, so multiple users see these ads while browsing the forum.

The campaign manager counts the number of signature appearances (and corresponding reward payments to the signature carriers). Some people specialize in designing the signatures for signature campaigns as Bitcointalk uses a special markup language with HTML tags and other proprietary format rules. Figure 9-7 shows an example of a Bitcointalk signature created for the signature campaign. Most of the content in the signature is hyperlinks, so when you click a particular area of the signature, you will be redirected to corresponding pages.

Figure 9-7. *Example of account signature specifically designed for signature campaign*

The campaign managers and designers are well paid from crypto project marketing funds. Campaign participants (users who carry the campaign signatures) receive rewards for advertising the projects. As with most other crypto bounty rewards, signature rewards can be paid in liquid currencies such as BTC or ETH, tokens that are being advertised (as crypto teams usually have plenty of them), or a mixture of the two. In any case, "professional" campaign managers and campaigners can receive quite generous payouts in exchange for their work.

Mining

Mining (or, more precisely, Bitcoin mining) was the first way to get free crypto, but it quickly became the most sophisticated. In addition, mining is far from free anymore, especially Bitcoin mining, which requires investment in expensive ASIC (application-specific integrated circuit) equipment and significant amounts of electric power.

Within a few years after the Bitcoin launch, mining was transformed from a geeky hobby to a professional business. I will not cover professional mining here, as there are books that already do this, but it's still worth talking about how mining is still available for mere mortals. Some cryptos, such as Monero, are designed to resist the creation of ASIC, making their mining more accessible to amateur miners.

Many cryptos require GPU (graphics processing units) such as those used in display cards to get meaningful revenue. But I have good news for you – it's still possible to mine some crypto for free, using your home computer's CPU! Bad news – you will not earn much money unless you have a bunch of computers and free electricity. But you can still do it as a scientific experiment – to "feel and touch" crypto and get something you harvested by yourself. It gives you a special emotional feeling like eating a fruit or vegetable you have grown by yourself in your garden!

Mining Monero

Since we already talked about Monero, let's try to mine it! To mine Monero, you will need the following:

- **CPU**, that is, desktop or laptop computer, or a virtual machine in a cloud. It can run any Windows, Linux, or Mac OS operating system.

- **Wallet** app supporting Monero (XMR).

- **Miner** – Software that runs on your computer and connects it with the mining pool.

For creating those instructions during my mining experiment, I used the following:

- **iMac** with Mac OS Monterey

- **Exodus** wallet running on iMac[8]

- **XMRig** miner[9] connected to **MineXMR** Monero mining pool[10]

You can easily adjust the following instructions to use Windows or Linux as both Exodus wallet and XMRig miner support all primary OS. You can use any mining pool that supports Monero but remember that they have different fees and hash rates. The higher the pool hash rate, the higher its chances of solving more blocks. However, such big pools usually come with a higher fee and a larger number of participants. The fee is the share of the block reward, which all participants pay to the pool after it solves the block. Keep in mind that the block reward is distributed between all pool users proportional to their contribution. So, the more users connect to the pool, the lower your portion of the block reward.

For the sake of the experiment, if you mine for the first time, I still recommend selecting a pool with a higher hash rate. You will get a very tiny amount, but at least you won't wait days or weeks to get the first reward, and within minutes you can prove to yourself and your friends that it works, and you have finally mined your first crypto. The MineXMR pool,[11] as shown in Figure 9-8, has the highest hash rate and solves most of the Monero blocks.

---

[8] www.exodus.com/download

[9] https://xmrig.com/download

[10] https://minexmr.com/miningguide

[11] https://miningpoolstats.stream/monero

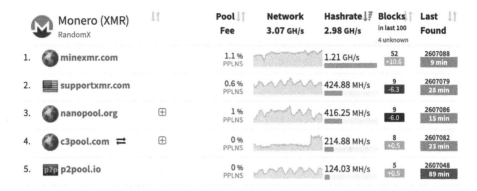

Figure 9-8. *Five top Monero mining pools*

Here are the steps to set up your mini mining rig:

1. Download and install the Exodus wallet from www.exodus.com/download if you haven't done so yet. Launch the wallet, set up the password, back up the mnemonic phrase, and search for Monero. Click the Receive button and copy the address. This address will be your ID in the mining pool, and it's where the pool will send your mining rewards.

2. Download the XMRig miner from https://xmrig. com/download. Double-click the downloaded file, which will unzip it into the folder with the same name. The full path to the file will look like this: /Users/slava/Downloads/xmrig-6.17.0/xmrig.

3. Launch the *Terminal* app, and run XMRig by typing
    the following command, after replacing slava with
    your computer home folder name (your username)
    and 4724cmJCCg4YjqS9yXZF5zaZaGsZTETRKLzo
    UTzSfpx9NoHtUy5wsjDTxpnzGkvmqFPQNZsM5J8
    pDQqsB1Jq3JrEPwtxNE4 with your Monero wallet
    address: /Users/slava/Downloads/xmrig-6.17.0/
    xmrig -o us-west.minexmr.com:443 -u
    4724cmJCCg4YjqS9yXZF5zaZaGsZTETRKLzoUTzSf
    px9NoHtUy5wsjDTxpnzGkvmqFPQNZsM5J8pDQqsB1
    Jq3JrEPwtxNE4 -k --tls

After several seconds, you should see one of the messages in the
Terminal window that looks like this:

```
cpu     accepted (1/0) diff 60805 (75 ms)
```

It means that the miner is working correctly, and the pool accepts the
hashes it's calculating.

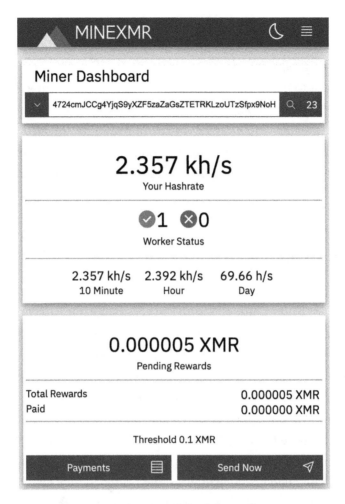

Figure 9-9. *MineXMR mining pool dashboard*

Now you can check the status of your miner in the pool dashboard –
go to `https://minexmr.com/dashboard` and enter your wallet address
(Figure 9-9). You should see your first pending rewards in the pool
dashboard within an hour. You probably won't be able to withdraw
anything for a few days because there is a manual withdrawal threshold of
0.004 XMR (about $1.12 in today's price) – a minimum amount you must

accumulate to be able to send it to your wallet. But at least you can be proud to contribute to the decentralization and stability of the most secure and private cryptocurrency!

If you want to increase your mining production, you can easily add more computers to your rig – just repeat the same steps on additional computers. There is no need to do any extra configuration as the pool will recognize multiple clients and automatically assign additional work to them, which will increase your hash contributions and subsequent rewards.

What's Next?

In this chapter, you learned how to get a small amount of crypto for free if you want to start and play with the ecosystem. Or you can earn a more substantial amount if you are ready to do some work helping new crypto projects with their marketing efforts. Another way to get crypto without actually buying it is mining, but this activity implies significant investments in computing power and electricity bills these days.

Now, after you have got a crypto wallet and, hopefully, some coins or tokens in it, it's time to move to the next chapter, where we discuss the holy of hollies in the crypto ecosystem – exchanges. Without exchanges, the crypto would be dead because they are the bridge to inject real money into the cryptosystem. We will discuss the different types of exchanges and how they work.

CHAPTER 10

How Crypto Exchanges Work

Civilization is the process of setting man free from men.

—Ayn Rand. *The Fountainhead.* 1943

Aqua regia (from Latin "royal water"), a mixture of three parts of hydrochloric acid and one part of nitric acid, is the only chemical substance with a unique and remarkable ability to dissolve precious metals such as gold and platinum. I am sure there are a lot of amusing tales related to aqua regia, but there is one interesting story that I think is somewhat related to our topic, not directly, of course.

When the Nazis occupied Denmark in 1940, Niels Bohr, a famous Danish physicist, was a director of the Institute for Theoretical Physics in Copenhagen, which he founded in 1921. Bohr, also a Nobel Prize laureate, helped his German colleagues Max von Laue and James Franck save their medals, which they received with the Nobel Prize in Physics, made of approximately 200 grams (more than six troy ounces) of 23-karat gold. They secretly sent their medals to Bohr because everyone on the territory of the Third Reich was required to surrender any gold they possessed to the government. But when the Nazis came to Denmark, if they found the medals with the names of the scientists who still stayed in Germany, Laue and Franck could be arrested by Gestapo the same day.

© Slava Gomzin 2022
S. Gomzin, *Crypto Basics*, https://doi.org/10.1007/978-1-4842-8321-9_10

Trying to hide the large, shiny medals was too risky. Hungarian radiochemist George de Hevesy, who worked with Bohr (and also became a Nobel Prize laureate later on), suggested using aqua regia to dissolve the gold... They placed the jar with the toxic, expensive liquid in plain sight, and the Nazis didn't suspect anything. In 1950, Hevesy reversed the chemical reaction and sent the raw gold to the Nobel committee, which recast the medals and handed them over again to Laue and Franck in 1952.

This fascinating story makes me think of an analogy with crypto. Like the gold that disappeared in aqua regia, fiat money is dissolved in crypto every millisecond on multiple crypto exchanges. What will happen if one day everyone decides to recast their medals? Perhaps, the answer to this question is out of the scope of this book, but at least you can learn how the chemistry behind it works.

If we try to set an analogy between the crypto ecosystem and the human body, the blockchains would be the blood and the flesh, and the networks of nodes would be the brain and the nerves. The exchanges are the heart of the crypto organism. Without exchanges, the crypto body would be dead because they are the ones who make the entire crypto market move with the speed of around $4 billion per hour, around the clock, without weekends. Unlike stock exchanges, which are linked to national financial markets, cryptocurrency exchanges don't recognize the borders (with some exceptions, which will be reviewed later). Therefore, they are open "24/7" – no night breaks, no weekends, no holidays.

Types of Crypto Exchanges

Spot, CEX, DEX, P2P, OTC... There are many terms associated with crypto exchanges – let's sort them out first.

There are two main kinds of crypto exchanges – centralized, also known as "spot," or CEX (from Centralized Exchange), and decentralized, often called "DEX" (from "Decentralized Exchange"). Both types have similarities – after all, they facilitate the trade of various coins, tokens, and fiat currencies between their users while generating revenues for their operators. But conceptually and technologically, CEX and DEX are very different.

Centralized exchanges are similar to traditional stock exchanges, except that they trade crypto instead of company shares. Centralized "spot" exchange is the most known, "traditional" form of exchange, where the price is determined on the spot by using the order book and multiple buy and sell orders.

Decentralized exchanges don't have an owner, making them more attractive to users who do not want to deal with corporations and endorse cryptocurrencies' independent, decentralized nature. Of course, both CEX and DEX have their advantages and disadvantages, which will become clear once we understand how they work.

OTC (over-the-counter) and P2P (peer-to-peer) exchanges come from traditional stock trading. OTC means that the trade is conducted between two parties via a broker. It provides enhanced privacy as the traders' identities and transaction details are only exposed to the broker.

In addition, OTC trading does not affect the market price because nobody knows about the transaction, so it is often used to trade for very large amounts without disturbing the market.

P2P is similar to OTC but does not even have a broker. More precisely, software plays the role of the broker in P2P exchange. OTC and P2P are often used interchangeably and can be either centralized or decentralized.

The overwhelming majority of crypto exchanges are spot CEX. However, various combinations are present on the market, with different advantages and downsides for each type.

How Centralized Spot Exchanges Work

Centralized spot exchanges use a single wallet to ingest all users' deposits; otherwise, they would waste a lot of money paying fees for numerous movements between multiple wallets. That's one of the reasons, by the way, for massive breaches associated with CEX. Depending on the blockchain, there are various techniques to manage multiple users with a single wallet. For Bitcoin and Ethereum, for example, they use subaddresses. Each Bitcoin or Ethereum wallet can have an unlimited number of subaddresses. It is impossible to say that these addresses belong to the same wallet without knowing the private key. So the actual crypto is deposited by all users to the same wallet, but CEX manages individual, separate virtual accounts for each user.

The actual trading happens between virtual accounts, not between the actual crypto wallets. It's similar to traditional banking, where a record represents each account in a bank database, but all the "real" money is stored in a single bank vault. As a result, it is impossible to tell that particular crypto was traded with another crypto by looking at the blockchain.

If you ever bought shares on the stock exchange through one of the retail stock brokers, you already know how centralized crypto exchanges work from the user viewpoint. Let's take our favorite example with Alice and Bob (Figure 10-1).

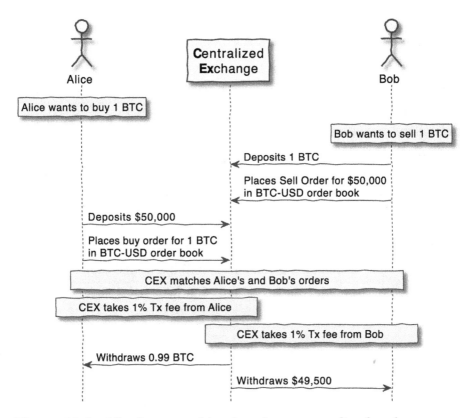

Figure 10-1. *Alice buys one bitcoin using a centralized exchange*

Alice wants to buy one bitcoin and pay in dollars, while Bob wants to do the opposite – sell one bitcoin and get paid in US dollars. They both go to CEX, sign up, and create accounts. Then, they both deposit the corresponding funds. Alice sends $50,000 from her bank account to the exchange bank account using ACH or wire transfer. Bob sends 1 BTC to the wallet address specified by the exchange. Once the Bitcoin transaction is confirmed within several minutes (sometimes, it can take hours), Bob creates a *sell* order for 1 BTC at a $50,000 price. It is also called a *maker* order because it makes the market by filling the order book.

The next day, once both deposits are confirmed (bank transfer will probably take longer, at least one business day), Alice goes to the BTC-USD trading pair and creates a *buy* (*taker*) order for 1 BTC. Alice will be prompted and will agree to place an order at market price, now set to $50,000 (by Bob's order). Once her order is submitted, the exchange will *match* the orders and *execute* the trade. Since all these actions happen inside the exchange *match engine*, which operates with the records in the database rather than real wallets or bank accounts, the assets (both BTC and dollars) will be available for withdrawal the next second after the trade is complete. Alice can now withdraw 1 BTC (minus fees), and Bob can withdraw $50,000 (minus the trading fees). Different CEXs have different user interfaces and various features, but the trading principle is the same.

Note   Not all CEX are necessarily available in your jurisdiction. For example, many exchanges block users from the United States and other countries because they cannot or don't want to comply with local regulations.

If you are in the United States, your options are limited if you want to trade on a high-rank, regulated exchange. You can check the exchange rank in the CoinMarketCap list. Typically, the lower the rank number, the better the exchange is. CoinMarketCap considers multiple parameters when calculating the rank.

If you are a US resident, I would recommend starting from Coinbase[1] which has a good reputation and a simple user interface for newbies. Don't confuse Coinbase exchange with its upscale professional version – Coinbase Pro[2] – aimed at more professional traders (we will chat on it in the next chapter). Kraken[3] will be another option if you want to play with the real exchange.

---

[1] www.coinbase.com

[2] https://pro.coinbase.com

[3] www.kraken.com

How to Become Your Own Exchange

Even though centralized exchanges account for most of the crypto trading, especially fiat-crypto pairs, they are all similar, and their technology is pretty trivial. I know exchange developers will disagree, and I understand why – it is not a simple task to implement a smoothly working order book and match engine that can process dozens of transactions and hundreds of API calls per second. But still, the design principles are pretty simple and similar to those already developed for stock exchanges. When it comes to decentralized exchanges (DEX), there is a wider variety of designs and technologies that are all novel and were never used before. It's good and bad because we know it takes time to bring new technology to a satisfactory level for retail customers, corporate investors, and traders.

Unfortunately, DEX is still unpopular compared to CEX. It reminds me of how democracies compare to autocratic regimes. Most of the world population still prefers to live without or with limited fundamental freedoms. But the situation is indeed better in favor of democracies than it was a couple of hundred years ago. Crypto is only 13 years old, so I am still optimistic.

Nevertheless, DEX has significant advantages over CEX:

- **Privacy** – While almost all CEX require you to create an account and disclose your real identity, with confirmation like sending the picture of your ID and your face, DEX doesn't ask you to do so, keeping your identity anonymous and your trade history private. Therefore, DEX helps you avoid identity theft and government surveillance.

- **Security** – With CEX, your assets are always at risk of being lost due to a data breach (hacker attack), exit scam, bankruptcy, or government crackdown. Whatever it is, it can forever wipe out your fiat and crypto assets. With DEX, you only rely on technology. It's not that technology does not fail, but at least you are protected (for the most part) from the human factor and intentional evil deeds as long as the DEX protocol is well known and tested enough.

- **Freedom, independence, and censorship resistance** – Any CEX is a private corporation that suffers from the same ailments as its older brothers – banks and stock exchanges. Therefore, CEX can decide to grant or revoke you or your favorite coin or token the right to trade, for *any* reason, *anytime*, without the ability to appeal. So, if we say about cryptocurrencies that *you can be your own bank*, for DEX, we can say that *you can be your own exchange*.

How Bisq P2P DEX Works

One of the issues preventing mass adoption of DEX is that most don't support fiat payments due to technological limitations. Currently, it's still impossible to process fiat payments using decentralized networks. Did you hear a tale about Walt Disney's will? Rumor has it that the legendary founder of the entertainment empire bequeathed a significant amount of money to a man who would be able to become pregnant. Most definitely, this story is untrue, but the idea is indeed entertaining. I think it would be great if someone bequeathed a few bitcoins to a person who will manage to design decentralized processing of fiat payments.

Someone familiar with the matter now can say, "wait, but there is Bisq!" Well, yes, there is a DEX called Bisq,[4] and, yes, they do handle fiat payments! Unfortunately, they don't qualify for the "pregnant man" prize, though, because they don't automate those payments which are processed "manually" or "out of band." But Bisq is still definitely a remarkable creature which is worth a little bit more detailed narrative. Let me show you how to buy your first bitcoins (in case you haven't done it yet) using Bisq DEX, that is, in a secure, private way.

As I said, Bisq provides a unique ability to buy Bitcoin and other cryptos using your local fiat currency such as dollars or euros. Since it is impossible to process decentralized fiat payments automatically, Bisq found an elegant solution: they do it "out of the band," that is, relying on the trade participants. Like in CEX, your transaction starts from the deposit, but unlike CEX, the destination and the purpose of the deposit are different.

In CEX, to buy bitcoins, you first need to deposit dollars (or other local fiat currency) to your exchange account. In Bisq, you need to make a security deposit first. Your future counterparty – the person selling you bitcoins – will need to do the same. This is required to ensure the security of the trade and deter scammers. If a transaction is not complete for any reason, it will be canceled, and one of the participants – the one who violated the agreement – will pay the penalty to another.

For example, if you started to buy bitcoins but refused to send dollars to the seller, you will pay the penalty. Or, if you sent your dollar payment to the seller, but they refused to confirm that they received your payment (which in turn automatically blocked the release of their bitcoin to you), they will pay some portion of the security deposit to you as compensation, plus the arbitrator will compensate you for the total dollar amount you spent on the failed transaction. The exact penalty amount will be determined by the mediator or arbitrator – two special roles in the Bisq network.

---

[4] https://bisq.network

Bisq algorithms work pretty well, but there is one nuisance I would like to mention. The fact that you need to make a security deposit to buy bitcoins creates a paradox: you need bitcoins to buy bitcoins. It's not an issue for experienced investors and traders, but what do you do when buying bitcoins for the first time? Well, there is nothing to do besides just buying a small number of bitcoins (at least 0.002 BTC) using different means.

There are various ways to get a relatively small amount of Bitcoin without a centralized exchange. While the Bisq team has their own suggestions,[5] I recommend using information from the previous chapter on how to get crypto for free. For example, you can earn some tokens or even bitcoins by participating in airdrop or bounty campaigns. In the worst-case scenario, buying a small amount of Bitcoin on CEX will not critically affect your security and privacy if you choose to conduct all subsequent trading using DEX.

Another thing worth mentioning is that at any step of the Bisq transaction, you never disclose your private keys to the network or any other third party. Everything is done using smart contracts and time-locked multisig transactions. Unlike CEX, where both parties delegate full control over their assets to the exchange, DEX trading is non-custodial, from the initial deposit to the order processing to the eventual withdrawal.

---

[5] https://bisq.wiki/Funding_your_wallet#How_to_Obtain_Your_First_Bitcoin

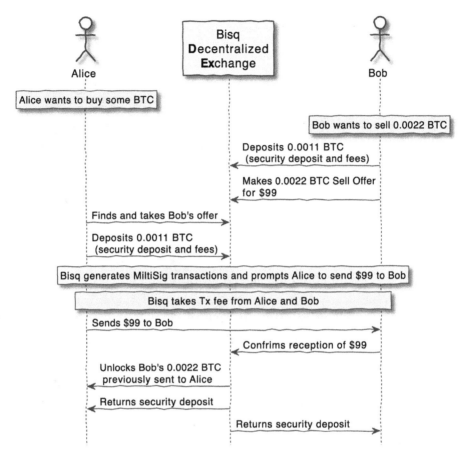

Figure 10-2. *How Bisq DEX works*

Let's go back to our transaction (Figure 10-2). Now then, I am going to buy bitcoins for dollars, and I have already transferred the BTC for the security deposit. Another thing I need to do is set up the payment method. I choose Zelle[6] as it is a convenient and fast bank transfer that can be done from almost any bank account. But you can choose more exotic and private (but less secure in my opinion) methods such as face-to-face cash payment or in-mail cash.

---

[6]www.zellepay.com

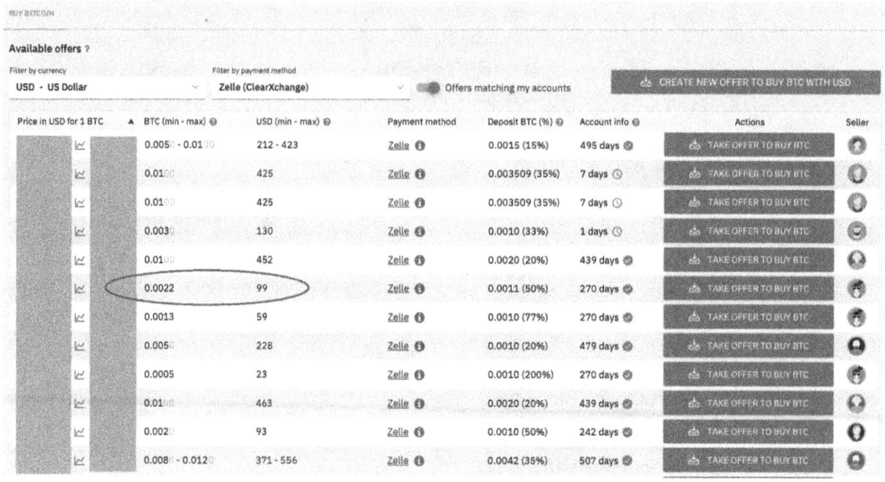

Price in USD for 1 BTC ▲	BTC (min - max) ⊕	USD (min - max) ⊕	Payment method	Deposit BTC (%) ⊕	Account info ⊕	Actions	Seller
	0.005 - 0.01	212 - 423	Zelle ⊕	0.0015 (15%)	495 days ⊘	TAKE OFFER TO BUY BTC	
	0.01	425	Zelle ⊕	0.003509 (35%)	7 days ⊕	TAKE OFFER TO BUY BTC	
	0.01	425	Zelle ⊕	0.003509 (35%)	7 days ⊕	TAKE OFFER TO BUY BTC	
	0.003	130	Zelle ⊕	0.0010 (33%)	1 days ⊕	TAKE OFFER TO BUY BTC	
	0.01	452	Zelle ⊕	0.0020 (20%)	439 days ⊘	TAKE OFFER TO BUY BTC	
	0.0022	99	Zelle ⊕	0.0011 (50%)	270 days ⊘	TAKE OFFER TO BUY BTC	
	0.0013	59	Zelle ⊕	0.0010 (77%)	270 days ⊘	TAKE OFFER TO BUY BTC	
	0.005	228	Zelle ⊕	0.0010 (20%)	479 days ⊘	TAKE OFFER TO BUY BTC	
	0.0005	23	Zelle ⊕	0.0010 (200%)	270 days ⊘	TAKE OFFER TO BUY BTC	
	0.01	463	Zelle ⊕	0.0020 (20%)	439 days ⊘	TAKE OFFER TO BUY BTC	
	0.002	93	Zelle ⊕	0.0010 (50%)	242 days ⊘	TAKE OFFER TO BUY BTC	
	0.008 - 0.012	371 - 556	Zelle ⊕	0.0042 (35%)	507 days ⊘	TAKE OFFER TO BUY BTC	

Figure 10-3. *Buy Bitcoin offer screen on Bisq DEX*

Anyway, we go to the Buy Bitcoin screen and select an offer with the amount we like (Figure 10-3). I chose $99 because I don't want to spend more on this test purchase which I definitely make with a loss. I will pay more than the current Bitcoin price because I need it right now; plus, there are no free meals, and privacy and security are no exception! When I double-click the $99 offer for 0.22 BTC, I will be prompted several times with all kinds of security and privacy warnings, and eventually, after I agree to all of them, it will show me the deal details (Figure 10-4).

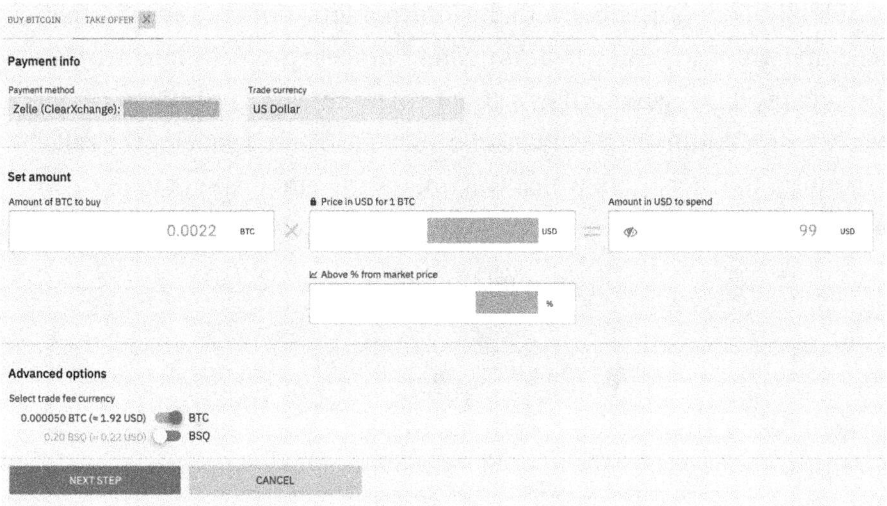

Figure 10-4. *Buy Bitcoin offer info on Bisq DEX*

After agreeing on the amounts and the rules, I get to the last confirmation screen (Figure 10-5).

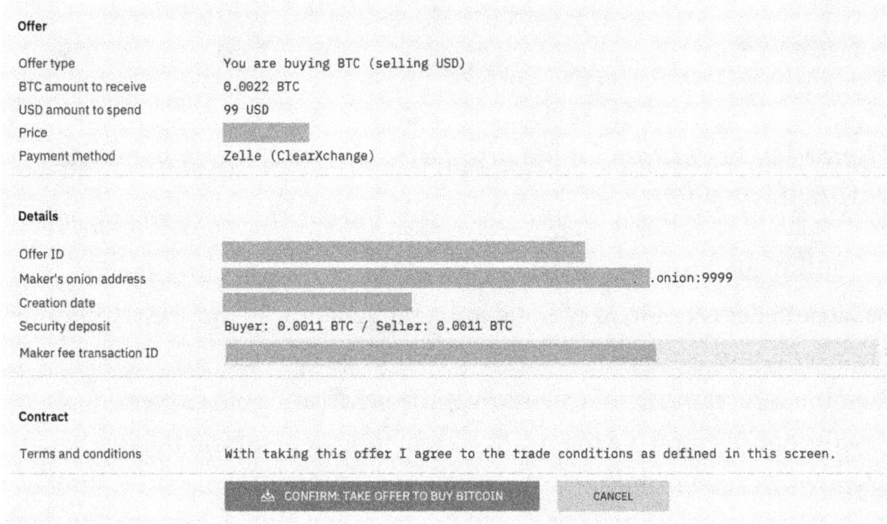

Figure 10-5. *Last confirmation screen with Bisq transaction details*

Finally, I am presented with the information about the seller's Zelle account (where to send 99 bucks). After I process the Zelle payment through my bank, which takes a couple of minutes, I confirm my payment by clicking a button on the transaction screen. Then, I wait for the seller to confirm the reception, which will unlock the bitcoins sent to me (Figure 10-6).

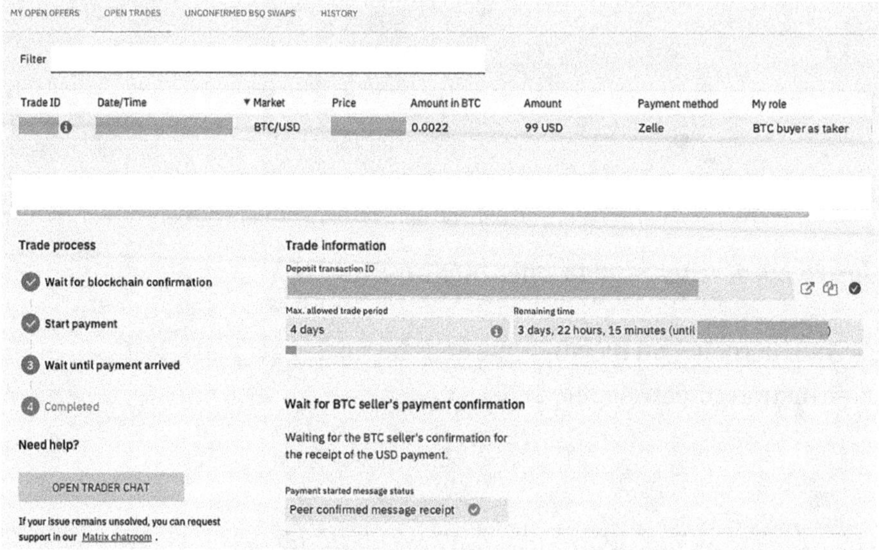

Figure 10-6. *Waiting for the Bisq DEX seller to confirm the dollar payment reception*

This final phase may take time, especially for the first transaction, because sellers are afraid of fraud and chargebacks, so they can wait until the last minute with confirmation, even though they already see dollars in their bank account. Bisq usually gives the buyer and seller several days to process out-of-band payments. The exact time depends on the method of payment. For Zelle, they offer four days to complete the trade. Eventually, the seller ensured the Zelle deposit was secure and hit the Confirm button, which unlocked the 0.0022 BTC transfer to my wallet and released our security deposits (Figure 10-7).

Trade ID	Date/Time	▼ Market	Price	Amount in BTC	Amount	Payment method	My role
❶		BTC/USD		0.0022	99 USD	Zelle	BTC buyer as taker

Trade process

✓ Wait for blockchain confirmation

✓ Start payment

✓ Wait until payment arrived

❹ Completed

Summary of completed trade

You have bought
0.0022 BTC

You have paid
99 USD

Refunded security deposit
0.0011 BTC (50.00% of trade amount)

Trade fee
0.000050 BTC (required minimum)

Total mining fees
0.00008388 BTC (3.81% of trade amount)

CLOSE

Figure 10-7. *Bisq Buy Bitcoin transaction is complete*

Finally, I would like to discuss a Zelle transaction's specifics briefly. One can say that the Zelle transaction is not private because it discloses the identity of the buyer and seller. That's true. But if you compare it with other payment methods, you can see that almost all of them disclose the identity in one way or another. Remember that this information is shared between the buyer, the seller, banks, and Zelle, so it is not visible to the public. But most importantly, the bank and Zelle do not know about the nature of this transaction, that is, they have no idea it is related to crypto. The only method that does not directly disclose the identity of the participants and does not leave a paper trail is face-to-face cash payment, but in my opinion, it is not safe, and thus it's not worth it.

How Uniswap DEX Works

Uniswap[7] is one of the most well-known decentralized exchanges; it's very reliable and works fast because the entire process is fully automated.

---

[7] https://uniswap.org

Unfortunately, Uniswap has two serious limitations. First, it only allows trading between ERC-20 tokens, that is, the tokens created on the Ethereum blockchain. No fiat and no other coins, including Bitcoin. Uniswap trading covers Ether (ETH) itself and one of the most popular stable coins – USDT – which would make Uniswap useful, if not the second issue: extremely high transaction fees.

I wanted to buy some USDT in exchange for 0.01 ETH to show you how Uniswap works but instead converted it to a demo of how useless Uniswap is for the average user because of the nonsense transaction fees. I hope Ethereum will fix this problem in the future, but for now, you should probably find a better exchange unless you operate with amounts large enough that such high fees begin to make sense. Figure 10-8 shows the initial screen for buying USDT with ETH.

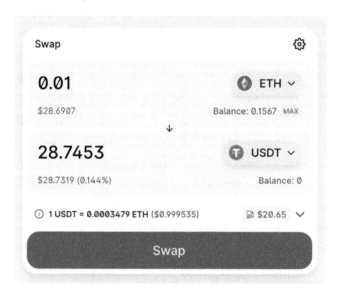

Figure 10-8. *Uniswap exchange transaction*

I previously linked my MetaMask wallet to Uniswap, which can be done with a few clicks. Credit must be given to the Uniswap (and MetaMask) designers. Despite the complexity of the exchange protocol,

which involves creating special smart contracts and liquidity pools, the
user interface is pretty understandable and intuitive. I also deposited some
ETH to my MetaMask account in advance. So now I select two tokens – the
one that I want to sell (ETH) and another one that I want to buy (USDT),
and the swap amount (0.01 ETH). The USDT price and the amount of
USDT I will get for 0.01 ETH will be automatically calculated from the
current ratio between the two tokens in their *liquidity pool* (Figure 10-9).

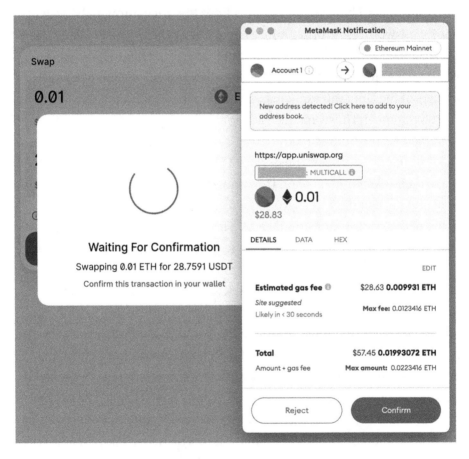

Figure 10-9. *Uniswap transaction with high fee*

Caution   Pay attention to the Uniswap transaction fee amount, which varies. In my example, it almost equals the amount of the swap, so this transaction would require paying nearly 100% transaction fee!

Let's hope the Uniswap fees will be normalized soon and see how Uniswap works. Unlike CEX, which defines the price through the order book, Uniswap has no order book. There is a *liquidity pool* instead, created by users who want to ensure the liquidity of a particular token (and earn some bucks on fees, of course). These liquidity pools are the market makers of the Uniswap exchange. Even though virtually any ERC-20 token can be traded on Uniswap, the trading is only possible after a liquidity pool is created for the trading pair.

If someone – let's say, the project XYZ development team – wants to make their token tradeable on Uniswap, they need to create the liquidity pool and deposit their fresh from the oven token along with the other token of the trading pair. To make XYZ liquid, they probably want it to be traded with ETH or USDT. To make it simpler to understand the numbers, let them start trading from USDT. So, they will need to create a new liquidity pool XYZ-USDT and deposit XYZ and USDT tokens there.

Now, this is the important part. By depositing the initial portion of tokens in a particular ratio, they define the initial trading price of their token. For example, they want their token price to start from ten cents, and they have a budget of $10,000 available for marketing. They create a liquidity pool and deposit 10,000 USDT tokens and 100,000 XYZ tokens. It sounds exciting (for the XYZ development team), but they shouldn't be excited too soon. The market will make its corrections. If they set the XYZ token price too high, no one will buy it, while users who already have XYZ (recent airdrop?) will be selling it quickly.

Here is what happens when someone sells XYZ on Uniswap. Let's say someone sells 10,000 XYZ and gets 1000 USDT. After the swap is complete, the XYZ-USDT pool, which initially contained 100K XYZ and 10K USDT, will have 110K XYZ and 9K USDT because the tokens that are being sold (XYZ) are getting into the pool, and the tokens that are being paid to the seller (USDT) are taken from the pool. As we said before, the price is calculated by the ratio of the two tokens in the pool; that's why the initial price was set to 0.1 USDT. So, the new price, which takes effect immediately after the first swap, will be calculated as 9K USDT divided by 110K XYZ, which equals around 0.08 USDT (Figure 10-10).

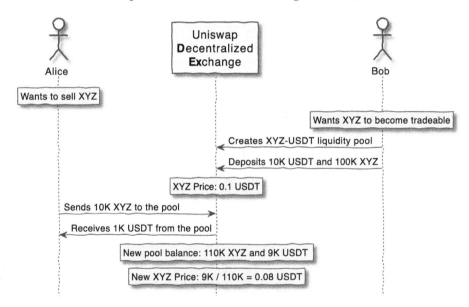

Figure 10-10. *How Uniswap DEX works*

The price dropped two cents after just one sale! If another user sells another portion of XYZ, the price will continue dropping until the pool is empty or the price begins to make sense, and people will start buying XYZ.

There is a way, however, to "correct" the price. If someone buys XYZ, the price will move in the opposite direction. This "someone" can be the same XYZ development team doing "buyback."[8] This way, the pool will be "recharged" with additional USDT. Some XYZ will be removed, which will restore the price in favor of XYZ. This also happens when the price is fluctuating around the "right" market price, so the number of sales compensates for the number of purchases, more or less. By the way, "buyback" is what some national governments do with their local fiat currency if they want to stop its devaluation if they have sufficient dollar and euro reserves.

What's Next?

Crypto exchanges, centralized and decentralized, play a vital role in the crypto industry as the primary means to acquire and spend coins and tokens. Next, we will see how developers, investors, and traders use and abuse crypto exchanges to make money.

---

[8] www.forbes.com/advisor/investing/stock-buyback

CHAPTER 11

Crypto Investment and Trading

> *Do not store up for yourselves treasures on earth, where moth and rust destroy, and where thieves break in and steal. But store up for yourselves treasures in heaven, where neither moth nor rust destroys, and where thieves do not break in or steal.*
>
> —The Bible

Tim Draper, a renowned venture capitalist and crypto proponent, has made a significant investment by buying 29,656 bitcoins confiscated by the US government from the Silk Road darknet marketplace site for $18.7 million ($632 per bitcoin) back in 2014. Even with today's Bitcoin price, which has seen better days, he's still made an enormous profit on crypto, incommensurable with returns on the stock market.

A few years ago, I participated in one of the numerous blockchain conferences where Draper talked about the future of Bitcoin and crypto in general. Several years after Bitcoin first saw the light of day in 2009, everything related to crypto was mostly called "blockchain." However, it's been changed since then because people realized that not every crypto is based on blockchain technology, at least not on blockchain in its original form. Even more importantly, there is a clear separation today between blockchain and crypto because some folks still think blockchain technology can successfully solve many problems outside the FinTech domain (which I doubt is true).

© Slava Gomzin 2022
S. Gomzin, *Crypto Basics*, https://doi.org/10.1007/978-1-4842-8321-9_11

Volatility

While speaking at that conference, Mr. Draper was asked about Bitcoin price volatility – how it affects the crypto market, investment, and adoption. He gave a fascinating answer. He said that if you think about it in the opposite direction – that is, it's not the Bitcoin price that fluctuates around a stable dollar but rather the dollar price that swings around stable Bitcoin – you will stop worrying about it… "These governments are trained to print more money to be more relevant. Well, we all know that as soon as I can buy my food, clothing, and shelter in bitcoin, I'm not going to want to hold – and neither will anyone else – any cryptocurrency or currency tied to any fiat political force," he also once said.[1] It's difficult to argue with a man who made more than half a billion dollars on Bitcoin. And it shows us that the volatility is irrelevant if you know that the general direction is growth (Figure 11-1).

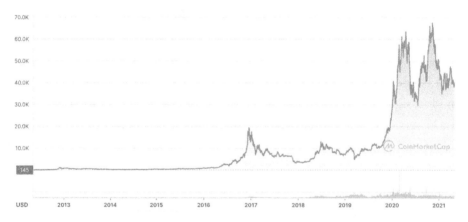

Figure 11-1. *Bitcoin price growth since its inception*

However, the trends and dynamics of the Bitcoin and other cryptos' prices are significant for both crypto investors and traders for different reasons. Investors, once again, leverage the general direction toward

---

[1] www.coindesk.com/business/2021/12/01/tim-draper-on-bitcoin-and-the-collapse-of-fiat

growth. They understand that the price of Bitcoin slowly but surely grows with time, despite the fluctuations, simply because, unlike fiat currency like the dollar, Bitcoin has a finite supply. At the same time, more and more people are involved in the crypto business daily. So the more people (potential investors) are exposed to the idea of crypto, the higher the Bitcoin price because the supply is growing slower than the demand. Don't forget about Bitcoin reward halving that happens every four years, when miners start getting 50% fewer bitcoins for each mining block compared to the previous four years.

Traders, however, have a different view of market dynamics. They don't care much about Bitcoin and crypto market growth but leverage the fluctuations. They can earn on both ups and downs of the market. It's easier to make money on trading when the market is moving up. But it does not mean you can't get gains when it's falling. There is a method called shorting, which works similarly to the stock market, and we will discuss it later. But now, let's see first how investors make money on crypto.

Why People Invest in Crypto

Before all, I should state that the process of crypto investment contradicts its main ideas of decentralization and independence. Investment is typically made by converting fiat currency to crypto using exchanges, and most exchanges are centralized, regulated corporations. But let's face it, crypto developers wouldn't be able to develop without investment, so this strange symbiosis of capitalists and cyberpunks exists and propels the crypto tech very fast.

The crypto market attracts retail (i.e., non-professional) investors for two reasons. The first one is the availability of crypto for virtually anyone in the world. Most people cannot become accredited investors who must have a particular income and starting capital. There are online discount brokers, of course, but they need you to submit all the paperwork to confirm your identity and citizenship. So for many people worldwide, the traditional investment platforms, even their most advanced versions, are still not accessible (Table 11-1).

***Table 11-1.** Different Accessibility of Investment Platforms*

	Accredited Investor Working with Broker	Discount Online Brokers like E-Trade	Retail Investment Apps like Robinhood	Crypto
Minimum investment	$50,000–$100,000	0	0	0
Minimum required income	$200,000 for two consecutive years	0	0	0
Full identity disclosure (legal name that matches government ID, email, address, social security)	Required	Required	Required	**Not** required
Residence in particular jurisdiction	Required	Required	Required	**Not** required
Typical trading fee	0–$50	0–$7	0	0–0.6%

And the second reason (perhaps it should be the first) is the high returns that the crypto market promises compared to the humble average of 10% returns delivered by the stock market (think of Tim Draper's example at the beginning of this chapter). On some crypto projects, investors get hundreds or even thousands of percent of returns in their investments.

The community of crypto investors is growing fast. 13% of US investors have traded cryptocurrency in 2020.[2] It only took four months for the crypto population to almost double from 106 million in February to 203 million in May 2021.[3] So, you can imagine how many people have already invested in crypto today. Such a speed can also be explained by a phenomenon called FOMO (fear of missing out). It happens when people learn about a new opportunity and rush to leverage it in the nick of time before (as they think) it's too late to get any gains. FOMO is a successful marketing technology employed by multiple crypto projects, especially those going through ICO (Initial Coin Offering).

I happened to meet the man who coined the term ICO on one of the social media platforms. J.R. Willett came up with the now-famous three-letter abbreviation back in 2013.[4] The word has its roots in the traditional stock market. IPO (Initial Public Offering) is an existing tool used by conventional startups to raise capital from institutional investors. Crypto developers took the heavily regulated IPO concept and teleported it into the crypto world, which did not have the burden of government control.

ICO and its derivatives, such as IEO (Initial Exchange Offering), IDO (Initial DEX Offering), and other forms of Initial "X" Offerings, seek to sell as many coins or tokens as possible. For many crypto projects, IXO is not just the only chance to sell their token to fund the development team but also their only purpose. Some don't even plan to do any development after the sale is made. So, when investing in an initial offering, you need to understand whether the project has any solid technical white paper and development road map besides just a commercial business plan.

---

[2] www.coininsider.com/13-of-us-investors-have-traded-cryptocurrency-in-last-year

[3] https://cointelegraph.com/news/crypto-population-doubled-to-over-200m-users-since-january-report-says/amp

[4] www.forbes.com/sites/laurashin/2017/09/21/heres-the-man-who-created-icos-and-this-is-the-new-token-hes-backing

Staking

The term DeFi (Decentralized Finance) was coined relatively recently and came into widespread use at the same time when *DeFi staking* became a new popular way of crypto investment. First crypto investors were HODLers (HODL stands for *Hold On for Dear Life*), meaning they buy crypto and hold it for a long time until it (supposedly) significantly raises in price. However, the HODL investment does not bring dividends, so it is more like buying gold or other precious metals than investing in stocks, which, in addition to the growth, provide periodic dividends paid to the shareholders.

Unlike "traditional" HODL ideology, DeFi staking offers a more pragmatic model of investment similar to short-term CD (certified deposits) provided by traditional financial institutions or even to the stock market, when you lock a particular amount of cryptocurrency ("stake") for the specific period in exchange to dividends paid to you by the network or by the financial institution such as an exchange.

The original form of staking, or DeFi staking, was provided by PoS and DPoS coins which required validators to deposit a *stake* to prove their loyalty to the network. The stakeholders received mining rewards and/or transaction fees as dividends generated by their stake. The DeFi staking process is usually based on smart contracts and can be fully decentralized. But centralized crypto exchanges, who constantly search for new revenue sources like any other commercial or financial institutions, liked the idea and started offering staking in collaboration with development teams of new crypto projects. This type of staking is not DeFi because it has nothing to do with decentralization.

The way "CeFi" (centralized finance) staking works is simple. The development team responsible for token XYZ usually owns a significant chunk of their overall token supply, generated by premining or other means and used for marketing, developers' salaries, and other expenses. The XYZ team partners with a centralized exchange and creates a staking offer by depositing a dividend fund. Investors in the staking need to buy a particular amount of XYZ and deposit it in an exchange account. After some time, as defined by the agreement and can be several months, the participants can unlock the tokens and get a reward from the dividend fund.[5]

It sounds slightly like a Ponzi scheme,[6] but it's not. The total supply of XYZ tokens is limited (usually), and both the XYZ team and the exchange leverage the fact that developers have a significant number of XYZ, which they generated out of thin air and which they need to sell to get paid for their hard work. Eventually, it's a win-win scheme for all participants. Developers sell and promote their tokens. Exchanges get the extra fees. Investors get their dividends, amounting to tens and even hundreds of percent.[7] They need to be lucky enough not to find the price of XYZ dropped to zero by the time they can unlock their stake and get their dividends.

Crypto Trading

Several different "interest" groups of people are involved in crypto, such as developers, investors, miners, and simple users. However, they have at least one thing in common: they are all traders.

When you start dealing with crypto, the chances are your very first experience looks like trading because you need to acquire some cryptocurrency by exchanging it for your dollars or any other fiat currency. There are ways to get some crypto without spending your money – we talked about it in Chapter 9. But at some point, you will need to trade sooner or later – just to cash out your investment revenue, invest in a "better" coin, or maybe simply "exit" and get your fiat money back.

---

[5] www.kraken.com/features/staking-coins

[6] www.investor.gov/introduction-investing/investing-basics/glossary/ponzi-schemes

[7] https://latoken.com/staking/fixed

A one-time exchange from dollars to bitcoins does not make you a trader. Most probably, your first experience will not be the best and most efficient one – you will pay a high fee and get a bad price. But at least you will get the idea.

I have never been a professional trader, so if you're looking for a serious crypto trading manual, this book is the wrong source. However, if you just need some info to start, you can get it here, as I have done some trading for fun. Let's start with the definition of what trading is.

Once again, if you just exchange your hundred bucks for some bitcoin – it's not trading; it's just a purchase. It might look like trading and have all the fancy attributes of trading, though, if you use one of the existing crypto trading platforms. Even if you buy a significant amount of crypto and pay much more than just a hundred bucks, it is still not trading – it is an investment.

You invest when you buy a crypto asset and wait for a long time until its value grows. But traders don't wait too long. You do crypto trading when you continuously and frequently exchange one cryptocurrency with another to earn revenue. The frequency ranges from several days, sometimes weeks, months, to milliseconds.

The most common trading method is buying a particular crypto asset when it's "time to buy" and selling it when it's "time to sell" – at a higher price. The science (or art?) of trading is just correctly determining (or guessing?) those two times. The right time to buy is when the asset is at a low price and just about to start growing. Accordingly, the right time to sell is when the asset is at a high price which is just about to stop growing and start going down. It sounds pretty simple, but it's not trivial at all.

First, it's not even clear whether trading is science or art. There are many "scientific" techniques to predict the price trajectory, and some of them are very convincing. But let's be realistic – if those methods were reliable, everyone could use them and become a millionaire. So, for many people, trading is still more art than science. It does not mean, however, that it's impossible to earn money by trading.

Trading is pretty straightforward when the entire crypto market continuously goes up ("bull market"). You just buy, wait, and sell. But when the market is going down ("bear market") like during uncertain times such as "crypto winter," trading might become too risky unless you *short* your positions. *Shorting* is a more sophisticated trading technique that allows traders to earn money when the price falls. It sounds counterintuitive, but it works well if you know what you're doing. I don't recommend starting from shorting if you're a beginner, but we can at least see how it works. So when the price is falling, how can you even earn anything?

The way shorting is usually done is the trader, instead of buying the asset, gets it as a loan (traders can use their own assets as well). Then you sell it at the current price, presumably about to go down soon, wait until the price falls, buy the same amount of asset at a lower price, and finally return the loan (the same amount of crypto assets you initially got from the loaner). Since you purchased the same amount of crypto for a lower price, you spent less than you got when you sold them. The difference is your trader's revenue!

Sounds interesting, but let's go back to the "standard" way of trading and see how to determine the right time to buy and sell. Surprisingly, there are people (professional traders) who can provide this information to you in the form of *signals*. Of course, in most cases, they want you to pay for this info as, in their opinion, it helps you earn big bucks so you can share your revenues with them to show your appreciation. There are buy and sell signals which tell you it's the right time to buy or sell particular crypto.

Trading Bots

Crypto trading bots are based on a straightforward principle of automated placement of buy and sell orders. To get some profit, you (or the bot) need to buy something at one price and sell it at a higher price (note that the bots can do *shorting* as well, but we simplify the use case). The difference between the buying and selling price multiplied by the number of coins/tokens is your revenue, as simple as that. The tricky part is determining the right time to buy and sell. Multiple techniques help traders answer those questions, and many use those methods successfully. But what if you don't want to spend a lot of time researching and monitoring the market but have significant assets and still want to utilize them for trading? Here come the trading bots – a software that allows you to "fire and forget," that is, set up the requirements and conditions and let the app do the work for you.

Unlike human traders, trading bots can work 24/7, which resolves the issue related to the fact that the crypto market is open around the clock and not just during specific work hours and days like the stock market. So how do trading bots know when to buy and sell? They are not that smart, but some people are. Experienced traders monitor the market using various indicators telling them whether it's time to buy or sell a particular asset. Once they are sure this is the time, they issue a signal to everyone who is subscribed to their service. Bots are configured to listen for particular signals, which come as free or paid subscriptions. The only work you need to do as the bot operator is to find the most reliable signal sources and set up your bot to follow them. The bot will do the rest.

Various crypto trading bots are available for free or as paid licenses or subscriptions.[8] You can choose the one that best fits your needs and your wallet. Some bots require much time to configure and set up, and you must host them on your machine (or cloud server if you want to ensure uninterrupted 24/7 operations). For a newbie trader, starting from a bot hosted by the owner is probably easier and requires minimum configuration and maintenance effort.

---

[8] www.guru99.com/best-crypto-trading-bot.html

Cryptohopper

Cryptohopper, in my opinion, is one of the best trading bots. It is hosted in the cloud, so the only thing you need to do to start trading is just create an account. You can even start with a free subscription if you want to play with it a little bit before starting serious trading. One exciting feature is called *paper trading*, which is an exchange simulator. You can test-drive your trading strategy, whether based on your own methodology or fully automated and based on signal subscriptions (Figure 11-2).

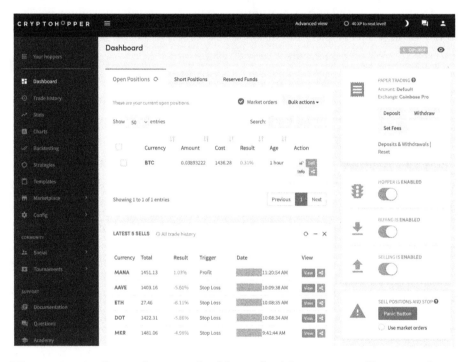

Figure 11-2. *Cryptohopper dashboard with paper trading template selected*

In any case, the advantage of paper trading is that you don't risk any real money besides just a relatively small fee for the Cryptohopper and signal subscriptions (unfortunately, paper trading is not included in the free Cryptohopper tier). Paper trading allows you to self-learn the basics and the nuances of trading before investing your real crypto assets. Once you feel confident and your trading strategy is polished, you can deploy the same rules to the actual exchange. Cryptohopper supports various exchanges[9], including the two I mentioned already – Coinbase Pro and Kraken.

To simplify initial setup, configuration, and ongoing maintenance, Cryptohopper developers introduced the concept of *templates, strategies,* and *signals.* When you create a new Cryptohopper account, it comes as bare metal, without any configuration. Since the bot has a lot of bells and whistles to play with, it's better to start with one of the predefined templates, which defines at least what exchange and base currency you will work with, along with some other essential parameters. For example, you want to connect to the Coinbase Pro exchange and start trading from US dollars (that's going to be the currency your bot will buy other currencies with and sell to). You can select a corresponding template that will enable Coinbase Pro as an exchange and USD as the base currency (Figure 11-3).

---

[9] www.cryptohopper.com/exchanges

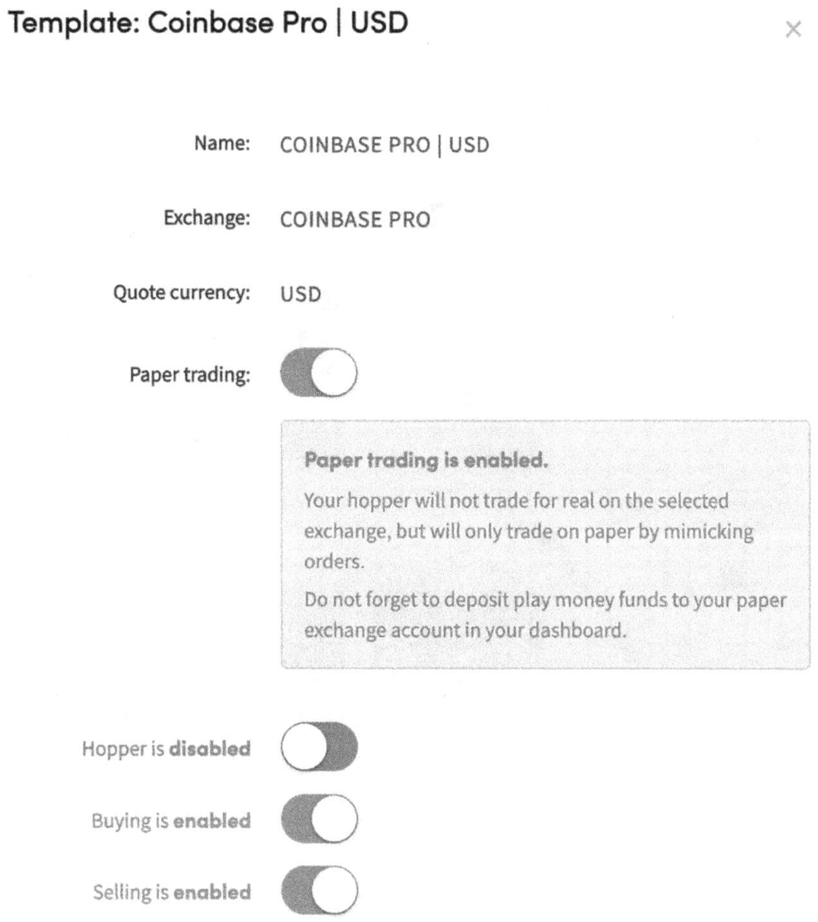

Template: Coinbase Pro | USD   ✕

Name: COINBASE PRO | USD

Exchange: COINBASE PRO

Quote currency: USD

Paper trading:

Paper trading is enabled.

Your hopper will not trade for real on the selected
exchange, but will only trade on paper by mimicking
orders.

Do not forget to deposit play money funds to your paper
exchange account in your dashboard.

Hopper is **disabled**

Buying is **enabled**

Selling is **enabled**

Figure 11-3. *Cryptohopper template for trading on Coinbase Pro
with USD*

Trading Strategy and Paper Trading

The next step is selecting your trading strategy. You can choose signals
only (if you rely exclusively on recommendations provided by the third-
party analysts), a marketplace strategy (if you want to have your own
strategy but initially buy it from a third-party expert), or a strategy you've
designed yourself.

You can select signals if you don't have time to learn all the nuances of numerous crypto projects and sit day and night monitoring their technical indicators. Templates, strategies, and signals are free or for sale on the Cryptohopper marketplace (Figure 11-4).

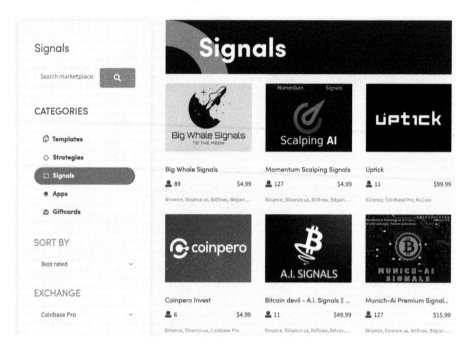

Figure 11-4. *Subscriptions for trading signals on Cryptohopper marketplace*

The Cryptohopper user interface is very intuitive and user-friendly, and there are a lot of instructions and training videos provided by the development team and third-party developers available for the users.

If you want to play with Cryptohopper, you can do the following:

- Start with a minimum paid subscription level that enables the paper trading feature.

- Select a template with the exchange and base currency that you would use in reality.

- Subscribe to free and paid signals that support your exchange, and deposit the amount of paper money equal to the one you would invest if it were actual trading.

- Play with it for several days or weeks until you see it's working out for you.

Paper trading is not the same as actual trading, but at least it will give you some idea of how it works and what to expect.

Fake Exchange Volumes

There is another interesting and important application area of trading bots, which is being kept out of the public eye for the most part. The fact is that many crypto exchanges use trading bots to create fake trade volumes. These bots differ from those that help traders, which we reviewed before. Their primary purposes are *market making* and *volume making*. Market making allows the exchange to create an effect of sufficient traders' interest by filling up the order book with buy and sell orders.

Let's say an exchange lists a new token that generates little to zero interest from investors. If they list such a token for trading with Bitcoin or USDT, there will be no or a few orders, especially buy orders, making it difficult to form the price, not to mention the bad impression. What exchanges do is ask the project development team to create a trading pair fund that would allow placing multiple *buy* and *sell* orders over the price spectrum to make it look like many buyers and sellers for the token. In some cases, the market-making bot can even help manipulate the price by spending more on buy orders and gradually increasing the buy order price.

Another type of trading automation used by exchanges is the volume-making bot. Trading volume is one of the main parameters used to rank exchanges, significantly influencing the exchange's reputation. The overall exchange trading volume is calculated as the amount of all trades for all trading pairs within 24 hours. If you look at CoinMarketCap, you can see billions of dollars in daily trading volumes for highly ranking exchanges. I must tell you the truth: most of these volumes are fake, even on very popular and top-rated exchanges. Even if the exchanges themselves don't fake the volumes, it's done by the project teams as many exchanges require them to maintain minimum daily volumes for their tokens. If the token or coin is not traded enough, the exchange does not make enough money on it and therefore can decide to pause the trading temporarily or even delist it permanently. That's why we (crypto users) better switch from CEX to DEX – decentralized exchanges don't have such demanding requirements, so their activities are more transparent, and their reports are more honest.

What's Next?

Cryptocurrencies are still one big technological and economic experiment. Most cryptos were created in an attempt to enhance Bitcoin, which is by far still a winner today. If not an absolute winner, then at least a strong leader, with just under half of the total crypto market capitalization (*Bitcoin dominance*) that includes several thousand altcoins and tokens.

But the stakes are still high. As it is sung in one famous song, *the winner takes it all.*[10] Those projects that do not offer new technological solutions exploit the trend. They elevate the overall cost of the FinTech revolution by taking somebody else's share of the financial crypto pie.

This chapter concludes the second part of the book, which talks about the practical aspects of cryptocurrencies. I believe you are well prepared to move to the final part, where I will walk you through the main steps of the crypto project and share some tips that will become handy if you decide to create your own money.

---

[10] IN FOCUS: THE WINNER TAKES IT ALL – THE STORY OF A MASTERPIECE. Abbasite.com. https://abbasite.com/articles/the-winner-takes-it-all-the-story-of-a-masterpiece/

PART III

Creating Your Own Crypto

CHAPTER 12

Creating a Token

Sometimes "good enough" really is.

—Tim Rayborn. *The Scandinavian Guide to Happiness*

I left Russia 30 years ago when the short period of democracy and liberalism just started, only to be effectively killed after several years by Putin's autocratic, nationalist regime, which led to the nightmare we all witnessed in Ukraine. I was born and raised in St. Petersburg, the second-largest Russian metropolis, but during my childhood, the name of the city was Leningrad, and the name of the country was USSR. Under the communist regime, the Soviet Union, fenced off from the free world by an iron curtain, was significantly behind the West in computer technologies. Unfortunately, the same will happen now with Russia under its current postmodern fascist rule.

Nevertheless, despite all the "inconveniences" associated with the communist regime ruling during my childhood, I was lucky enough to have access to recent advancements in the computer industry, both Soviet and American. Thanks to my dad, who was a professor and an executive in one of the most prestigious universities, I had an opportunity to get student side jobs that allowed me to work on various big and small computers, both as part of my duties and during after-work hours, day and night. But many, perhaps most, Soviet people were not so lucky back then. Imagine the world before the Internet and without an affordable personal computer.

© Slava Gomzin 2022
S. Gomzin, *Crypto Basics*, https://doi.org/10.1007/978-1-4842-8321-9_12

The invention of the Internet and the mass production of home computers changed everything. People from the countryside and big cities now have equal chances to become a programmer. Bitcoin created a similar revolution in the financial sector. People who previously could not afford a bank account or credit card can now become investors, traders, and account holders. Software developers can become entrepreneurs without the mediation of haughty angel investors and venture capitalists.

But this is just the beginning. The Bitcoin white paper was published only 13 years ago. Only a selected population of lucky plugged-ins could benefit from crypto in the first years after the blockchain revolution. But more and more people join the club, and now crypto does not belong only to geeks anymore. Everyone these days can create their own cryptocurrency, and you don't even need to be a programmer.

Coins vs. Tokens

We already learned about the difference between coins and tokens, but let's repeat it for clarity. Coins are the result of creating a whole new ecosystem, including a new blockchain and network of nodes. Some coins also become a platform for creating tokens. The most known example of a token platform is Ethereum, which has its coin Ether (ETH). But there are others, less known but sometimes more efficient and less expensive, such as Solana (SOL), Polygon (MATIC), and Klaytn (KLAY).

As a token platform, Ethereum carries many custom-created tokens that can be generated by recording a transaction containing a smart contract in a blockchain. Designing smart contracts requires programming skills outside this book's scope. But fortunately, some tools allow nontechnical people to create smart contracts and their own tokens.

How to Create a Token Without Coding

Even though the token generation process requires writing a smart contract code, there are applications created by third-party developers that allow unsophisticated users to make their own tokens with no coding at all. ERC-20 is the most popular standard for custom fungible tokens, that is, tokens that can become a cryptocurrency.

As you probably realized already, there is almost nothing free in the crypto world, so if you want to create your own token, which can become your own money, you better get ready to pay some money for it up front. To simplify the task, we will refrain from creating a token directly on the mainnet and do it on the testnet instead. Using a testnet is the best practice for any software development activity, and a smart contract is nothing but a new code deployed on the distributed blockchain network. Therefore, creating a new token means new software development and deployment, so it's better to be tested on the testnet before mainnet deployment.

Another reason for using a testnet first is financial, as you don't want to spend real money on something you haven't tested yet. Testnet tokens, which you need to pay for your token's smart contract, can be obtained for free. Unlike real Ether, getting a testnet Ethereum coin is very simple. Let's use the *Ropsten testnet* for our experiment. The Ropsten testnet has a functionality close to the Ethereum mainnet, so you can get a similar experience for free.

Setting Up the Wallet and Getting the Testnet Coins

Let's use the MetaMask wallet as that's the one that can contain both test tokens and our future real crypto. I have installed MetaMask as an extension to the Chrome browser. Do not forget to switch from the mainnet to the Ropsten testnet – the current network's name is on the top of the MetaMask wallet screen, so it is difficult to miss (Figure 12-1).

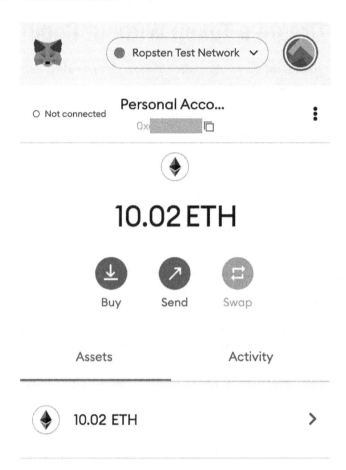

Figure 12-1. *MetaMask wallet connected to the Ropsten Ethereum testnet*

To get Ropsten Ether, you go to the *Ropsten testnet faucet*[1] and specify your wallet address. You get 10 ETH within a few minutes (Figure 12-2). I wish getting ten real Ethers was that easy!

---

[1] https://faucet.egorfine.com/

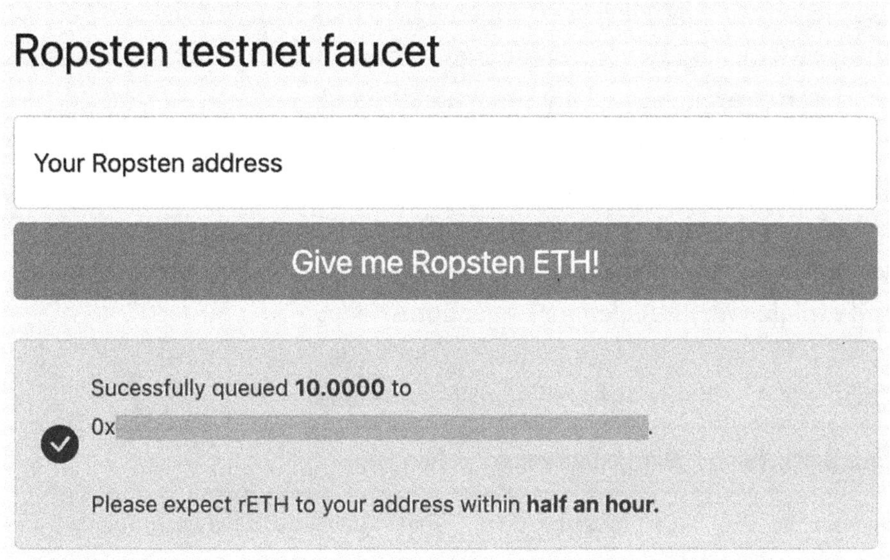

Figure 12-2. *Ropsten testnet faucet*

Generating ERC-20 Token

Now, when we get more than enough test coins to pay for Ethereum transactions, we can create a smart contract. To do that (without coding), you go to the Student Coin website.[2] Despite its .org domain, which is typically supposed to mean that this is a noncommercial organization, Student Coin is actively promoting its own token called... Student Coin (STC).[3] I will not comment on it because the only thing we care about now is their ability to generate an ERC-20 smart contract without a single line of code, which they do well.

So, you just go to the Student Coin website and find *Create your token* button and click it. Welcome to the centralized, incorporated world of decentralized, free cryptocurrencies: you will be prompted to create a

---

[2] www.studentcoin.org/
[3] https://coinmarketcap.com/currencies/student-coin/

user account. Okay, we'll get through this to make our lives easier. But in fairness, I must note that you can make a token without sacrificing your privacy; however, you will have to write the code.

After creating an account, you will be prompted to connect to the MetaMask wallet, so just click that MetaMask logo. Once the wallet is linked, you will be prompted to enter the token name and other token parameters. Table 12-1 shows the parameters I chose for my experiment and explains why I made those selections.

Table 12-1. *Crypto Basics Token Parameters*

Parameter Name	Parameter Value	Reason
Token name	CryptoBasics	That's the name of the book! You can choose any name but try to find the unique one that was not taken before
Token symbol	CRBT	This is the abbreviation for Crypto Basics Token. You can select any capital letters; typically, it's three to five letters. You can check if yours is the unique one by looking it up at the CoinMarketCap website. If you choose the token name or token symbol that is in use already, it will create a lot of confusion for you and the users
Capping	Capped supply	This is typical for IXO tokens as investors don't like uncertainty. The uncapped supply can lead to inflation and abuse. The max supply can be any number. Bitcoin has 21M so I simply set it to 21M

(continued)

Table 12-1. (*continued*)

Parameter Name	Parameter Value	Reason
Supply	Initial supply	This is the simplest and most straightforward one. You can choose vesting to appease your potential investors
Initial supply amount	21000000	Can be any number between 0 and the max supply. But if you set a number less than the max supply, you will have to come up with a tricky way to issue the rest
Sale	No sale	You can sell it later using Uniswap or other exchanges
Supply adjustments	Unchecked	Using those options will make things too complicated. Keep it simple and transparent
Transaction tax	Unchecked	It would be very tempting to get paid for every transaction with your token, but I don't think it is suitable for most use cases, especially for IXO

Now you are ready to hit the *Contract summary* button to get to the next screen, which will show the summary of the token parameters you have selected, the network (which should be set to Ropsten Test Network), and the Transaction Fee (shown in Figure 12-3).

Transaction Fee

In short, gas fees help keep the Ethereum network secure. By requiring a fee for every computation executed on the network, we prevent actors from spamming the network.

Figure 12-3. *Transaction fee for token generation on the Ropsten testnet*

Note that the actual fee will be much higher, and you can see it if you switch to the mainnet. On the mainnet, it would ask me to pay ~0.1435 ETH, which is around $287 at current prices. So, I better go back to the testnet, click the Deploy Token button, and confirm the transaction in the MetaMask wallet (Figure 12-4).

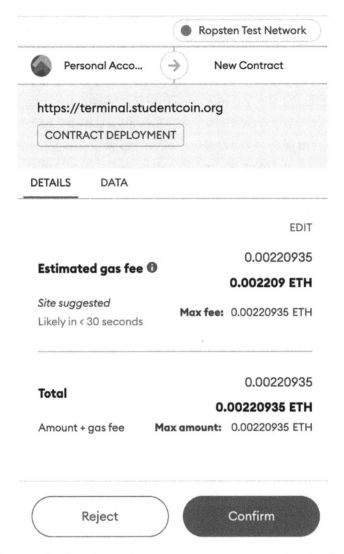

Figure 12-4. *Confirming token generation transaction in the MetaMask wallet*

Viewing Your Token in Wallet and Block Explorer

That's pretty much it; you have got your own token. Of course, it's not real, but it could be very much concrete if you switched to the mainnet and paid 287 real bucks. Write down and store the Token and Transaction addresses – you will need them later. Then click the Add tokens to wallet button to see the new token balance to your MetaMask wallet. You should see your token in the MetaMask wallet now, and not just see it but be able to send it to anyone who also has a wallet like MetaMask that supports ERC-20 tokens (Figure 12-5).

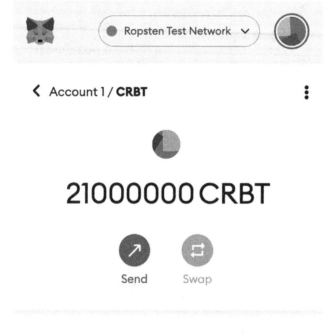

Figure 12-5. *CryptoBasics (CBRT) balance in the MetaMask wallet*

To check the status of your token's smart contract, you can use the Ethereum blockchain explorer, for example, *Etherscan*. Note that since we use the testnet, you should not go to the main Etherscan website but open the test one[4] and enter the Transaction Address. If you switch to the Contract tab, you should see the smart contract details (Figure 12-6), including the source code.

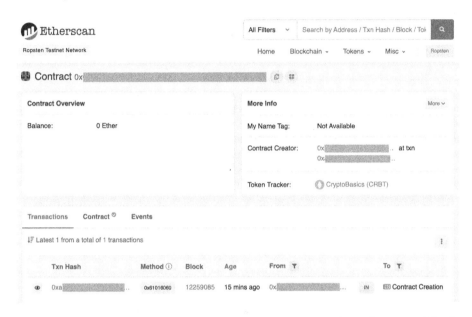

Figure 12-6. *CRBT token smart contract view in the Etherscan block explorer*

You still need to do a couple more things to make your token "alive," like registering it with the CoinMarketCap and CoinGecko[5] websites and listing it on exchanges. We will see how to do it in the next chapter because some preconditions should be satisfied before you can apply for those listings.

---

[4] https://ropsten.etherscan.io/
[5] www.coingecko.com/

Token or Coin?

Before starting your own crypto project, you need to answer the central question of whether you should create a token or a coin. You just learned about one of the possible options to generate a token. As we discussed already, a new coin means creating a new blockchain, which sounds scary, but let's see how difficult it actually is.

The fact is that there are two main ways to create a new blockchain. The first one is designing and writing the new code from scratch, which is the most challenging method, but it might give your project a better chance to become successful if it's based on an original, brilliant idea. Most successful platforms are coded from scratch. Most top coins on CoinMarketCap are original designs such as Bitcoin (obviously), Ethereum, XRP, Cardano, Solana, etc. To code from scratch, however, you must have a good team of engineers with a deep understanding of blockchain tech, a unique vision, and original ideas. Note that *core development* (another fancy name for coding from scratch) also requires a lot of time and funding, so be prepared for serious fundraising.

The second way – forking – is also common and sometimes very successful. Forking has a dual meaning as some crypto projects fork the source code, enhance it, and start a new blockchain, while other projects fork the existing blockchain while starting from some point on the original chain. The main idea of forking is reusing the design and source code of the existing, often already successful cryptocurrency such as Bitcoin.

Some well-known examples of cryptos created by forking are Bitcoin Cash (BCH) and Ethereum Classic (ETC). Forking can be as easy as just copying the code repository of the original project, renaming some functions, and adjusting some constants. For experienced programmers, it can be, if not a weekend project, at least something that can be done within a very reasonable time.

Table 12-2 compares different ways to develop your own cryptocurrency.

Table 12-2. *Comparing Different Ways to Create Your Own Cryptocurrency*

	ERC-20 Token	Forking Existing Crypto Project	Designing and Coding from Scratch
Does not require coding at all	Yes		
Short time to market	Yes	Yes	
Does not require developers involved	Yes		
Small initial costs	Yes	Yes	
Does not require maintaining infrastructure like seed nodes	Yes		
Can be placed on DEX immediately	Yes		
Easy (and less expensive) to list on exchanges	Yes	Yes	
Possibility to attract supporters and investors from existing platforms		Yes	
Possibility to attract serious investors			Yes

The comparison shows that probably the easiest way to create your crypto is the ERC-20 token, while designing it from scratch is the most difficult one, although it has some benefits that other methods lack. If you fork an existing project and plan to enhance it, such a move can attract supporters and investors from the original project if they like your ideas.

The bottom line is that if you decide to launch your own project, you should use the method that best fits your goals, capabilities, and circumstances. My mission is just to show that a variety of options are available.

Doing It the Hard Way

If you still decide to do it the hard way, that is, create your own coin by forking the existing crypto or writing a new code, you should be aware of several important things.

First, you will need to decide whether to go PoW or PoS. In previous chapters, we have reviewed the advantages and disadvantages of both consensus algorithms. If you are going to fork, the decision would be as simple as just selecting your project of preference based on other features. The consensus algorithm will be just one of those features, perhaps not even the most important one.

If you select to write your own code, however, I suggest going PoS or DPoS as they are more promising than the widely desecrated PoW. The PoS coin is also easier to manage as you don't need to fight the continuous emission. Still, on the other hand, without mining, you will need to solve the problem of motivating the node operators. In PoS, the node operator can get rewards in the form of transaction fees.

Another essential factor you need to consider is node hosting expenses and maintenance effort. When you create a token, you piggyback on the existing network, such as Ethereum, which does all the hard work of managing the nodes for you. But if you start your own coin, you must establish a new distributed network of nodes.

Each new crypto network starts from the seed nodes that are the primary go-to sources of truth for new nodes which just joined the network. You will have to host and maintain those seed nodes for the entire period of the project. For redundancy, there should be at least three to four powerful servers as seed nodes. In case one or two nodes go down due to hardware failure, hacker attack, or overwhelming from the network traffic jam, you should still have some redundant backup nodes up and running.

For PoS and especially DPoS projects, you may need more than four nodes to ensure the initial quorum and network stability. In general, the more seed nodes you have, the better for network safety. When the project gets traction, you can rely on other node operators and gradually reduce the number of your nodes. But ensure that somebody still hosts the seed nodes whose addresses are typically hardcoded in the node initialization code.

The easiest way to host the nodes is using a public cloud such as AWS or Azure. You can get a free tier from either provider, but it will not be enough to host multiple nodes. AWS also provides significant credits to startups (up to $100,000). They used to give those credits directly, but now the only way to do it is to join their Activate program through third-party providers. You will need to apply for a membership with one of such providers.[6]

How to Create NFT with No Coding, for Free

A chapter called *Creating a Token* would not be complete without mentioning NFT, which has become a superhot thing nowadays. Although NFT is not directly related to creating a crypto project, why can't we still see how to create NFT? Maybe building your own cryptocurrency, which must always be a fungible token or coin, is too heavy a lift for you. But you still want to join the army of clever people who benefit from crypto differently but also creatively by designing their own **non**-fungible tokens.

---

[6] https://aws.amazon.com/activate/portfolio-detail/

NFTs are different from coins and fungible tokens by their uniqueness. Each NFT instance has some unique properties, for example, a unique image associated with it. By the way, imagery NFT is the most popular and sellable category. Many artists today sell their artwork attached to NFT, and buyers are paying a lot of money – sometimes, millions and tens of millions in a dollar equivalent![7]

Creating NFT is as easy as creating regular fungible tokens such as Ethereum's ERC-20. And similar to ERC-20, NFT is a smart contract, which can also be generated without a single line of code using special tools provided by third-party developers. Let's use *OpenSea*,[8] a popular NFT marketplace, to develop our own NFT.

The NFT generation process is even easier than the ERC-20 one, and OpenSea developers managed to do it *off-chain* without paying a fee. They call it *lazy minting*, which means the token is only recorded in the blockchain when it is sold or transferred for the first time. This is an excellent feature because it allows you to create an unlimited number of NFTs without spending a dime. You only pay a one-time fee to initialize your account.[9] To implement the lazy minting functionality, OpenSea developers used a special type of NFT token standard called ERC-1155.[10]

The NFT Artwork

To make the long story short, let's create an NFT together. For example, I decided to create an NFT that would contain the picture of my previous book cover as an artwork component. Since such artwork is not unique

---

[7] www.forbes.com/sites/jeffkauflin/2022/02/14/how-azukis-suddenly-became-the-worlds-best-selling-nft-collection

[8] https://opensea.io

[9] https://support.opensea.io/hc/en-us/articles/360061699514-Who-pays-the-gas-fees-when-using-Ethereum-on-OpenSea-

[10] https://opensea.io/blog/announcements/erc1155-marketplace/

as it's used in multiple books, I added an image of my signature to add some uniqueness to my NFT, making it a digital equivalent of a signed book. To make it even more unique and reserve an option to create more NFT instances in the future (more "copies" of the signed book) while keeping each one of them exclusive, I added a number to the signature (Figure 12-7).

Figure 12-7. *The NFT art with book cover, signature, and unique serial number*

Now, when my beautiful artwork is compiled and ready to be attached to the token, I will generate the NFT itself. By the way, they accept various image file formats like JPG, PNG, GIF, etc., but instead of an image, you can also use video or audio files or even a 3D model.

Linking a Wallet

Another remarkable and pleasant detail about OpenSea: Although they offer to register a user account, they don't force you to do so. OpenSea is a peer-to-peer marketplace, meaning the tokens belong to their owners throughout token creation, listing, and selling. The process is still arranged by the centralized entity, but they use your crypto wallet address instead of your identity to link the tokens to you.

Note that you can still create your NFT using the ERC-721 smart contract directly on the Ethereum blockchain, without the "man in the middle," but this is a pretty complex process that requires coding. Since NFTs, especially the ones created as collectibles and containing the artwork, are often loosely linked to their creators' identities, in this particular case, I would say let's ignore any potential privacy issues. In addition, even if you register your account entirely, you don't have to use your primary email and your real name if you want to keep your identity private – there is no identity verification on this website.

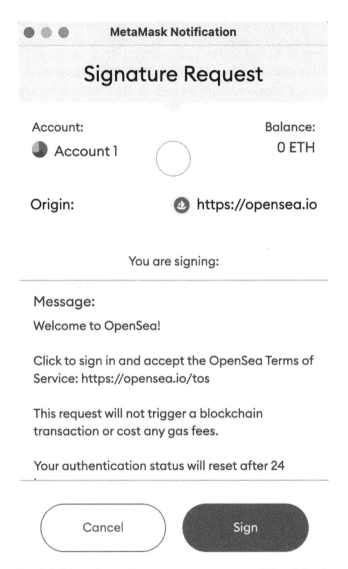

Figure 12-8. *Linking OpenSea account to your MetaMask wallet address*

So, when you go to the OpenSea website and try to hit the Create button for the first time, it will prompt you to link your wallet and sign their terms of service (Figure 12-8). Unfortunately, unlike Student Token, OpenSea does not allow creating tokens on the testnet, so you will have to link a wallet connected to the Ethereum mainnet. But don't get too upset about it – you can connect a wallet with zero balance because they don't charge any fee up front and even allow you to create a token before paying the initiation fees. However, you will be prompted to pay when you try to list your NFT for sale.

Generating the NFT

After I linked my MetaMask wallet installed as a Chrome extension for the previous exercise with the ERC-20 token and signed the OpenSea terms of service, I could finally hit the Create button and go straight to the business of designing my NFT. But before doing it, I did another step, which is optional, and designed my *collection* where I am going to place all my tokens. You can skip that step for now and use a default collection if you just want to experiment with a single token. Once in your collection, you can hit the Add Item button to create an NFT (Figure 12-9).

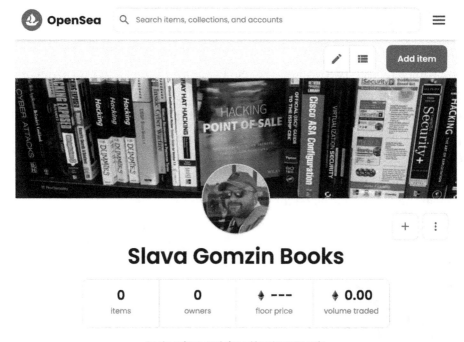

Books written and signed by Slava Gomzin

Figure 12-9. *My new NFT collection on OpenSea*

So, after I clicked the Add Item button in the collection (the same as the Create button on the website's front page), I got into the new token page. I uploaded the image I prepared and specified a few token parameters such as name, description, and properties like Author and Publisher (these are the custom properties you add by yourself, any number of them). I hit the Create button, and that's it! I have got my NFT for free! Note that you can still edit some parameters, even the token's name.

Listing the NFT for Sale

The next step is to sell it (if you want to). When you click the Sell button, you will be offered two options: Fixed Price and Timed Auction, which are self-explaining. With a fixed price, you set your price and wait until someone buys your token at that price. With time auction, you set an initial price and let people bid for the best price – similar to eBay. By the way, I set Creator Fees for my NFT to 10%, which means that every time my token is sold, I will be getting a 10% commission. Figure 12-10 shows the NFT's appearance when it is listed for sale (on auction).

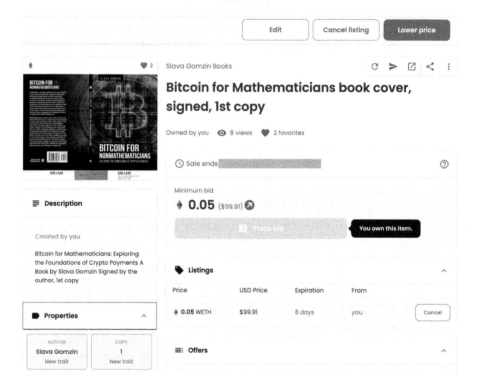

Figure 12-10. *My NFT listed for sale on OpenSea*

When you put NFT on sale, as I said, you will be prompted to pay the initiation fee (actually two fees, one after another), which can be in total anywhere from a few bucks to $30–$40, depending on how crazy Ethereum network traffic is. Once the transaction is completed, the NFT is listed, and anyone can purchase it (or bid if you selected the auction option). Note that now if you want to create more NFTs, as many as you want, as I said, you won't need to pay anything. As promised, the NFT design and selling process is (almost) free and does not require coding!

What's Next?

Designing your own crypto can be extraordinarily difficult or simple. Coin or token, new code or fork – there are many options. It depends on what level of technology your idea demands. The irony is that the financial success of cryptocurrencies does not necessarily have a direct link to technological complexity.

Creating a token can be easy. In this chapter, you have learned how a token can be generated without a single line of code. But developing a crypto project is a different story. Next, we will see how to start such a business.

CHAPTER 13

How to Start the Crypto Project

Never marry for money, but marry where money is.

—Alfred Tennyson

Tsar Peter the Great was a remarkable person not just because he was a powerful emperor. Peter was a great tyrant. Trying to bring Western civilization to Russia, he oppressed millions of people and forced them to change their habitual lifestyles, for better or worse.

Peter the Great founded St. Petersburg – the biggest city in the world north of the 60th parallel, which also goes through Greenland and Alaska – not necessarily the most comfortable place to live a normal, healthy life. Many people (some sources say as many as 30,000) died while building the new capital on swampy terrain. Another example of tsar cruelty is related to Streltsy[1] regiments, which were analogous to the national guard under Peter, who revolted in 1698. The uprising was brutally suppressed by the tsar and ended with the execution of 2000 soldiers.

So why do many Russians still remember and admire Peter the Great? Maybe because he also was a visionary. The first museum, science library, public theater, public newspaper, regular army, and navy are a concise

---

[1] Shooters, riflemen in Russian

© Slava Gomzin 2022
S. Gomzin, *Crypto Basics*, https://doi.org/10.1007/978-1-4842-8321-9_13

list of the novelties he brought from Europe. The great tyrant also was Bill Gates, Steve Jobs, and Elon Musk of his time, and that's the part that amuses people with imperial ambitions, who ignore, unfortunately, the grim details behind his deeds.

Like many innovators, however, Peter was not an inventor. The invention is often a surprisingly small part of the innovation process. Bill Gates did not invent computers. Steve Jobs did not invent smartphones. Elon Musk did not invent electric cars. They *made* a product desirable to many consumers, taking the idea through the steep and thorny way of design and implementation to the actual result.

All cryptos are innovative, some more, some less. But only a few of them are also inventions. The mix of these two ingredients usually determines how successful the project is. The success of crypto is mainly measured by one parameter: market capitalization. It's similar to the stock market – the market capitalization of companies traded publicly. The higher the market capitalization, the better the price of the shares. Think about it: right after the crypto is created, it has a zero value. Then, it's listed on the exchange, and trading starts. People start to buy. Crypto becomes money. But why do they buy? That's the million-dollar question.

Finding the Niche

Each (successful) crypto has its niche. Bitcoin, for example, became a digital equivalent of gold. People buy bitcoin for the same reason they buy gold. Ethereum became the go-to platform for smart contracts, custom fungible tokens, and NFTs. People buy it because they believe there will be more and more use cases for smart contracts and tokens, and demand will continue to grow. There are other, more unique yet essential niches.

Monero is the leader in privacy-centric transactions. If you are a ransomware hacker, drug cartel member, or merely care about the privacy of your finances, the first thing you think about is Monero. I guess you can see the trend. The most popular cryptos are the "go-to" ones. If I need to do X, I use crypto Y. Creating Y is not a problem – you have already seen how easily it can be done. Finding the right X and making your crypto the go-to for X, or at least one of the go-to for X (it does not necessarily need to be unique as there is a competition for virtually anything these days) – that's the real problem the crypto creator must solve.

Projects win if they make sense and have a practical application. Elon Musk's Tesla wins because the transition from fossil fuel to electric power makes sense for many people who want to use clean energy. Bitcoin wins because a decentralized currency makes sense for many people who need access to an unregulated financial system. But let's face it – blockchain will not replace all relational and NoSQL databases, and decentralization is unnecessary for every type of business. Use common sense and look for practical applications.

In previous chapters, we already spent some time reviewing Bitcoin, Ethereum, and Monero. Now let's look at other crypto niches as these three seem well known and too crowded already. One of the most exciting and, in my opinion, promising niches, although very preoccupied already, is stable coins. Tether and USDC are the boldest examples. The idea behind a stable coin is simple. Bitcoin and similar crypto coins have very volatile prices. What if you like the concept of crypto (decentralization, etc.) but don't like the possibility of losing 30% of your assets one day after buying it? No problem, here comes the stable coin.

The team behind the stable coin tech "guarantees" that its price is tethered to US dollar price. Meaning 1 USDT will always equal (more or less) 1 USD. This is great not just for investors (it's bad for investors because of dollar inflation), but this is also good, for example, for merchants who do their business mainly in dollars and want to receive their payouts (proceeds from purchases made in crypto) in dollars or the crypto equivalent of dollars. So how do stable coin creators make money? They do it similar to banks: on fees, loans, and investments. In fact, they are banks. They are centralized organizations as only centralized companies can back tether currency.

The Project Steps

Many previous chapters in this book can be considered a preparation for this one. I am not sure it's even possible to formalize the process of crypto project creation because it comes to too many individual circumstances. But I will try at least to describe what to expect so you won't be too surprised if you still decide to go on this road. Several steps summarized in Table 13-1 can be used as a quick guide on starting the crypto project.

Table 13-1. *How to Start the Crypto Project – Quick Guide*

Step/Action	Description
Generating the idea	This is the very first step for obvious reasons. You need to decide what you do. Your options are
	Creating a token using one of the token platforms, such as Ethereum
	Forking an existing crypto project
	Designing a new blockchain and network from scratch
	I already discussed this step in the previous chapter and other chapters throughout the book
Assembling the team	Find the co-founder. Find other core team members to lead software development, marketing, etc. Don't forget to invite advisors

(*continued*)

Table 13-1. (*continued*)

Step/Action	Description
Writing the white paper	Put your ideas on paper. This is an essential step because the white paper will form the perception of your project by the public. You can create a technical white paper, a business white paper, or both, depending on your project type. If you create a token, you need to focus on the business. If you write the code from scratch, you must write a very detailed technical document
Creating the website	The website is the face of your project. It can be as simple as a one-pager, with links to other sources of information such as GitHub, doc site, social media, etc.
Announcing the project	Start telling the world about your project in the very early stages. Create Bitcointalk announcement thread and social media channels
Building the community	Create a main Telegram user group for English speakers, but don't forget that crypto is a worldwide thing, and there are many people who don't speak English, so add local community groups in different languages
Incorporating your business	If you have an appetite to create a serious business, you will need to incorporate, i.e., create a company. Many exchanges require to provide info about incorporation as part of the listing process
Select the financing strategy	Decide on how you are going to fund your project – using your own savings, by selling your tokens on an exchange or over the counter, or conducting an initial coin offering, initial exchange offering, or something else

Using this quick guide, you can find things you are not familiar with yet and research them in greater detail. Important note: Most of the actions described in this chapter can be done for free or with a minimum expense that does not require an extraordinary investment. It means, therefore, that virtually anyone can start their crypto project, which is excellent. However, once you are done with the initial steps, you get to the point when you need to decide how to continue running your project, meaning you need to find the sources to fund the software development and the marketing. That's why the last step in this guide is determining the funding method. Beyond this point, the activities described in the next chapter will depend upon more significant expenses.

If you read this sentence, you are interested in getting a little more detail on the steps listed in the quick guide. Let me walk through the quick guide items and add some specifics as the devil is in the details, as they say.

Generating the Idea

I don't have much to add to what we have discussed previously. You can read again the "Finding the Niche" section earlier and the "Token or Coin?" section in the previous chapter. The idea, of course, is much bigger than just a simple choice between generating a new token or designing a new blockchain. But still, it eventually comes to that selection, no matter how brilliant your idea is.

There is one more thing that I would like to add: don't be embarrassed even if you feel that your idea is not very original or not technically super cool. Fortunately for some people, and unfortunately for many folks, there are stupid ideas that became very successful projects, and vice versa – there are sophisticated inventions that could not find proper support and acceptance. Most importantly, you must be confident that your idea is the best.

Assembling the Team

The first thing you must do after you have a brilliant idea, or even before, is finding a co-founder. Yes, there are many examples of successful solo entrepreneurs, but working alone in this business is challenging. There is nothing terrible in sharing your triumph with other people who have the same motivation to make your project a champion. With the co-founder, you can divide your responsibilities based on personal preferences and skills, and it's easy to keep up with thousands of things going on 24/7.

You may not need that many team members in the initial stage because you have nothing to pay them. But if you do a significant development, you will need serious developers as a co-founder or a member of the core team. Also, you'd need the head of marketing unless you or your co-founder will manage it by yourself.

Finally, do not underestimate the importance of advisors. You may need people who have deep expertise in crypto, payments, software engineering, business development, or other areas closely related to your project. Advisors do not participate in the project directly; therefore, they can take a more sober and unbiased look at the state of affairs. On the other hand, since advisors are usually compensated for their participation in the form of token or coin stake, they have enough motivation to give you the right advice.

Another critical function of advisors is marketing. A single famous person on the advisory board can significantly influence the community, attract many new followers, and convert them to believers in the idea of your project. If you cannot secure a public figure as an advisor, at least make sure your advisors have a significant social media presence; a solid, impressive resume on LinkedIn; or some unique achievements – in other words, something that would stand out and inspire confidence.

Writing the White Paper

After you have the idea and the initial core team, you next must write the project white paper. If you or your co-founder have never written anything like this before, it won't be easy to launch a project. You don't have to be the writer or published author, however. If you can write good technical documentation, in many cases, that's what is necessary for a successful tech-centric project.

There are various white paper formats, and which one is suitable for you depends on your project and taste. While some founders prefer geek-oriented GitHub-like markup documents, others create more business-oriented, pitch deck–like, illustrated brochures. By the way, creating both is another option. You can write a humble but detailed technical specification and post it on GitHub and, in addition, create a rich document in an investor pitch deck format and publish it on your website.

Many crypto projects translate white papers into multiple languages to reach a larger global audience. Many crypto enthusiasts worldwide don't speak English fluently and can easily skip your project just because the next one offers more materials in their native language.

Creating the Website

Websites are an essential element of every business, not just crypto projects, for obvious reasons: all the information about the project is concentrated on the website. However, it's not necessarily located on the website. Many projects create a blog where they post announcements and updates on development progress. The blog posts are typically duplicated on other media platforms like Twitter and Telegram channels. The website also must have links to the white paper (and its translations), the GitHub (where the project's source code and documentation are located), and the social media channels.

Including the project development road map to show the previous achievements and plans is essential. The document site can be separate from the main project website. You can use third-party tools for rapid document site design such as GitHub Wiki[2] or GitBook,[3] which is a very easy-to-use and, at the same time, powerful documentation tool. Both tools are free.

There are many ways to create a website these days, from fully codeless WYSIWYG (What You See Is What You Get) website builders such as Square's Weebly[4] to more professional tools such as WordPress.[5] I used both, and I can tell you that both methods are worthwhile, depending on your goals, budget, and skills. Weebly allows you to build the website with no or very minimum coding, but you are somewhat limited in design options and functionality. If you want a low-maintenance, free, rapidly created website, go this route. But if you want something that looks more professional, with state-of-the-art design, go for WordPress, with self-hosting in the cloud.

WordPress can host your website as a service, but it is not free and still somewhat limited. With a self-hosted website, you get complete control over the website and WordPress features. If your project is token based and you don't need to host anything in the cloud, you can use a free tier from AWS or Azure sufficient to cover the cost of a virtual machine to host a lite WordPress website for a while. However, you or your co-founder should have some technical expertise to do that.

For the same reasons the white paper should be translated into multiple languages, it is recommended to offer the website transactions. It will help build an international community.

---

[2] https://docs.github.com/en/communities/documenting-your-project-with-wikis/about-wikis

[3] www.gitbook.com/

[4] www.weebly.com/

[5] https://wordpress.org/

Announcing the Project

So, you have written the white paper and designed the website. Now you are ready to tell the world about your intentions. Once you make the announcement, the communication becomes a two-way road. People will start reaching out to you, offering their services, looking for work, or asking questions about your project to see if there is an investment opportunity.

One of the most important ways to announce the crypto project remains to create a Bitcointalk announcement thread. You create a Bitcointalk account (use the project name as the username) and create a new thread in `Bitcoin Forum` ➤ `Alternate cryptocurrencies` ➤ `Announcements (Altcoins)`. The subject of the thread should have a prefix [ANN], for example, *[ANN][BMR] BitMonero - a new coin based on CryptoNote technology - LAUNCHED*. By the way, this is the Monero announcement thread (BitMonero was Monero's original name). You can duplicate your blog posts in that thread to keep it on top of the forum. The latest post or reply in Bitcointalk pushes the thread to the top of the forum, immediately grabbing the visitors' attention when they visit the website. Thus, simplistically, the more posts and replies you and your readers publish in the thread, the more attention (and potential followers) you get. The frequent posts and replies work like an excellent free promotion.

Telegram Channels and Groups

Suppose you are unfamiliar with Telegram[6] like many people unrelated to crypto or political opposition movements. In that case, you will be interested to learn about the history of this social media platform. Telegram was created by Pavel Durov, who was previously famous for creating VK, or VKontakte,[7] a Russian copycat of Facebook. VK was so

---

[6] `https://telegram.org`
[7] `https://vk.com`

successful that it pulled over most Russian Facebook users.[8] Of course, such a platform could not be left without the attention of the authoritarian state. The Putin regime's special services could not miss the easy opportunity to control the local media giant and eliminate all opposition voices. Durov resisted but lost the battle and was forced to leave Russia in 2014, saying "the country is incompatible with Internet business."[9] In 2013, Durov founded a new social communication platform called Telegram, which became popular among political opposition groups and crypto communities.

These days, almost every crypto project has some Telegram presence in the form of *channels* or *groups* – the two styles of Telegram media. A channel resembles a Twitter feed, with the posts composed by the channel owner and reactions such as likes and replies made by the followers. The project typically has a single channel for making announcements. Unlike channels, groups are more like online forums where any participant can express their opinion in the form of conversation with other participants. Crypto projects typically have multiple groups, for example, local groups in different languages for supporting communities speaking a particular language or located in a specific county. Also, many Telegram groups are not associated with a particular crypto project but promote (for a fee) various coins and tokens.

You won't be able to moderate all your channels and groups, especially local groups in different languages, by yourself, so you will need to find moderators and community managers. While you build your community, some of your supporters might offer you help to moderate the forums or manage the community groups. Usually, they receive rewards in the form of a project's token or coin.

---

[8] www.forbes.com/2009/07/13/facebook-vkontakte-russia-technology-internet-facebook.html

[9] https://techcrunch.com/2014/04/22/durov-out-for-good-from-vk-com-plans-a-mobile-social-network-outside-russia/

Incorporating Your Business

Incorporation is another step in the project launch, which initially seems optional but may be required if you want to get VC (venture capital) investment or list your token or coin on solid exchanges. Before incorporation, the first decision you need to make is jurisdiction, meaning creating a local business vs. an offshore company. While local companies are easier to set up and intuitively make more sense, offshore registration might provide some legal benefits as there are countries[10] that are more supportive of crypto than others, but it is more complex and expensive. Every founder has different circumstances, and I am not a lawyer, and this book is not legal advice, so I want to tell you that you have other options.

If you are located in the United States and decide to create a US company, one of the favorable options for the US entrepreneurs is incorporation in Delaware. According to common opinion, Delaware has very fair laws for businesses. Many startups register their corporation in Delaware, which can be done quickly and does not cost too much.[11]

You can hire a law firm to register your corporation or do it yourself if you want to pay a fraction of what lawyers will charge you. There are also online agencies that can do the registration for a decent fee if you are looking for a compromise between the law firm and DIY.

Selecting the Financing Strategy

So, you are all set with the preparation steps and ready to move forward. One of the most important decisions you need to make is how you fund your project. In general, there are four options and their combinations available to you, besides the apparent self-funding option:

---

[10] https://coinmarketcap.com/alexandria/article/where-are-the-worlds-crypto-tax-havens-in-2021

[11] www.forbes.com/advisor/business/incorporating-in-delaware/

Presale

IXO

Exchange listing

VC investment

Almost all of them require *premining*, which most crypto projects do in some form. The original meaning of premining comes from the PoW coins, where you can *premine* some number of coins at the time of the mainnet launch.

Let's say you are launching a new PoW blockchain XYZ with the total maximum supply of 21 million coins. XYZ is PoW and therefore is minable, meaning that the coins are gradually created with each new block as the reward for mining node operators. But instead of starting with zero circulation, you decide to generate 20% of the coins (4.2M) in advance and transfer them to a wallet that belongs to your development team. So, the remaining 80% of the total supply will be mined during the following years. However, 4.2M will be available immediately after the launch and can be used for the project funding and the rewards for developers and other contributors. The same concept can be applied to PoS coins and tokens, even though they are technically not minable. Such coins and tokens can be fully premined, that is, their entire total supply is generated up front.

Presale

Presale is usually done directly by the project team, without listing on the exchange. This is the easiest way because listing on the exchange is costly, and the founders might not have enough funds to cover such an initial cost. The problem with presales is the limited audience, as with an absence of the broad exchange userbase, the project can advertise only using its social media or paid ads (which also require funding).

Note that the price of the coin or token being presale is artificial and set by the founders rather than defined by the market, which means that it can go in any direction once the coin or token is listed on the exchanges. This attracts buyers because they hope the price will rise significantly (sometimes multiple times) once the crypto is listed and open for trading.

IXO

IXO stands for multiple forms of *initial offerings* such as ICO, IEO, etc., which we briefly reviewed in Chapter 11 about investment and trading. The founders should find an exchange that offers ICO or IXO services and the exclusive sale of the coin or token on that exchange. During the ICO or IEO, the coin or token is usually only available on one exchange, making it difficult to sell and stimulating the buying. Also, similar to the presale, the price is generally fixed rather than defined by the market (because the market for the coin or token does not exist yet).

Note that most IXOs have to avoid US buyers because of the SEC (Securities and Exchange Commission) view of crypto being sold through IXO as security, with all the possible consequences associated with this fact. You can try to run the Howey test on your crypto to determine whether it will be classified as a security by SEC.[12] But no matter what result you get, it does not guarantee their outcome will be the same.

Exchange Listing

Exchange listing is the way to get some funding without the complex and uncertain process of presale and IXO. The coin or token is listed on an exchange and traded like any other crypto. This way, the market determines the price; therefore, this method seems more honest than

---

[12]www.investopedia.com/terms/h/howey-test.asp

278

presale or IXO, where the valuation can be artificially overpriced. I will provide more details on the exchange listing process in the next chapter.

VC Investment

VC (venture capital) investment is traditional startup financing through angel investors and other venture capitalists. Unlike other forms of crypto funding, the conventional investment gives the investors the company share. Such investment requires incorporation so the investors can get their shares in the form of the company stock. It isn't easy to get VC investment for crypto projects for various reasons, but you can still try, and, who knows, maybe you will be lucky.

What's Next?

So, your crypto project is set up and ready to go and move to the next, active phase. In the next and last chapter of this book, we will talk about development, *tokenomics* (a portmanteau of "token" and "economics," the discipline that is focused on supply, demand, and emission policy of cryptocurrency), and marketing.

CHAPTER 14

Running a Crypto Project

If you can't ride two horses at once, you shouldn't be in the circus.

—Proverb

His music breaks the heart. It is unbelievable how such incredible creations could be forgotten for almost a hundred years. But justice prevailed, and he was remembered. And not just remembered but erected on a pedestal and made nearly a saint. But during his lifetime, he was not a saint. He was an ordinary man, a church organist. He had a large family with many children and worked hard to earn a living.

One day, he wrote to a friend and complained in a letter about insufficient earnings and explained the reasons: *My present income is about 700 thalers, and if there are more funerals, my additional income rises; but if everyone is healthy, there are not so many funerals. Last year, I earned 100 thalers less than usual due to this fact.*[1]

Even such great creators as Johann Sebastian Bach are not without human weaknesses, and their lives, just like ours, also depend on money or, rather, on their quantity. The goal of most post-Bitcoin crypto projects,

---

[1] Hans Conrad Fischer. Johann Sebastian Bach: His Life in Pictures and Documents. Hänssler (2000).

© Slava Gomzin 2022
S. Gomzin, *Crypto Basics*, https://doi.org/10.1007/978-1-4842-8321-9_14

one way or another, is to earn more money. Some of them need it to be able to spend on development and ultimately bring their product to perfection. Others need it just to live well. Other ones pursue both. In any case, every crypto is heavily tied to money; therefore, *tokenomics* is an essential component in addition to technology. And marketing, of course, is simply necessary to promote the project.

So, you have set up your crypto project. What's next? I assume you have got some initial seed funding, or maybe not. In any case, you'd want to move forward to the implementation phase if you are still reading this. You will need to take care of several aspects of the projects to make your crypto alive. Just as all coins are different, no two crypto projects are the same. Thus, no one can provide you with a universal formula for running a crypto project, but this chapter at least will equip you with several tips.

Tokenomics

Tokenomics is the crypto jargon word for everything related to the management of token financials. Let's review some of its elements.

Remember the sample CryptoBasics token I created in Chapter 12? I set up the *max supply* to 21 million for the straightforward reason – that's the number used by Bitcoin. But I could set up virtually any number.

The max supply defines the maximum number of your crypto that can be ever created, that is, how many coins or tokens can be released into circulation. Don't confuse it with the *total supply*, also called the *circulating supply*, which shows how many tokens or coins are circulating right now. So how do the crypto creators define max and total supplies? The rule is that there are no rules.

Some designers copy the key numbers and algorithms from existing crypto; others come up with their own, sometimes crazy, concepts. Note that no matter how high or low the max supply number is, the market will determine the market capitalization, the total supply multiplied by the token price. The price of a single token or coin does not matter. What matters is how many tokens out there can be sold at this price.

For mineable coins like Bitcoin, Ether, and Monero, the circulating supply increases as more blocks are generated and new mining rewards are paid to the miners. This growth can be shown as a graph called the emission curve. Using an emission curve, you can predict how many coins will be there at any given moment in the future. Figure 14-1 shows the Bitcoin emission curve.

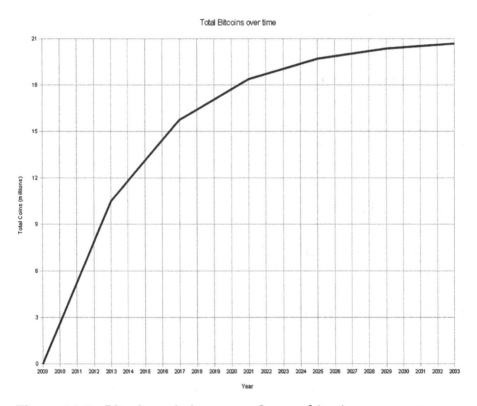

Figure 14-1. *Bitcoin emission curve. Source: bitcoin. stackexchange.com[2]*

---

[2] https://bitcoin.stackexchange.com/questions/161/how-many-bitcoins-will-there-eventually-be

You can see that the Bitcoin protocol ensures continuous inflation because more and more coins are minted with every block. But the increase gradually degrades every four years when the mining reward is halved according to the Bitcoin protocol.

Unlike fiat money, whose supply is replenished periodically by the governments printing new money, the total number of bitcoins will remain the same once it reaches the max supply number. In practice, it will never reach 21 million but will be close. Note that many coins are already lost and will continue to be lost as people forget their wallets' private key or seed mnemonic phrases. Such lost assets will be missing from the supply forever, increasing the value of a single coin even more.

If you have premined crypto assets and want to sell them, you need to consider that your reserve of premined coins or tokens is not the only source for sale. New coins or tokens are continuously injected into circulation if your crypto is mineable. If your crypto is openly tradeable on exchanges, the miners will "compete" with your sale by constantly selling their newly mined assets. To prevent it, you need to make your sale exclusive by either not listing your cryptocurrency before the sale on any exchanges or striking a deal with a selected exchange to do something like IEO so that other sales will be prohibited.

Listing on Exchanges

Listing on crypto exchanges is critical in every crypto project. The listing converts your coin or token from a theoretical project to a real tradeable asset and gives it a price. Listing is relatively simple if you have much money because exchanges want the crypto developers to pay them well for making their baby tradeable. There are at least two reasons for this.

One reason for the high listing costs is that exchanges have one-time and ongoing expenses associated with the listing. For each new asset being traded, they must pay their developers for integrating with the new crypto tech and for hosting the wallet and the node infrastructure. Depending on your project's technology, these expenses can range from zero to thousands of dollars.

Another reason for exchanges to charge ridiculously high fees for listing is that this is their good income source in addition to trading fees. Imagine an exchange that fakes most of its trading volumes – they don't earn much on trading, so the listing is where they can get their livelihood. A few new crypto projects are popping up (and dying) every day, so this income source has all characteristics of a recurring revenue stream.

If your crypto is an ERC-20 token, most exchanges are already integrated with Ethereum and support other ERC-20 tokens, so their listing expenses are nearly zero. But if your project is a brand-new blockchain, its developers need to learn your protocol, connect to your block explorer, host your node, and integrate with your wallet's API. Such work will take time and will cost them. The exchange listing fee varies from zero (if you are lucky and catch some extremely rare promotion) to hundreds of thousands of dollars for top exchanges, so be prepared.

Don't forget about DEX listing – this is less significant than CEX but also an option. If you have created an ERC-20 token, you can easily list it on Ethereum DEXs such as Uniswap. There are plenty of articles on how to do that online, so I will not duplicate them here.[3]

Market Making

Market making is the way to inflate the trade volume of crypto assets artificially. Exchanges often do it to raise their rating on CoinMarketCap and other ranking sites and attract more traders.

---

[3] https://hackernoon.com/how-to-list-your-defi-token-on-uniswap-d4s3w7s

Some crypto exchanges do market making by themselves for all their trading pairs automatically, but others may ask you to do it for your crypto trading pairs, which is not a legitimate request. Since exchanges cannot require you to conduct the market making directly, they may add a clause in the listing agreement regarding your trade volumes. They can put on hold the trading of your asset or even completely delist it if the trading volumes fall below a particular number, which is typically pretty high for new, unknown crypto.

If you want to go down the market-making path, you can use the services of one of many providers of market-making bots, or you can do the bot yourself.

How to Detect Listing Scammers

If you decide to go on the journey of creating your crypto project, you will never be alone. You will be accompanied by an army of scammers throughout the process, from the beginning, when you have nothing that can be stolen yet, to the more mature stages, when you will have an asset that automatically becomes a target for hackers and scammers. Every day you will be getting offers to help you with sales, marketing campaigns, development, listing on exchanges, managing your community, creating YouTube videos, and much more (Figure 14-2).

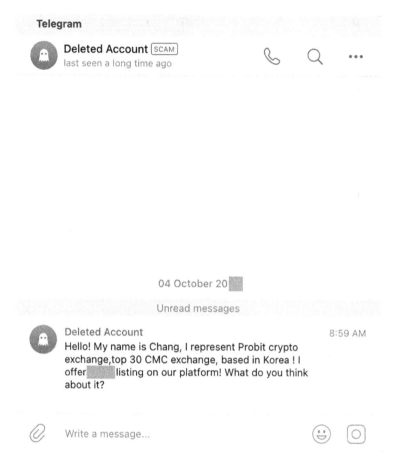

Figure 14-2. *Scammer pretends to represent Probit exchange*

On Telegram, you can report the user as a scam, but who knows how many victims will be out there until the reports are processed, and the account is banned? Scammers are as creative as developers of cryptocurrencies!

I'm not saying everyone who reaches out to you is a scammer, however. There are honest people, of course, in the crypto industry, trying to earn their share of the hype. But the percentage of rogues is very high compared to traditional business, which is related to the entire virtual nature of the crypto industry.

So, be prepared for scammers – there will be many of them. You will get offers through email and social media to list your crypto for a decent fee. Some of these people will be legitimate representatives of the exchanges, but most are scammers. If you are not interested in the listing, just ignore them. But if you are, you will need to validate their identity.

The most straightforward way to verify the identity is to ask the person to send you an email from their corporate email address. Every exchange has a corporate structure with an email system linked to its primary domain. Let's say someone reached out to you on Telegram with an offer to list your crypto on the P2PB2B exchange.

First of all, if they say they can "help" list your crypto, but they are not exchange employees, just ignore and ban them. If this person says they are an employee of P2PB2B, they must have a corporate email address, so ask them to send the offer through email to your work email from their corporate address. You can verify the exact domain name of the exchange by going to CoinMarketCap and searching for the exchange record. The domain name for the P2PB2B exchange is `p2pb2b.com` (Figure 14-3).

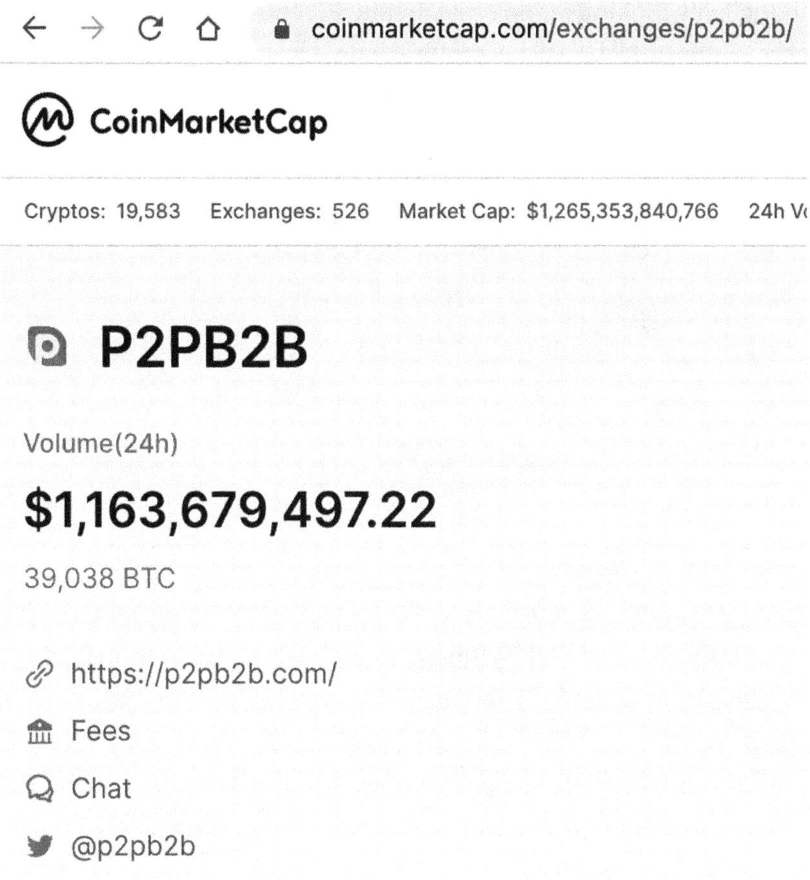

← → C ⌂   🔒 coinmarketcap.com/exchanges/p2pb2b/

Ⓜ CoinMarketCap

Cryptos: 19,583   Exchanges: 526   Market Cap: $1,265,353,840,766   24h V(

🅿 **P2PB2B**

Volume(24h)

$1,163,679,497.22

39,038 BTC

🔗 https://p2pb2b.com/

🏛 Fees

💬 Chat

🐦 @p2pb2b

*Figure 14-3. P2PB2B exchange record with the domain name on
CoinMarketCap*

If you don't get a response within hours, this person is a scammer, so
you just ban their Telegram account and move on. If you have an email, it
can still be a more persistent scammer, so you need to verify the sender's

authenticity by looking at the email header. If you are using Gmail, you can hover over the small arrow next to the recipient's name and click it to show the details. You should see the text similar to the following one:

from:	Listing Rep <listing@p2pb2b.com>
to:	XYZ Info <info@XYZproject.com>
date:	Jan 1, 2022, 1:00 PM
subject:	Re: Listing verification request
mailed-by:	p2pb2b.com
signed-by:	p2pb2b.com
security:	Standard encryption (TLS)

From and *Signed-by* are the most important fields: the email should be originated from and signed by the p2pb2b.com domain. In this case, this is a legitimate email, and the person behind this offer is the real rep of the exchange.

Another secure method of identity verification is sending an email to the address displayed on the exchange's official website (usually in the main page's footer), such as team@p2pb2b.com. You can ask to confirm that the Telegram account of the person who made you an offer belongs to the exchange employee. If you get a reply to your email with the confirmation, you can continue working with this person. Also, in the footer of the exchange website usually, there is a link to the listing applications so that you can apply for a listing on all exchanges through the CoinMarketCap's exchange list.

Listing on small exchanges costs less, but it is inefficient because they don't have a big enough userbase to kick off the significant trading for a new token. Trading volumes are probably fake in most cases. It's better to list on one top exchange than several small ones.

Marketing Scammers

You can use the same steps described earlier to detect other scammers, but it becomes more complicated if people offering you their services are individual entrepreneurs. For example, some video makers on YouTube propose creating a marketing video for your project, which can be helpful. But how do you know they are not scammers?

First of all, such a video maker should have a channel on YouTube that you can check out to evaluate the quality of their work. They should have their email or Telegram username published on that channel. If they reach out to you through Telegram but don't have a Telegram username published on their channel, send an email to the address posted on the channel and ask them to reply to confirm their identity. Please don't ask them to send you an email; only respond to it; otherwise, they may try to trick you!

Another important tip: Do not pay anyone up front. Make an arrangement to pay after the work is done. If they disagree, pay some small portion of the payment in advance, and the rest after the project is finished. In many cases, you won't be satisfied by the quality of the work, but if you paid already, you would never get your money back.

How to List on CoinMarketCap and CoinGecko

Once your coin or token hits the mainnet and is listed on one or several exchanges, you need to tell the world of crypto fans that it's officially there for them to take. It's difficult to imagine real crypto that would be not listed on CoinMarketCap or CoinGecko websites, which became de facto world registries for cryptocurrencies. Their role is similar to ICANN's (the Internet Corporation for Assigned Names and Numbers) role for Internet domain registration.

At first glance, it may seem that listing on CoinMarketCap and CoinGecko is a difficult task, but in reality, it's straightforward – as long as your token or coin has all the attributes of the real crypto project. You will have to provide the following details:

- Incorporation (the name, location, and address of the company)

- Website address

- Block explorer (for coin)

- Community info (media channels)

- Bitcointalk announcement thread

- Social media channels

- Published white paper

- The team of developers and advisors with public profiles

Once you have all these attributes, you just go to the website and apply.

For CoinMarketCap, there is a `Request Form` link at their website footer under the `Support` menu. You should select the following request type: `1 - [New Listing] Add cryptoasset`. On the CoinGecko website, the `Request Form` link is located under the `About CoinGecko` menu. There will be many questions, almost all of which are straightforward, and many are optional. If you have a legitimate project, it will be listed quickly.

Telegram Trolls

You will get many supporters in your community who like your project and sometimes even offer gratuitous help. But at the same time, there will be people who continuously criticize your project, argue, and even harass you and your followers. The mistake you will probably make is starting a dialog with them. Don't. You won't be able to convince them because there is a person who just looks for an argument for any reason.

Sometimes, people work for or invest in a competing project and are financially motivated to criticize your project. These people are called *trolls*. Don't waste your time on trolls; just ban them. If they are not real trolls and they still want to participate in the project, they can reach out to you via DM (direct message) to admit their mistake so that you can unban them.

AMA Sessions

Even if you don't have enough funds to hire a marketing professional, there are many things you can do by yourself and sometimes even for free or a minimal fee that can be paid with your project's crypto. One of such marketing tools is the *AMA* (Ask Me Anything) session which can be done in various formats. One popular form of AMA is the Telegram session, organized and moderated by crypto communities. Many such groups on Telegram have thousands and even hundreds of thousands of followers.[4]

The owners of these groups earn money by promoting new cryptos by posting ads and organizing AMA sessions. There are many local groups in different languages; they translate AMA questions and answers in real time to and from English. The average time of an AMA session is one hour. All the questions and answers are usually scripted, that is, they are prepared in advance and released one by one during the session to avoid surprises.

---

[4] https://blockwiz.com/community-management/crypto-telegram-groups

AMA moderators also take questions from the public through Twitter and Telegram, but the AMA host and guest have the right to select the questions that will be answered. Participants of the AMA receive rewards, typically in the project's coins or tokens, but can be in "hard" crypto such as ETH or BTC.

Development Team

In the previous chapter, we talked about the team already. That was the core team, that is, in most cases, co-founders and advisors. Now you need to do the actual work – write the code – so you must find developers. IRL (In Real Life) developers are a rare case in crypto, so don't waste your time and money on the office space and local recruiters but go full remote right away. A few years ago, remote work was exotic for many employers, but now, in the post-Covid world, it has become a new norm. So, you will have to learn if you are not used to it.

In crypto, everything is done remotely by teams geographically spread worldwide. Most of the time, teammates and business partners communicate only through chats and never see or even speak to each other, which is usual practice in crypto. In one project, I had some developers I had never seen on the video, although at least I have spoken to them over Skype. On another project, I had team members I had never even spoken to, only communicated to them on Telegram.

Remote communication is not an issue – you have free Skype, cheap Google, or fancier Zoom. Skype worked well for me, but this is up to your taste. A few tips, however.

First, hold daily status meetings, even if you are not following a formal agile/scrum methodology. If you don't have daily communication, you lose control over the situation quickly.

Second, use video. Every device has a camera, so there is no excuse for anyone to keep their video off. If they do it once, that's completely fine – everyone has their moments. But if they do it all the time, they hide something.

Third tip, forget about the first two if your project is small and informal. You can do well without daily formal meetings and video if it's just you and another guy or two. But if you have a team of ten, try implementing numbers one and two from the beginning.

One way to find developers is by looking at GitHub. You should check projects similar to yours. It is especially easy if you create yours by forking another crypto. You can also check projects that were also forked from your code origin. Almost every developer has a website or email on their profile so that you can contact them, and they will be happy to respond if they are interested in your project.

Another option to develop your code is outsourcing. Many development outsourcing companies would be happy to help you if you have money, so prepare your wallet if you want to go this route. Individual developers can be interested in a project and work for the stake of your crypto, but outsourcing will require "real" payments, fiat in many cases.

Relationship with Developers

Beware of business owners, managers, or employees who pretend to be your family. When bosses talk about their employees as a family, this is hypocrisy. Maybe they even mean it when they say that, but believe me, they will forget it when the time comes. Business is all about money. I am not saying you can't make friends at work. Of course, you can, with your colleagues. But it is a mistake to think about your employer as a family; unfortunately, there is so much proof.

Most of us have some family – children, spouses, parents, grandparents, cousins – any combination of them is your real family. And your close relatives will not throw you out on the street if some temporary financial difficulties suddenly arise or their business plan and budget change. But your boss will and won't even bat an eyelid.

If you are in a position to create your own business and hire people, don't lie to them and don't give them empty promises. It does not mean you have to tell them that you have enough money only to pay their salary for 12 months, but at least hire them as contractors.

When you hire someone as a contractor, it gives that sufficient awareness about uncertainty. You don't promise too much, and people don't build false expectations. As compensation for risk, developers can get rewards in the form of bonuses and shares paid in crypto.

Partnerships

When I say *development*, I usually mean *software development*. That's likely because I am a software developer in my background. But development in any business, including crypto projects, also means *business development*. Finding some partners in the early stages is essential to demonstrate that your ideas are finding support among mature businesses.

If you manage to secure a *partnership* with a well-known company, it will add many bonus points to your project. Partnerships are one of the best marketing tools in crypto.

PoC vs. MVP

There are two concepts in software development that you are probably not familiar with if you are not a developer: *PoC* (proof of concept) and *MVP* (minimum viable product). These are two initial stages of software development.

PoC is the first software release that typically does not do much besides just showcase some fundamental product features that will work in the future. For example, it can be a crypto node that processes transactions but does not have the finished implementation of the consensus algorithm or complete network communication. Hence, it only works as a single node.

Unlike PoC, MVP can already be offered to first users. It has the basic features implemented and working, but it does not look fancy and still has bugs. An example is the alpha release of the wallet without a proper, good-looking user interface design but already doing some basic functions like send and receive.

PoC is an excellent tool to show your progress to the community and prove that your project is moving in the right direction. If you want to offer something to VC investors or potential partners, you better have MVP.

Open Source License

Another aspect of crypto software development that would be important to review at the beginning of the project is the open source license. First, let's clarify – there is no place for proprietary code in crypto; this is the base assumption. It can be not easy to accept if you come from the traditional commercial software industry, but you will have to. If you make your crypto software proprietary, it will cause multiple issues.

First of all, there will always be a suspicion about the quality and readiness of your software. Crypto projects can hide many things but cannot conceal what they have done in the code. It gives users some peace of mind.

Second, the DeFi is primarily based on technology. Unlike traditional banking, there are no human safeguards in the decentralized crypto world, and everyone's finance depends entirely on the software's quality and security. The only way to prove that the software is reliable is to open it so independent researchers and hackers can test and validate it.

Assigning a license to your software from the beginning of the coding is essential. I am not a lawyer, and this book is not legal advice, but I can refer you to an example of a suitable license that works for Bitcoin and many other crypto projects. The *MIT License*[5] does not restrict other developers from using your code. Still, it requires the users of your code to do two things:

1. Release it under the same license, that is, they cannot convert it to the proprietary software.

2. Include your copyright into their license, so your name or the name of your project will appear on all derivatives of your code.

Another essential function of the MIT license is protecting the developers from liability claims for any harm the software can do. This will become important if someone decides to sue you. Figure 14-4 shows an example of an MIT license.[6]

---

[5] https://opensource.org/licenses/MIT

[6] https://github.com/LYRA-Block-Lattice/Lyra-Core/blob/master/LICENSE

```
22 lines (18 sloc)   1.09 KB                                    ...

  1    The MIT License (MIT)
  2
  3    Copyright (c) 2019–2022 Slava Gomzin
  4    Copyright (c) 2019–2022 Wuzhou Yang
  5
  6    Permission is hereby granted, free of charge, to any person obtaining a copy
  7    of this software and associated documentation files (the "Software"), to deal
  8    in the Software without restriction, including without limitation the rights
  9    to use, copy, modify, merge, publish, distribute, sublicense, and/or sell
 10    copies of the Software, and to permit persons to whom the Software is
 11    furnished to do so, subject to the following conditions:
 12
 13    The above copyright notice and this permission notice shall be included in
 14    all copies or substantial portions of the Software.
 15
 16    THE SOFTWARE IS PROVIDED "AS IS", WITHOUT WARRANTY OF ANY KIND, EXPRESS OR
 17    IMPLIED, INCLUDING BUT NOT LIMITED TO THE WARRANTIES OF MERCHANTABILITY,
 18    FITNESS FOR A PARTICULAR PURPOSE AND NONINFRINGEMENT. IN NO EVENT SHALL THE
 19    AUTHORS OR COPYRIGHT HOLDERS BE LIABLE FOR ANY CLAIM, DAMAGES OR OTHER
 20    LIABILITY, WHETHER IN AN ACTION OF CONTRACT, TORT OR OTHERWISE, ARISING FROM,
 21    OUT OF OR IN CONNECTION WITH THE SOFTWARE OR THE USE OR OTHER DEALINGS IN
 22    THE SOFTWARE.
```

Figure 14-4. *Example of open source MIT license*

Conclusion

Learn from the mistakes of others. You can't live long enough to make them all yourself.

—Eleanor Roosevelt

Our life activities are driven by two opposite forces, which are contradictory and complementary simultaneously, like magnetic poles or electrical charges. One force is fatalism ("we are all going to die anyway"). Another is pragmatism ("we need to think about our future and plan accordingly"). Even though pragmatism better fits our basic instinct of self-preservation, I think the truth is somewhere in the middle. If all people were driven by fatalism only, there would be no progress – no technology, no social justice, etc. After all, what's the point of doing anything if we know how it will end in advance? But on the other hand, if everyone were pragmatic, there would be no progress either, as no one would want to take any risk.

Any attempt to implement an innovative idea implies a massive risk for your future by affecting your career and personal life. So if you are thinking about a new adventure, think about all sides and possible outcomes. There is an old Russian proverb that initially referred to handicraft but is still relevant even in the virtual world: measure seven times, cut once.

And finally, if you ask me to characterize crypto in one sentence, I will give it a try: brilliant technology which opens up unheard-of opportunities for universal accessibility, individual freedom, and privacy but has a shady economy and enormous opportunity for abuse. I hope my attempt to reflect this definition in this book will help you navigate the crypto ocean. May you have fair winds and following seas! Ahoy!

© Slava Gomzin 2022
S. Gomzin, *Crypto Basics*, https://doi.org/10.1007/978-1-4842-8321-9

Index

A

Account-based payment
processing, 144, 145
Airdrops, 187, 189
Altcoins, 62–64, 142, 238
Amount commitments, 132
Apple Pay, 140–142
Ask Me Anything (AMA)
session, 193, 293, 294
Asymmetric (Public Key)
encryption
classification, 14
digital signatures, 17–19
Attacks
blockchain protocols,
80, 91–92
ransomware, 88–90

B

Bank transaction, 34, 36, 38
Bisq P2P DEX, 210–217
Bitcoin
advantages *vs.* flaws, 64
vs. plastic payment card
privacy, 99
problems solving, 28, 29
TOR nodes, 114, 116

Bitcoin blockchain
vs. bank transaction
ledger, 36–38
cash and bank
transactions, 34–36
fractions, 42–44
simplified blockchain
transaction, 39–42
transaction pool, 44, 45
Bitcoin block header, 49
Bitcoin Cash (BCH), 252
Bitcoin Core GUI wallet, 111, 112, 114
Bitcoin standard, 98
Bitcointalk, 188–191
account rank requirements and
signature limitations, 195
Bitcointalk announcement, 188,
189, 190, 269, 274, 292
Bitcointalk signature
campaigns, 193–196
Bitrefill, 159, 160
Block, 7, 13, 37, 38–42, 44, 45,
47–55, 64, 65, 66, 68–74, 94,
95, 132, 133, 134, 146, 151,
198, 225, 251, 283, 284
Blockchain, 38
vs. bank transaction
ledger, 36–38

© Slava Gomzin 2022
S. Gomzin, *Crypto Basics*, https://doi.org/10.1007/978-1-4842-8321-9

CPSIA information can be obtained
at www.ICGtesting.com
Printed in the USA
LVHW080423290922
729567LV00005B/138